# THE AGRICULTURAL REVOLUTION
## Changes in Agriculture 1650–1880

# Documents in Economic History

DOCUMENTS IN ECONOMIC HISTORY

*General Editor: Professor Sidney Pollard, University of Sheffield*

# THE AGRICULTURAL REVOLUTION

## CHANGES IN AGRICULTURE
### 1650–1880

EDITED AND WITH AN INTRODUCTION BY

## G. E. MINGAY, Ph.D.

ADAM & CHARLES BLACK
LONDON

First published 1977
A. & C. Black Ltd., 35 Bedford Row, London WC1R 4JH

© G. E. Mingay
ISBN 0 7136 1703 9

Designed by Richard Sadler Ltd.
Halfpenny Furze, Chalfont St. Giles,
Buckinghamshire

Made and printed in Great Britain by
The Garden City Press Limited
Letchworth, Hertfordshire SG6 1JS

# ACKNOWLEDGEMENTS

In preparing the introductory survey for this volume I have drawn on the work of many scholars; I am particularly indebted, however, to Dr E. J. T. Collins of the University of Reading who kindly read the survey and made many valuable suggestions. Mrs M. Waring of Rutherford College, University of Kent, gave invaluable help in preparing the final typescript.

My thanks are due also to the following who have kindly given permission for the reproduction of documents:

Cambridge University Press for Documents IV and XV;

the Oxfordshire County Record Office for Documents XIX and XXII;

University of Michigan Press for Documents XX and XXXI;

George Routledge & Sons, Ltd for Document XXIX;

Penguin Ltd for Document XXXII;

Mr Rex C. Russell for Document XL.

G. E. MINGAY

# CONTENTS

# THE AGRICULTURAL REVOLUTION

## 1. INTRODUCTION

To an earlier generation of economic historians the familiar term 'agricultural revolution' had a clear and well-understood meaning. To them it conveyed in shorthand form a complex of changes—involving farming techniques and enclosure of open fields, commons, and wastes—which resulted in a transformation in farming efficiency, all of which occurred in the course of under a hundred years, the span of time, in fact, between the earlier pioneer work of innovators like Jethro Tull and Turnip Townshend and the subsequent advances fostered by Robert Bakewell, Arthur Young, and Coke of Holkham. It was recognized that the pace of agricultural change was normally slow, and indeed it was thought that, apart from the enclosures of the sixteenth century, there had been few developments of real significance since the Middle Ages. It was the assumption of general backwardness and near-stagnation in farming techniques which gave the work of the eighteenth-century pioneers its dramatic quality, and together with the rapid sweeping away of open fields justified the treatment of the period as one of revolution.

This view was reinforced by an exaggerated idea of the revolution's achievements. While Tull produced his seed-drill and pointed out the advantages of having land sown in drills rather than broadcast, Townshend by marl and turnips converted a sandy waste into productive fields. Bakewell then transformed livestock by applying the principles of selective breeding, and Coke put into practice the famous 'Norfolk system' of large farms let on long leases to farmers who rotated wheat and barley with turnips and clover, thereby raising his rent-roll ninefold. The work of these leading innovators was publicized by the pen of Arthur Young, and the spread of the new practices and improved livestock was greatly speeded up by the enclosures which finally put paid to the grossly inefficient anachronism of open-field farming. An interpretation which (despite the contrary evidence offered by the much-consulted contemporary writers, Young and

Marshall) saw the Norfolk system as something new, ultra-productive, and easily imitated, held that the breeds of Bakewell and his followers transformed the size, weight, and quality of livestock, and believed that no advances in farming could be introduced in open fields, had little difficulty in concluding that the total of these changes constituted an 'agricultural revolution'.

In several respects the old-established concept of an agricultural revolution ran parallel to that of an industrial revolution in the same period. Both revolutions were seen as beginning about the middle of the eighteenth century, and were thought to be well advanced by the early decades of the nineteenth; both involved the abolition of archaic and inefficient methods of production, and for this achievement depended heavily on the efforts of a limited number of great pioneers; both brought about very remarkable, if vaguely estimated, increases in the level of output, and assumed the existence of expanding markets to absorb them; and both resulted in a transformation in the character of work and social life in the occupations affected.

Modern re-interpretations, based on a much wider range of information and research than was available to earlier historians, have stressed by contrast the long period of development which preceded what one authority has described as the 'great discontinuity' of the later eighteenth century. Also emphasized today are the limited extent of the economic activities which were affected, the generally gradual pace of change, and the circumscribed nature of the effects which followed. In the case of the agricultural revolution it is now well understood that some major innovations, including the introduction of new fodder crops and the reduction of bare fallows, were already widespread in some areas in the later seventeenth century. Turnips were being grown when Townshend was still a child, and the four-course rotation, large farms, and long leases were features of the nearby Holkham estate at least a quarter-century before Coke drew breath. Experiments in selective breeding were carried out by forerunners of Bakewell in the early decades of the eighteenth century, and as for the moribund open fields, many of them showed flexibility and progress in their cultivation, including the introduction of the new fodder crops, for a long period before their eventual eclipse. If the supposed achievements of the eighteenth-century pioneers have proved to be less real than used to be thought, the unsolved

problems of agriculture, equally, remained serious long after the
days of Arthur Young and Coke of Holkham. Cheap, efficient,
easily-repaired machinery became widely available only with the
improved designs and techniques of specialist manufacturers of
farm equipment in the middle decades of the nineteenth century.
The shortage of manures, despite the larger flocks and herds
carried on improved pastures, had long obliged farmers to draw
on supplies of 'town muck', coal ashes, seaweed, and other
materials; this difficulty was eased by the imports of guano in the
1840's, and more satisfactorily met only by the availability of
inorganic fertilizers from the early years of the same decade.
Similarly, the effective under-drainage of heavy clay soils awaited
the invention in the 1840's, of machines for making cheap tiles and
pipes while veterinary science, like human medicine, was only
beginning to take on its modern form in the later nineteenth
century. Many other key advances, such as tractors, machinery
powered by electricity, more effective fertilizers and pesticides,
more prolific and disease-resistant strains of seed, preventive
veterinary treatment, and a host of other developments belong to
the post-1914, and even more, the post-1939 era.

Considered in the broadest sense, the development of modern
farming can be seen as stretching back into the sixteenth and
seventeenth centuries, gathering pace in the later eighteenth and
nineteenth centuries, and proceeding at its fastest in the present
century. It is hardly surprising, therefore, that recent historians
have produced a profusion of agricultural revolutions, one for the
two centuries before 1750, another emphasizing the century after
1650, a third for the period 1750–1880, and a fourth for the
middle decades of the nineteenth century[1]; and no doubt there is
also much to be said for calling the post-1914 changes revolutionary. Earlier periods, too, could well lay claim to the term in
respect of such obscure but fundamental advances as the
discovery and systematic cultivation of grain crops, the invention
of the plough, and the domestication and management of the
various species of livestock. Such beginnings, however, occurred

---

[1]E. Kerridge, *The Agricultural Revolution* (1967); E. L. Jones, *Agriculture
and Economic Growth in England 1650–1815* (1967); J. D. Chambers and G. E.
Mingay, *The Agricultural Revolution 1750–1880* (1966); F. M. L. Thompson,
'The Second Agricultural Revolution 1815–1880', *Economic History Review*
(2nd series), XXI, 1 (1968).

over a period of we know not how many centuries, and it seems historically sound to draw a distinction between the evolutionary progress of pre-history together with the slow and limited changes which followed, and the relatively rapid development which has marked the past three centuries. A further distinction is also needed, for the most recent changes which had their origins in the middle or second half of the nineteenth century should be separated off as different in kind, and as revolutionizing the whole technological basis of agriculture. The dependence of these most recent changes on modern discoveries in chemistry, botany, medicine, oil technology, and other areas of scientific investigation places them in a different category from the earlier developments, which were essentially the result of trial and error, not based on clearly understood or valid scientific principles, in what was a relatively simple and slowly changing technological environment. The beginnings of modern agricultural chemistry and rapid improvement of farm machinery in the middle decades of the nineteenth century mark the close of one phase of agricultural change and the opening of another.

The pace of technical change in the pre-scientific period 1650 to *c.* 1850 was generally slow (although exceptions should be made for the rapid spread of convertible husbandry in light soil areas and the great outburst of enclosure between 1790 and 1820). Leisurely by twentieth-century standards but relatively fast by reference to what had gone before, this change may be seen as a particular kind of agricultural revolution, in rather the same way as the age of steam power and steam railways may be seen as different in kind from the present industrial world of oil, electricity, motor vehicles, air transport, and computers. If this distinction is accepted, the question arises of how the pre-scientific revolution in agriculture should be defined and delimited. A basic difficulty here lies in the matter of chronology.

In the field of agricultural history, as in other branches of history, the chance survival of records and the problems of their interpretation often make it difficult to date with precision or certainty the earliest introduction of a new practice, as for example in the introduction of the new fodder crops into arable rotations. There is also the matter of distinguishing between haphazard experimentation and systematic development of an innovation: for instance, some attempts were made at improving livestock by crossing breeds in the Middle Ages, but the professional undertaking by specialists of selective breeding on a systematic basis, directed towards producing animals with specific characteristics, seems to have appeared only about the beginning of the eighteenth century. As we move forward in time the greater availability of records makes more accurate dating possible, so that it is possible, for instance, to fix on the date for the first imports of guano, the patenting of various designs of reaping machines, and the first shipments of frozen meat.

To give any very clear idea of when an innovation became a significant influence on production is also problematical. It will be generally accepted that the period of widespread adoption (however defined) of a new practice or machine is more significant than the earliest known date of its introduction. However, we do not know with accuracy just when clovers or turnips were grown by a substantial number of farmers, when improved breeds of livestock had considerably affected the quality of livestock, or precisely when as much as, say, a half of the wheat crop was cut by mechanical reapers; and there could be argument as to how the words 'substantial' and 'considerably' in this sentence should be defined. A problem attached to the question of dating the widespread adoption of improved methods in farming is that many of the innovations had, within the technological restrictions of the period, only a limited sphere of application. The cultivation of roots and legumes, as in the Norfolk rotation, was difficult, sometimes impossible, on badly drained clay soils. Progress in the cultivation of such soils rested on the introduction of cheap and effective methods of drainage, which did not occur until nearly two centuries after the first application of these crops to light-soil areas. Similarly, the successful adoption of field machinery in the middle nineteenth century was often held back by the conservatism and limited resources of small farmers, and the existence of small, uneven fields where movement was restricted by obstacles such as hedgerows and trees. This kind of situation led to innovations being adopted much more rapidly in some areas than in others, a state of affairs which was also influenced by the attitudes of landlords, farmers, and labourers, the availability of markets, the level of prices, supply of labour, conditions of relief and climate, and many other factors.

The pace of change was therefore often slow and erratic.

Wooden ploughs drawn by clumsy teams of oxen were still to be seen in Sussex and elsewhere as late as Caird's tour of 1850–1 (and indeed much later still), and in some upland areas farmers long made use of a form of sled for moving their produce. At the same time other more enterprising cultivators had mechanized many of their operations by means of steam engines, and even conveyed their produce from the fields by wagons running on portable railway tracks. These were two extremes, but it is possible to say that by 1850, or somewhat earlier, the major part of English farmland was being cultivated in a manner very different from that which had generally prevailed in the seventeenth or early eighteenth centuries. The agricultural revolution of this period, then, consisted in the adoption over the larger part of the farmland, in the course of about a century and a half, of methods of production significantly more efficient than those which formerly prevailed. This is an unsatisfactorily vague definition, but it is perhaps as good a one as can be formulated in the existing state of knowledge.

We turn next to the question of measuring the increase in production which the changes of *c.* 1700–1850 brought about. The accurate measurement of improvement in grain yields is made difficult by the doubtful accuracy of eighteenth-century figures. If Deane and Cole are correct in deducing that yields of wheat increased by only about 10 per cent in the course of the eighteenth century, this suggests a figure of 22 bushels per acre in 1800, which seems reasonably well in line with the middle nineteenth-century estimates of 24–27 bushels and the official figure of 29·3 bushels for the years 1885–94. Over the whole period between 1700 and 1850 it seems that yields of wheat may have improved by about 25 per cent, and grain yields as a whole by rather less. However, the main factor in the increase in grain output was not the improvement in average yields but the large extension of the area under grain. This may have risen by as much as 50 per cent or even more. One way of estimating the total increase in output of grain is by reference to the growth of population. The British population was about three times as great in 1850 as in the first half of the eighteenth century, and allowing for imports, it appears that between 16 and 17 million people were fed from home-produced grain in the 1840's as compared with nearly 7½ million a century earlier, indicating an increase in output of rather over 100 per cent. These figures are compatible with the estimates we have of yields and arable acreage.

With livestock we are on even more uncertain ground. Estimates suggest that numbers of sheep rose sharply in the eighteenth century but declined subsequently. Cattle numbers may have been stable or even falling in the eighteenth century, but probably increased substantially thereafter. Some estimates for 1741 and 1870 suggest an overall increase in sheep numbers of only about 30 per cent in the interim, while some figures for the shorter period 1779 to 1870 indicate an increase of about 25 per cent in cattle. There were, however, imports of cattle from Ireland and the Continent, and the total supply of meat was also affected by the increase in average size and weight of the animals brought about by selective breeding and better feeding: it seems that cattle may have increased in weight by about a quarter over the eighteenth century.[2] In the light of all the evidence it appears likely that the estimates just mentioned are much too low. Between the middle of the eighteenth century and the middle of the nineteenth population trebled; and if, as many historians believe, there was an improvement in average real incomes, leading to a higher *per capita* consumption of meat, then it appears that the total meat supply must have grown more than threefold. Even if there was no increase *per capita* consumption, and allowing for imports, the home-produced element in the supply must have considerably exceeded the growth of cereal output.

To sum up the conclusion of these very rough estimates, it seems likely that grain output rose by about 120 per cent in the period 1700–1850, and livestock, taking sheep and cattle together and including the increase in average carcass weight, rose by something of the order of 150 per cent. It is difficult to say what happened in the dairying sector, or in the minor branches of agriculture such as market-gardening, fruit, poultry and hops. There was certainly expansion, but in the sectors other than dairying, probably at a rather lower rate than the increase of population, perhaps a markedly lower rate.

[2]Phyllis Deane and W. A. Cole, *British Economic Growth 1688–1959* (1962), pp. 67–75; C. S. Orwin and E. H. Whetham, *History of British Agriculture 1846–1914* (1964), pp. 39, 121, 251–2, 381; J. Caird, *English Agriculture in 1850–51* (1851), p. 522.

It seems likely therefore that, though substantial, the rise in output of the two principal branches of agriculture was not at all spectacular by modern standards. The modest results reflect nevertheless a marked acceleration in the pace of agricultural advance when compared with the performance in previous periods. At the end of the Middle Ages English farming supported a home population of some 2½–3 million, and in addition provided a surplus of wool for manufacturing into cloth and for export, as well as moderate and fluctuating exports of grain. By 1700, on the basis of a larger cultivated area, farming was supporting a population of about 5·8–5·9 million, again with a surplus of wool and grain, but with some assistance from Scottish cattle and imports of cattle and dairy produce, mainly from Ireland. In the course of the next 150 years the agricultural resources of England and Wales, again with considerable assistance from Scottish cattle and Irish produce, and for the first time substantial imports of grain, were supporting a population that had increased by more than 12 million or a little over 200 per cent. It is possible that when the rapid increase in numbers got under way in the second half of the eighteenth century there may have been some reduction in average food consumption standards, particularly among the poorer classes. Historians are divided on this issue. Nevertheless, given the nature of the agricultural improvements of the period and the obstacles in the way of their application, the feeding of an extra 12 million was still a remarkable achievement. It is true that England changed from an exporter of grain to an importer, but the rise in grain imports was fairly slow and the amounts limited, and this was true even in the two decades following the repeal of the Corn Laws in 1846. At mid-century home-produced grain still supplied about 80 per cent of the British population.

It is worth reiterating that, compared with the increases in agricultural productivity obtained in the twentieth century, the results of the classical revolution of 1700–1850 were not very impressive. The achievement appears the more moderate when it is remembered that the major part of the increase in output was obtained by a large expansion in the cultivated acreage, and that improvements in yields and in average weight of livestock accounted for perhaps only about a third of the total increase. In the twentieth century the effect of scientific discoveries in agriculture has been to bring about impressive expansion of output on a *reduced* acreage. The fall in total agricultural land (excluding commons and rough grazing) amounted to over 3 million acres, or over 11 per cent, between 1901 and 1966. Figures for the United States, show increases in output averaging $2\frac{1}{2}$ per cent per annum between 1935 and 1960, and a rise in average product per man of 165 per cent between 1935 and 1961—considerably greater than the rise in non-farm labour productivity. In Western Europe, too, recent decades have been marked by great improvements in agricultural productivity. If regard were had solely to the highest rate of increase in productivity, then it would have to be said that the true agricultural revolution has occurred in the past fifty years, and is still proceeding.

Nevertheless, the period 1700–1850 did see an increase in output which, even if small by present standards, was undoubtedly significant both in maintaining a rapidly expanding population and in facilitating the growth of industrial towns. Not only were increased supplies of food produced, but also important gains were achieved in raw materials needed to feed major industries, such as wool, leather, tallow, and timber. There was also a remarkable growth in the supply of horse fodder. This last item, though often overlooked, was no mean one. In addition to all the horses engaged in husbandry, great numbers were used in land carriage, canal haulage and industrial works, as well as for haulage in the towns and private carriages; and to these have to be added the many thousands of horses employed by stage coaches on the main roads, and those kept for hunting and pleasure. According to Nathaniel Kent a horse employed on the roads consumed annually in hay and oats the produce of five acres of land. As late as 1902, at the height of the country's dependence upon horse power, no fewer than $3\frac{1}{2}$ million horses were kept, absorbing the produce of some 15 million acres at home and abroad.[3]

In addition to the produce of agricultural land, the capital and enterprise of many landowners and farmers played a major part in the development of mining, iron production, brick-making, quarrying, and other estate activities, and were also prominent in fostering turnpikes, river improvements, canals, harbour developments,

---

[3] N. Kent, *General View of the Agriculture of Norfolk* (1794), p. 141; F. M. L. Thompson, *Victorian England: the horse-drawn society* (Inaugural Lecture, Bedford College, London, 1970), p.19.

and early railways. The increase in the output of agriculture was achieved only by some expansion of the total numbers employed on the land: the numbers engaged continued to rise at a fairly slow rate until the 1850's; the census of 1851 showed the British total of farmers, graziers, labourers and farm servants to amount to 1,788,000 males and 229,000 females. At that date the male labour force in agriculture formed 27·3 per cent of the total number of males in employment, and the total agricultural labour force of over 2 million represented 21·5 per cent of the whole—far and away the largest single group of occupations. But not very long before this, agriculture had been even more predominant, with as much as a third of the labour force in 1811, and probably over 40 per cent in the later eighteenth century. The agricultural expansion was thus brought about with a much reduced *share* of the nation's labour, so that a rising proportion of the working population could be diverted to other occupations in industry, transport, commerce, and personal services, where the productivity of labour was probably, on average, considerably above that in agriculture. This transfer of labour resources from a sector of relatively low labour productivity to sectors of higher productivity made an important contribution to the economic advances achieved by the country in this period.

One of the striking characteristics of the changes in agriculture was that so large a proportion of the increase in output—we have suggested a tentative figure of two-thirds—was brought about by expansion of the cultivated acreage, with only the remaining third arising from improvements in average output per acre. Of course, the expansion of the cultivated acreage, probably amounting to some 6–7 million acres, or perhaps a third of the 1700 area, was in itself no mean feat, involving as it did a very heavy capital expenditure by landowners and farmers in legal, surveying, and administrative costs, as well as in outlays on fencing, roads, buildings, drainage, and land clearing. This aspect of enclosure, however, has received less than its due share of attention from historians. And, in view of the emphasis given by contemporaries to farming techniques and experiments, it may well be asked why the improvement in output per acre in terms of yields, higher stocking capacity of pastures, and weight of livestock, was not greater than it was. What were the limitations to technical progress in the century and a half after 1700?

There is no simple answer to this question, but a number of factors may be readily indicated. In the first place, the obtaining of an increased output per acre often depended on prior changes in land use, and thus on reform of the structure and organization of farming. The farming of open fields and commons had first to be modified, and then eventually replaced, by individual cultivation of enclosed farms; land had to be turned to its most efficient use, and taken out of the hands of inefficient producers and transferred to those who were more capable and enlightened. Substantial amounts of capital had to be invested in providing the fundamental conditions for better farming: in enclosure and reorganization of holdings, drainage of wet soils, improvement of local means of transport for easier access to markets, and modernization of farm buildings—to say nothing of the increased sums which farmers had to lay out on superior breeds of livestock, more efficient implements, and fertilizers and labour. None of these changes individually contributed more than a fraction of the increased output of the land, though the two most costly of them—enclosure and drainage—probably accounted between them for a major part of it. For real progress to be made each advance was dependent on progress being made in others, and as a result this complex chain of interdependent advances took time to become fully effective. One difficulty was that the changes involved both interference in property rights and the finding of large sums of money; and also involved were the individual efforts of many thousands of landowners and farmers, whose interest in progress frequently turned on the existence of profitable conditions for farming.

A second limitation to technical progress was the farmers' receptivity to new ideas. For the lengthy process of reorganization, investment, and modernization to achieve its full results there was needed the enthusiasm of enlightened farmers commanding a sufficiency of capital. Contemporaries complained of much conservatism among farmers, and a cautious attitude to new developments may well have been connected with the prevalence in some areas of small farmers who lacked adequate resources and unquestioningly accepted the wisdom of traditional practices. Most of the agricultural experts of the day had nothing good to say of the little farmers, men who were obliged to bend all their efforts towards securing a subsistence from the soil, and had neither time nor money for experiments. Arthur Young bitterly attacked the 'goths and vandals' of the open fields, though he occasionally recognized instances of progress in open-field farming. He firmly believed that the farmers from enclosures were of an entirely different breed from the narrow-visioned, suspicious, open-field cultivators. The latter, he argued, had to pass away before new ideas could become generally established.

However, there were quite often rational reasons for apparent conservatism. Contemporary writers who advocated new methods were often attacked by other self-styled experts as ill-informed, impractical, or too theoretical. In any case, they showed a tendency to exaggerate the extent of backwardness and ignorance among the farmers, and to overlook the very real difficulties and disadvantages attached to the introduction of new techniques. Variations in soils, relief, climate, and access to markets had much to do with a reluctance to shift from existing practices. Furthermore, the financial returns of improved methods might easily be over-estimated, and their profitable introduction might well depend on better market conditions and higher prices.[4] In fact, there is much evidence that farming techniques were rarely static for very long periods but gradually evolved in order to achieve higher production or adapt to changing markets. Many innovations were known to at least a few long before they were generally applied, which suggests that, apart from the limitations affecting the diffusion of new ideas, the economic and technical environment might be the crucial factor in their adoption. In some instances landowners and farmers were wise to hang back and doubt the supposed technical and economic advantages of an innovation. Some of the practices discussed by the experts were controversial, such as paring and burning of the turf to improve the fertility of old grasslands—a method advocated by Young but criticized by his opponent, Thomas Stone; other practices, like the hoeing of turnips, were costly in labour and practicable only on sandy or loamy soils; while some basic improvements, such as drainage, might be too expensive unless the tenant was assisted by his landlord, and even then the results were often uncertain. Again, many farmers were in the hands of labourers who were

---

[4] See C. Peter Timmer, 'The Turnip, the New Husbandry, and the English Agricultural Revolution', *Quarterly Journal of Economics*, 83 (1969), p. 391.

accustomed to a leisurely pace of work. Gloucestershire plough-teams, for instance, with their oxen and great heavy ploughs took seven hours to plough three-quarters of an acre, and on the Essex clays an acre a day was all that could be managed in the 1880's. In Norfolk, on the other hand, a light wheel-plough drawn by only two horses and one ploughman could cope with two or three acres a day, though admittedly on much lighter land. As Young complained, where cumbersome ploughs and teams of excessive size were the rule it was usually the labourers who opposed any change.

It is true, however, that the instruments of agricultural education were weak. With a few exceptions, like Young's *Farmer's Kalendar*, which had gone through thirteen editions by 1823, farming books and journals had only a limited circulation among a restricted circle of improving landowners and wealthy gentleman-farmers. It was the same sort of educated agriculturalists who made up the regular attenders at the annual 'sheep-shearings' or private shows held at Woburn and Holkham (see Document I), and who were the mainstay of the numerous agricultural societies, such as the Dublin Society founded in 1731, the agricultural committee of the Royal Society of Arts (1754), and the Smithfield Club (1798) (Document II). In the nineteenth century the membership of these societies, even the famous ones, was a restricted one, and was unrepresentative of farmers as a whole. The Bath and West of England was doing well to be able to boast of some 1,200 members in the 1850's, and in 1854 the Royal Agricultural Society distributed only 635 copies of its *Journal*.[5] The societies relied heavily on the enthusiasm of a few well-to-do enthusiasts, and their publications tended to be highly technical and scientific. Their shows however were usually well attended, and were valuable in bringing to notice new types of machinery and advances in livestock and crop varieties.

Most of the early local societies probably had very little influence on improvement. Young, who in his day was an honorary member of many such societies, held them in contempt, and attacked them for wasting time on irrelevant trivialities and theoretical controversy instead of encouraging worthwhile practices among practical farmers. A number of societies revived,

---

[5] Kenneth Hudson, *Patriotism with Profit* (1972), pp. 3-4, 46-7, 99.

however, in the 1820's and 1830's when they were able to attract a larger and more active membership interested in the new types of fertilizer and novel forms of machinery. The first Board of Agriculture, founded in 1793, followed from one of the suggestions for agricultural education put forward in 1790 by Young's rival, William Marshall (Document III). The Board, however, proved ineffective as a means of accelerating agricultural progress. It lacked official status, was inadequately financed, and poorly managed. It did not have the facilities to do very much in encouraging practical experiments, and its county reports, often badly prepared by ill-qualified authors, failed to attract a wide audience. The Board's one achievement, the General Enclosure Act of 1801, proved to be only a half-measure which offered too little too late. Hampered by disagreements among its aristocratic oligarchy, and by the slackening drive of its secretary—Young himself, who by 1811 was seventy years old and blind—the Board failed to act as the needed forum for advanced ideas, and gradually relapsed into somnolence and obscurity.

Although there were the suggestions of Marshall and others for the foundation of specialized institutions for agricultural education, and Young, for instance, advocated the appointment of a professor of agriculture at every university, little was done in these directions until well into the nineteenth century. Something, however, was achieved on a personal, individual basis. Young himself accepted foreign pupils at Bradfield, and he took visitors on tours of the best farming to be seen in East Anglia, where strangers were surprised by the knowledge, enthusiasm, and intelligence of the farmers. Possibly a good deal of useful information was gathered and valuable ideas exchanged by those who went on Young's excursions or journeyed to the private sheep-shearings (Document IV). Among the enthusiasts there was a great deal of farming talk at the dinner table, and Young loved a gathering where toasts were proposed to the plough or the success of a new pamphlet on manures. The ideas introduced at Woburn or Holkham, and discussed over the port at Bradfield or at Euston, the Duke of Grafton's mansion, sometimes filtered down to the farmers through the medium of landowners' home farms and demonstration plots. Landlords' stewards, or agents, also, played a role in the process of dissemination by passing on suggestions to tenants, and in some farm agreements the tenants were bound to follow the advice of the steward. In the nineteenth century some agents learned their business in the estate office of one of the leading estates, and took to their subsequent posts an enthusiasm for drainage, improved farm layouts, and higher standards generally.[6]

The Royal Agricultural College, founded at Cirencester in 1845, was the first institution established specifically to provide systematic courses of theoretical and practical agriculture, but most of its students came at first from the landowning and professional classes and not from the ranks of the farmers. The big advance in formal agricultural education began only in the last quarter of the nineteenth century (though a Chair of Agriculture had been founded at Edinburgh as early as 1790); degrees in agriculture were offered by a growing number of British universities, as well as at Cirencester, and full-time courses were provided by private colleges established at Downton in Wiltshire and Aspatria in Cumberland. The county councils, subsequently, employed travelling instructors in butter and cheese-making and in dairy hygiene, paralleling the similar work of extension agents in the United States. In the middle of the century, meanwhile, scientists employed by the Highland and Agricultural Society and the Royal Agricultural Society, along with the private Rothamsted team of Lawes and Gilbert, succeeded in making progress in fertilizers, soil analysis, silage, and plant and animal physiology. There was from this time a marked growth in specialized journals and farming magazines, and the new scientific agriculture began to have practical effects. However, as C. S. Orwin and E. H. Whetham remark, most farmers and their men still learned their trades by the traditional way of working on the land: 'the stockman's eye, the ploughman's skill, the grazier's judgment of beast and grass, the ability to make a profit from the complex mixture of soil, climate, crops, animals and men still could not be taught in schools and colleges . . .'[7]

The relatively late application of scientific knowledge to the improvement of agriculture helps to explain why the technical

---

[6] See G. E. Mingay 'The Eighteenth-Century Land Steward' in E. L. Jones and G. E. Mingay (eds.), *Land, Labour and Population in the Industrial Revolution* (1967), pp. 26–7; David Spring, *The English Landed Estate in the Nineteenth Century: its Administration* (1963), pp. 102, 108.

[7] Orwin and Whetham, *op. cit.*, pp. 31, 281–2.

advances of the classical agricultural revolution made only a secondary contribution to the increase in output as compared with that resulting from the expansion of acreage. Eighteenth-century experiments in farming were scientific in spirit, in that they were frequently conducted under controlled conditions so far as was possible, with a normal plot cultivated as a check on the advantage gained by the innovation. Improving farmers went in for careful measurement of inputs and outputs, and calculated the financial costs and benefits of particular practices, as is evident from the accounts given to Young on his various tours (Document V). Many leading farmers, like Young himself, had their 'experiment grounds' for trying out fodder crops or assessing the qualities of different breeds of livestock. They also assembled collections of implements for purposes of comparison, and sometimes made new ones to their own design.

But all this was done in the absence of any real understanding of soil chemistry, the physiology of animals and plants, or the nature of plant blights and animal disease. Indeed, the combating of insect pests like the carrot fly, mildew or rust in wheat, or liver-rot and rinderpest among livestock remained essentially a matter of folklore and trial and error. One of the most obvious technical weaknesses of the age—the inadequacy of knowledge for dealing with pests, blights, and diseases—was one of the last to be remedied. We can have little precise idea of how much production was lost through this cause, but from the legislation concerned with controlling the movement of cattle and the slaughter of diseased animals during the cattle plague (rinderpest) of the middle eighteenth century and in the severe outbreaks of rinderpest and pleuro-pneumonia of the 1860's, we can guess that it was at times disastrous. Furthermore, the fact that some severe fluctuations in yields of crops were put down to blights, the attention given by agricultural writers to the problem, and the frequent appearance of patent nostrums, all suggest a serious and recurrent need for effective means of treatment. Veterinary science, like agricultural chemistry, developed late. The London Veterinary College was established in 1791 (as a result of the interest shown by the Odiham Agricultural Society), but at first devoted its attention to horses. The Royal College of Veterinary Surgeons, which gave status to a new profession, was not founded until 1844, a year earlier than the Royal Agricultural College.

Until the middle nineteenth century the development of improved farming techniques rested almost entirely on empirical experimentation and informal dissemination of the results. Progress was confounded, too, by the wide variety in existing conditions of soil, climate, and relief, and by the practical difficulty of acquiring new varieties of seeds, implements, and livestock, to say nothing of skilled supervisory labour. Numbers of gentlemen, for instance, wrote to Young asking him to send them seed or some new design of implement, or requesting the recommendation of a skilled bailiff. Furthermore, it was not always easy to fit a given innovation into an existing farm system without making wholesale changes which might well involve heavy expenditure. Livestock which were well suited for one purpose might be inappropriate for another. Farmers on Romney Marsh, for example, hung on to their local breed of sheep in preference to other 'improved' breeds because their sheep's native hardiness made them best fitted to survive winter weather on the exposed terrain.

The varied conditions and diverse farming systems of England, therefore, also help to account for the slow and limited adoption of techniques which could only be tested by trial and error. Improvements in implements could not be rapid until locally made ploughs and harrows were readily replaced by the products of such specialist firms as Ransome of Ipswich and Garrett of Leiston. In time iron and steel replaced wood, and factory-made machines offered ease of repair and replacement of worn parts. By the middle nineteenth century farmers could select from a wide variety of ploughs, scarifiers, harrows, rakes, drills, rollers, threshers, winnowers, seed dressers, hay-tedders, and chaff- and turnip-cutters. But before this time horse-drawn or steam-powered machinery had made little progress except in Scotland and northern England. Seed-drills, despite the pioneering work of Jethro Tull, had never come much into favour except in light-soil areas, and the principal example of the use of machinery in agriculture was the threshing machine, a labour-saving device which was adopted in arable areas of Scotland and the north during the labour scarcity of the Napoleonic Wars, and spread more widely in the subsequent decades. In the late eighteenth century steam power was being used for drainage in fen country, and in due course it came into vogue for driving threshing machines and other types of barn machinery. Arthur Young in 1804 described the first steam engine used for agricultural purposes in Norfolk, and possibly in England. Designed to replace the horses used in driving the threshing machine, it cost £600 and threshed nine bushels of wheat on one bushel of coal.[8] By the 1840's mobile steam engines that could move under their own power from field to field and farm to farm were coming in, and experiments were made with steam ploughing, though this never became very common. The bulk of farm machinery continued to be horse-drawn and still required a considerable labour force: even the steam-powered thresher, for instance, required a dozen hands to operate it. The main advantage of machinery, in fact, was the flexibility it gave to farm operations, and especially the opportunity of taking maximum advantage of good weather for harvesting and haymaking. Before the later decades of the nineteenth century economy of labour was not a very considerable factor, especially as the areas of arable farming, for which the greater number of machines was devised, usually had plenty of cheap labour which could be supplemented in busy periods by hands hired from neighbouring towns and gangs of itinerant Scots, Welsh and Irish. Indeed, the cheapness and availability of labour, together with the improved efficiency of hand tools in harvesting, were factors retarding the introduction of machinery; and there were also such considerations as the small size of the majority of farms and lack of capital of the farmers, the limited area and ill-drained nature of many fields, the existence of obstructions such as streams, hedges, and trees, uneven surfaces, the hostility of labourers to machines like threshers which reduced winter employment, as well as questions concerning the cost, efficiency, and reliability of the machines themselves.

The advances in agriculture occurred, therefore, on a number of fronts—techniques, machinery, land use, reorganization of farms, education—and tended to be interdependent—the lack of adequate drainage, for instance, delaying the reduction of bare fallows, discouraging the introduction of more valuable livestock, and retarding the use of machinery. When due weight is given to the complexity of the problem it is not surprising that the progress of the age was relatively slow and uneven, and that for

[8] A. Young, *General View of the Agriculture of Norfolk* (1804), p. 73.

the main fruits of the agricultural revolution the country depended on the work of the enclosers rather than all the patient efforts of the Tulls, Bakewells, Cokes and Youngs.

The progress in agriculture, it must be remarked, necessarily involved consequences for the nature of rural society and the character of village life. The consequences varied greatly from one area to another, and indeed from village to village, depending on local conditions and circumstances. Simple generalization about such changes is neither sensible nor feasible. And to the social effects of shifts in land use, enclosure, the introduction of farm machinery, and alterations in employment on the land must be added those powerful, and eventually more pervasive, influences arising from the forces of industrialization and urban growth—influences which, tentacle-like, spread out through the country-side to affect the wages, living conditions, availability of work and possibilities of migration of rural inhabitants. If it is to be discussed at all, this large and complex subject deserves a full-scale treatment: we have thought it best in a volume of modest proportions to confine our consideration to the changes which occurred in farming itself, touching on social questions only where they are directly related to the largely technical issues which sprang from the response of agriculture to the economic demands of an industrializing environment. Like farming itself, village society of the later nineteenth century had seen remarkable changes over the preceding century or so, but these changes derived from a much wider spectrum of forces than merely those involved in the agricultural revolution. And since we are concerned primarily with this revolution, it is to the new methods of farming that we turn next.

## 2. NEW METHODS OF FARMING

In the light of the preceding discussion it is perhaps surprising that the myth of rapid technical change occurring in the eighteenth century should still be current. Nearly forty years ago in her *The Agricultural Revolution in Norfolk*,[9] Naomi Riches

---

[9] N. Riches, *The Agricultural Revolution in Norfolk* (1937, 2nd ed. 1967), pp. 84, 88.

pointed out that the use of clovers and turnips was at least vaguely understood by later seventeenth-century writers such as John Worlidge, and that both crops were known to have been cultivated in Norfolk towards the close of that century. In a much more recent work Dr Kerridge has stated that sainfoin, and clovers used in mixtures with rye-grass, were being sown even earlier—by the middle of the seventeenth century—while turnips had appeared in Suffolk about 1650, and in east Norfolk by 1670. Another valuable crop, rape or coleseed, was being cultivated in the midlands by 1686, cabbages were evident in the 1660's, and potatoes, grown in Lancashire by 1650, were commonplace by 1690.[10] Imports of clover and rye-grass seed came in regularly from Holland after 1620, and it seems likely that the field cultivation of roots and grasses was stimulated by observations of Flemish husbandry made by English landowners when on the grand tour, and also during their enforced exile at the time of the Civil Wars. One such exile was Sir Richard Weston, whose discovery of the value of clover and turnips for cultivating poor soils was related in his *Discours of Husbandrie used in Brabant and Flanders*, first published in 1650 (Document VI); on his return to his Surrey estate Weston proceeded to put his Flemish knowledge into practice. Andrew Yarranton, whose little book *The Great Improvement of Lands by Clover* appeared in 1663, noted that the seed could be bought for seven pence a pound, and he listed twenty-nine people who sold it in the west midlands. The intensive cultivation of thin, sandy soils had long been developed in the Low Countries, using fodder crops and heavy manuring in order to avoid the necessity for regular fallows, and employing bed and row cultivation in order to achieve high yields. It was natural that in due course these methods should be transferred across the North Sea and adopted in those areas where conditions favoured them. In both Holland and England a shift towards livestock and application of more intensive methods of arable cultivation were evident in the periods of low corn prices in the later seventeenth and first half of the eighteenth century when arable farmers were under pressure to become more efficient.[11]

---

[10] Kerridge, *op. cit.*, pp. 270–80.

[11] B. H. Slicher Van Bath in J. S. Bromley and E. H. Kossmann (eds.), *Britain and the Netherlands* (1960), pp. 132, 139, 142, 150; *The Agrarian History of Western Europe A.D. 500–1850* (1963), pp. 213–15.

In England the new legumes and grasses were used to produce highly nutritious pastures in grazing areas, and for cutting for hay. Together with the roots, they were eventually introduced into rotations on arable land as a means of reducing bare fallows and of providing fodder for additional stock. Heavier stocking, and the action of legumes in fixing nitrogen in the soil, had the effect of improving fertility, and made it possible to achieve heavier yields of grain, especially in the light soils which were well adapted to the cultivation of turnips. Thus both grazing and arable benefited from the greater variety and increased output of feed, especially where sainfoin and lucerne were grown, for these crops were twice as nutritious as the natural grasses. Coupled with the widespread use of water-meadows, described by Dr Kerridge,[12] farmers were able to utilize the new crops to over-winter more stock, and put them out to pasture earlier in the spring.

Roots and clovers were beginning to be grown on a small scale, even in some unenclosed districts, in the middle and later seventeenth century. However, the evidence for their diffusion and adoption on larger acreages has only recently begun to be investigated in detail. Turnips were first grown as a field crop in a few isolated areas in central Norfolk and high Suffolk, and it seems that the small acreages of roots were intended primarily as additional cattle feed or as a substitute for the hay crop and a safeguard against its failure. It was only in the middle decades of the eighteenth century that turnips spread to the 'improvable sands' of north-west Norfolk and became incorporated as a major element in the rotations for the purpose of feeding large flocks of sheep. Where other sources of feed for stock had been developed, turnips were never much favoured: in east Kent, for example, the farmers of Thanet specialized in producing beans and took little interest in the turnip. The spread of the turnip was influenced by its liability to pests and to damage by weather, while to secure a good crop it was necessary to have a rich or well-fertilized soil, well-limed, and in addition plenty of spare labour for hoeing the roots and keeping up a good tilth. There were thus some powerful restraints on its more widespread adoption.

By the middle eighteenth century, however, the development of

---

[12] Kerridge, *op. cit.*, ch. VI.

rotations in which cash crops of grain were neatly integrated with the keeping of stock fed on clovers and turnips was a remarkable feature of the northern districts of Norfolk. There was some dispute among contemporaries as to precisely what 'the Norfolk rotation' was. William Marshall, writing with north-eastern Norfolk in mind, referred in 1787 to a rotation of wheat – barley – turnips – barley – clover – rye-grass as having been practised 'for at least a century past'.[13] But Arthur Young, who also knew the county very well, thought the true Norfolk rotation to be a simpler four-course system of wheat – turnips – barley – clover, and its home to be in the sandy district of north-western Norfolk. Other characteristics of the Norfolk system, said Young, were the large farms held under long leases at low rents by farmers of capital, who could then afford to spend the large sums required to enrich the thin soils with marl at an outlay of £125 or £150 per acre. In his *Southern Tour* of 1768, and later in the *Annals of Agriculture*, he elaborated on these points, and gave some striking details of the huge farms to be found on the 'improvable' (as distinct from 'poor') Norfolk sands, farms which stretched to two, three, four or even five thousand acres[14] (Document VIII). In practice, the rotations were varied widely to meet price changes and local conditions, and especially so as the soil began to show marked symptoms of becoming 'clover-sick' and of producing diseased turnips. On Coke of Norfolk's estates the four-course rotation described by Young was only rarely used in the 1790's, and spread rapidly only in the first two decades of the nineteenth century, to become almost universal by the 1850's.[15]

So far as the introduction into rotations of leys, or temporary pastures of legumes and grasses, is concerned, this was an old practice that went back in some areas to before 1560, and spread rapidly between 1590 and 1660, according to Dr Kerridge.[16] Ley-farming involved a succession of grain crops followed by a grass ley of variable length to rest the soil and support stock, the ley being broken up again in due course for a new succession of

---

[13] W. Marshall, *Rural Economy of Norfolk* (1787), I, p. 132.

[14] A. Young, *A Six Weeks Tour through the Southern Counties* (1768), p. 23; *Annals of Agriculture*, XIX (1793), pp. 441–98.

[15] R. A. C. Parker, *Coke of Norfolk: A Financial and Agricultural Study* (Oxford, 1975), pp. 138–42, 156.

[16] Kerridge, *op. cit.*, p. 194.

grain crops. The system was a highly flexible one, the crop cycle lasting between two and nine years (but mostly three or four) and the ley between six and twenty years (mostly between seven and twelve years),[17] though the higher figures suggest that the system was hardly a 'rotation' in any systematic sense. Marshall wrote of ley-farming in an area of the midlands as something rather unusual, and the practice there was for the arable cycle to take the course oats – wheat – barley, followed by a ley of six or seven years, a nine- or ten-year course in all. The grass ley, he said, was used for 'the breeding of heifers for the dairy, dairying, and the grazing of barren and aged cows; with a mixture of ewes and lambs for the butcher . . .' A feature of this system which Marshall found distinctly novel was the practice of preserving the grass seeds in the soil during the cropping cycle, the new turf being 'raised out of the ruins of the old'.[18] (Document VIII.)

Dr Kerridge calls this system 'up and down husbandry', and makes a great deal of its productiveness, claiming that it doubled the yield of arable crops and quadrupled the quantity of grass nutrients, so making possible heavier stocking while at the same time improving the structure of the soil. By 1660, he believes, it affected half the farmland. This statement, if taken literally, seems to overlook the existence of extensive areas of permanent pasture, the hill and vale districts devoted to sheep and corn husbandry, and the large proportion of arable land still cultivated in the open fields at this time—and Dr Kerridge seems to think that up and down husbandry was not found in open fields until the eighteenth century.[19] Nineteenth-century figures, compiled after the completion of enclosure of open fields, indicate that the system then affected only some 30 per cent of the total *arable* area, and of course a much smaller proportion of the total area of arable and permanent grass put together. In the eighteenth century, with much of the arable still under the old two crops and a fallow, and other large areas under some variant of the Norfolk system, it seems quite impossible that up and down husbandry could have extended as widely as has been suggested by Dr Kerridge.

---

[17] *Ibid.*, p. 197.
[18] W. Marshall, *Rural Economy of the Midland Counties*, I, pp. 184, 187; II, p. 42.
[19] Kerridge, *op. cit.*, pp. 96, 194, 205–8.

What is undoubted, however, is that improved farming involving the conversion of arable to grass and back to arable again, the introduction of crops providing more nutritious fodder, and the reduction of bare fallows, was expanding in a number of districts in the seventeenth and eighteenth centuries. An excessive importance was perhaps attached to the 'Norfolk system', and to its supposed chief protagonists. Lord Ernle, whose classic work *English Farming Past and Present* so long dominated our understanding of agricultural history, was principally responsible for spreading the idea that Turnip Townshend in the 1730's initiated the Norfolk rotation and revived the marling of light soils in Norfolk, thereby converting into fertile farmland his 'rush-grown marshes or sandy wastes where a few sheep starved and "two rabbits struggled for every blade of grass" '.[20] Ernle, no doubt, based his account on the suppositions of Nathaniel Kent and Arthur Young,[21] which have proved to be unfounded, though it may be that Young was correct in attributing the enclosure of much of the Raynham estate to Townshend (Document IX).

The famous Coke of Norfolk, equally, was said to have taken the Norfolk system into the sands of the north-western district of the county, introducing on his estate the long leases of twenty-one years containing strict husbandry covenants, the drilling of seeds, and use of oil-cake for feeding cattle, and bringing to light the value of sainfoin as a fodder crop.[22] All these 'innovations' were well-established practices in the area when Young made his *Southern Tour* in 1768, at which date Coke was still only fourteen and was to see another eight years before he succeeded to the Holkham estate. Indeed, a number of the practices formerly associated with Coke can be traced back to before the beginning of the eighteenth century. Yet, as Dr R. A. C. Parker has pointed out, Coke was still an important pioneer, if not for his supposed transformation of north-western Norfolk, his long leases, and the mythical ninefold increase in his rental. Leases of twenty-one years were in use on the Holkham estates in the time of the first Lord Leicester in the early decades of the century, although Coke's agent, Blaikie, did extend and improve the husbandry

[20] Lord Ernle, *English Farming Past and Present* (6th ed. 1961), p. 174.
[21] N. Kent, 'On Norfolk Turnips and Fallowing', *Annals of Agriculture*, XXII (1794), p. 24; A. Young, *ibid.*, V (1786), pp. 120–6.
[22] Ernle, *op. cit.*, pp. 217–20.

covenants contained in them. The practice of investing substantial sums in farm improvements was also of long standing, and both the large farms and the use of clovers and turnips in the rotations went back to well before Coke's time. Nevertheless, Coke played an important role in establishing the Southdown sheep in the area, replacing the old Norfolk sheep with 'backs like rabbits'. He introduced and championed the Devon breed of cattle, and improved the Suffolk breed of pigs by crossing them with pigs specially imported from Naples. In addition, he helped to spread the drilling of seeds, and took an interest in fertilizers, such as gypsum, bone manures and saltpetre. He greatly extended his home farm, and his 'sheep-shearings' or private shows enabled him to display his model farming and stimulate imitation of his methods. The sheep-shearings were also an opportunity of giving encouragement to his tenants, who mingled freely with the distinguished company, and Coke himself proudly pointed out their achievements.[23] Among those who made a frequent pilgrimage to Holkham was Arthur Young, and his account of Coke's own husbandry was published in Volume II of the *Annals of Agriculture* in 1784 (Document X).

It is more difficult to assess the role of Jethro Tull in the improved arable farming of the period. As is well known, Tull advocated the planting of seeds in rows or drills, with sufficient space between the rows for regularly hoeing, so keeping the soil friable and free of weeds (Document XI). This worked well enough for root crops, though Tull was in error in supposing that regular hoeing could obviate the need for manure. In any event, the idea of sowing in drills was far from new, having long been practised in the intensively cultivated smallholdings of the Low Countries for valuable horticultural crops as well as for coleseed, hops, madder, and tobacco.[24] Apart from ensuring a better crop, drilling also economized in expensive seed; on the other hand, however, it was time-consuming and costly in labour as compared with the traditional method of sowing broadcast. Tull also turned his attention to the production of a horse-hoe and a mechanical drill, designed to make a furrow and deposit the seed in one operation. Again, the idea of the mechanical drill was not novel,

---

[23] Parker, *op. cit.*, pp. 114–24, 152–61.
[24] Slicher Van Bath, *Agrarian History*, pp. 241–2.

for John Worlidge had produced his design for such a machine in 1669, some thirty years before Tull's invention. And Worlidge, in turn, had criticized the 'sowing engine' devised by Gabriel Plattes as early as 1600. Plattes's machine seemed too complicated for it to be adopted, though as Worlidge conceded, 'to ingenious men it is plain enough, but to others, this and everything else besides the plain Dunstable-road is intricate'.[25] However, Dr Fussell argues in a new study that Tull could claim to be the first to design *and construct* a *practical* working machine.[26] At all events, the use of the mechanical drill and the horse-hoe, as distinct from the hoeing by hand of hand-sown root crops, made little headway before the appearance of improved designs in the early decades of the nineteenth century, even in areas of progressive farming. Prior to this Marshall found that there was 'not perhaps a drill, a horse-hoe, or scarcely a horse-rake, in East Norfolk'.[27] The continuance of hand methods was not irrational. Machines were difficult to obtain, had serious technical weaknesses, and were particularly unsuitable for wet and heavy lands, as Young argues in Document XII.

More serious in an age of cheap labour than the deficiencies of machinery were the problems of soil fertility and the long-term viability of rotations employing clovers and turnips. The solution to the first depended on the eventual development of effective drainage, and suitable soil dressings and manures, and these matters are considered in subsequent sections; the second problem was perhaps the more immediately vital. Even in 1768, when Young made his first tour of Norfolk, difficulties arising from clover-sick soils and diseased turnips were already matters of concern. The turnip crop was unreliable, being easily damaged by rapid changes in weather, and was in any case restricted to districts of free-draining soils. An answer was found in diversifying the rotations, using sainfoin, lucerne (alfalfa) or other alternatives to clovers, and introducing the hardier Swedish turnip (swede) and mangel-wurzel in the place of turnips. Rotations perforce became more flexible, both in the crops employed and in

---

[25] John Worlidge, *A Compleat System of Husbandry and Gardening* (5th ed. 1716), p. 81.
[26] G. E. Fussell, *Jethro Tull: His Influence on Mechanized Agriculture* (Reading, 1973), p. 121.
[27] W. Marshall, *Rural Economy of Norfolk* (1787), I, p. 59.

the duration of the cycles. The emphasis might be shifted also to take advantage of market trends, now leaning towards a higher proportion of grain crops, then towards reliance on heavier stocking and fattening. As new sources of fertilizers were developed progressive cultivators invested in heavier inputs of soil dressings and manures, and as machinery improved in efficiency and availability so drills, hoes, rakes, rollers, cultivators and manure spreaders came into use. More effective drainage methods improved the condition of the claylands and made them easier to work. The grand objects of advanced cultivation were amelioration of the soil, more intensive cultivation, and maximization of yields. By the 1830's this 'high farming' was well in vogue in areas dominated by the capitalist occupiers of large arable holdings, and the most remarkable area of high input–high output arable production was to be found in the Scottish lowlands, particularly in the Lothians as described in 1855 by a visiting French expert, Léonce de Lavergne (Document XIII).

## 3. LIVESTOCK

Though most authorities of the time gave pre-eminence to the progress and problems of arable farming, grass and livestock had always been major features of British farming. Much of the west and north of the country, with bleak, wind-swept uplands and moist but milder valleys, were naturally suited to grazing, while even in the cornlands of the east and south sheep played an important role in crop production, and cattle were fattened in the rich midland pastures and the marshes of Lincolnshire, East Anglia, and Essex.

In the grasslands there had long been a strong tendency towards specialization, with some districts concentrating on dairying and others on rearing and fattening. The mountains of Wales and Scotland were primarily rearing areas, and the young store cattle were driven south and east to lowland pastures for fattening and the market. Rich grazing districts in Lancashire, Cheshire, and the west country were given over to dairying, although farmers everywhere kept a few cows to supply themselves and the immediate neighbourhood with milk. Until the railway age was well advanced milk and much of the butter had to be locally

produced. But long before then the specialist dairying districts
sold their cheeses at a distance and had a valuable sideline in pigs
fattening on the waste products. The famous English cheeses—
Cheshire, Cheddar, Gloucester, Stilton—were conveyed long distances to London and the major provincial ports and industrial
cities. Whether it was that dairying for the market was generally
the *forte* of small-scale family farmers, and appeared to offer little
scope for radical improvement, the agricultural writers usually
gave it little attention. William Marshall, however, noted its
importance in the west country, and has left us a valuable detailed
account of the dairies of north Wiltshire (Document XIV).

Much more space in farming treatises was reserved for the
current advances in breeding, mainly because these had an immediate impact on the period required for fattening and tended to
emphasize the peculiar characteristics which suited certain breeds
to particular environments. Before the deliberate creation of new
breeds each district had its own local varieties of livestock, and
farmers attached considerable pride and attention to such trivial
points as the colour of the skin or length of horn. These animals,
however, were often extraordinarily well suited to the purposes
required, whether manure, wool, meat, or milk, and through
natural adaptation were acclimatized to the local habitat. Through
the centuries there had been attempts to improve the native breeds
of cattle, especially by crossing with stock from the Low
Countries, and some landowners kept herds of improved cattle
carefully segregated in their parks. Cattle were brought in from
the Low Countries, Denmark, and the Channel Islands, and in
the later eighteenth century shorthorns were still known as the
'Dutch breed'. Merino sheep were also brought in from Spain for
trial by the royal farmer, George III. However, the general
standard of beasts, often grazed in common, and sired indiscri-
minately by whatever bull or ram was available, remained low.
Only about the beginning of the eighteenth century did specialist
breeders emerge on a scale sufficient to bring about a gradual but
radical improvement in existing stock, and to produce entirely
new breeds.

The most famous of these breeders was the celebrated Robert
Bakewell, though, as Marshall remarked, his area of the midlands
had 'for many years abounded with intelligent and spirited breed-

ers'.[28] Bakewell, born in 1725, exhibited an absorbing interest in farming matters as a young man, and by the 1770's had emerged as the country's best-known livestock expert. His achievements, however, were a natural extension of the work of earlier breeders, and his advances were complemented and improved upon by contemporaries and successors like the Culleys, the Collings, John Ellman, Jonas Webb, Thomas Bates, the Booths, Lord Somerville, and many others. The history of livestock improvements is indeed long and tangled, and in many respects obscure. New breeds were developed by a variety of hands, were popularized by leading fanciers, and then were superseded as further breeds appeared or needs changed. Much of the promotion of the new breeds was due to sponsorship by aristocratic landowners, and knowledge of them was spread by the private shows held by Coke of Holkham, the Duke of Bedford, the Smithfield Club founded in 1798, and from 1839, the shows of the Royal Society.[29]

Bakewell was undoubtedly a man of many talents. He travelled widely in pursuit of agricultural knowledge, and his reputation brought him a numerous and distinguished acquaintance (Document XV). His interests embraced not only cattle and sheep but also grassland irrigation, the design of ploughs, water transport and road-making, and the cultivation of cabbages. Some of his time was devoted to experiments in these matters, as well as the breeding of pigs and the shire horse. His pre-eminence rested primarily, however, on his achievements with the improved longhorn cattle and the Dishley or 'New Leicester' sheep.[30] As is now well known, both his cattle and his sheep had their defects: his new longhorns were deficient in milk and fecundity, and, like his sheep, fattened quickly but mainly with the result of producing masses of low-priced fat. He did succeed, however, in his main object of producing animals that could be made ready for market much more rapidly, and which had a high proportion of saleable flesh to the unsaleable portions of the carcass (Document XVI). Contemporaries were well aware of the deficiencies of his

---

[28] W. Marshall, *Rural Economy of the Midland Counties* (1790), I, pp. 270, 295, 381, 392.

[29] See the standard work on the subject by Robert Trow-Smith, *A History of British Livestock Husbandry* (1959).

[30] See H. Cecil Pawson, *Robert Bakewell: Pioneer Livestock Breeder* (1957).

animals, and his new breeds had many critics and opponents (Document XVII). There were, however, some noted advocates. George Culley, who played a large part in popularizing Bakewell's sheep in Northumberland, wrote that while Dishley mutton was not inviting 'to weak appetites', 'it finds a ready market amongst the manufacturing and laborious part of the community, whom necessity has taught to lay out their money to the best advantage, and who have found by experience, that a pound of bone is not so nutritive as a pound of mutton; and of course they always endeavour to buy that which has the least bone and most flesh'.[31]

The Dishley longhorns soon disappeared, and the Dishley breed of sheep, though more durable, was valuable mainly for crossing with, and improving, other breeds. More important, Bakewell's methods had a lasting influence on the course of livestock improvement, and their adoption by his followers led eventually to a great general advance in the quality of herds and flocks, and to the foundation of an important industry producing pedigree stock for home and overseas markets (Document XVIII). Bakewell showed that by breeding in and from selected stock it was possible to produce animals with desirable characteristics while breeding out undesirable ones. He overcame the existing prejudice against consistently uniting animals of the same breed (though the principle had been accepted for racehorses, game-cocks, and dogs, and as Culley noted, had not impaired the quality of the famous herd of wild cattle confined in Chillingham Park for centuries). Indeed Bakewell's doctrine and its results formed an early influence on the development of Darwin's ideas.[32]

Owing to differences in terrain, climate, and feed, and the varying needs of different types of farming, a wide variety of breeds remained essential. Local breeds might be improved by crossing with Dishley sheep or Collings' shorthorns but they could not be entirely superseded. Some sheep, for example, did well on the thin grass of exposed hillsides, while others made the most economical use of rich lowland pastures. These and many other considerations had to be taken into account. The Lincolnshire graziers for instance, clung to their local sheep,

---

[31] George Culley, *Observations on Live Stock* (4th ed. 1807), p. 108.
[32] Roger J. Wood, 'Robert Bakewell (1725–1795), Pioneer Animal Breeder, and his Influence on Charles Darwin', *Casopsis Moravského Musea*, LVIII (1973), p. 239.

which though excellent for wool were regarded as 'very tender', and produced a coarse-grained, big-boned type of mutton. The Lincolnshires, however, were well-adapted to the rich feeding of their native marshes, where they fattened well.

Progress in livestock depended not only on the efforts of the breeders and breed societies, but also on the work of a multitude of interested landlords and farmers who tried out different var- ieties and ascertained which were best suited to their local cir- cumstances. The old Norfolk sheep, for example, with their massive horns, were widely used for folding on roots, but were eventually replaced by the improved Southdowns, partly through the trials made by Coke of Norfolk, the Duke of Bedford, and other leading agriculturalists.

All this took time, and over a great area of the midlands the adoption of better breeds was held back by the survival of common grazing rights and a deficiency of closes for the segregation of improved stock. Disease spread easily among stock grazed in common, and periodically the herds and flocks of open- field farmers were decimated. Many enclosed pastures, however, were badly drained, and formed a potent source of loss. Veterin- ary knowledge was primitive, and though a variety of symptoms could be recognized, the precise causes remained unknown. The destructive sheep rot, for example, was known to be associated with wet pastures, but for a long time understanding of its causes did not go much beyond Plattes's theory that too much moisture dissolved the sheep's liver, so that the animal became 'replete with noxious and waterish humours; thereby causing death and destruction to the bodies thus distempered'.[33] And, as in human medicine, the anxious demand for remedies spawned local quacks and patent medicines (Document XIX). Again, breed improve- ment was costly. One of the rules of Bakewell's Dishley Society, founded in 1783, was that no member should let a tup for less than the then considerable sum of 10 guineas; Bakewell himself promised not to let his tups to anyone within a hundred miles at less than 50 guineas, and in 1789 his ram 'Two Pounder' alone brought in fees totalling 1,200 guineas. Charles Colling was able to get as much as 100 guineas for one of his shorthorn cows, and

---

[33] Gabriel Plattes, *Practicall Husbandry Improved: or A Discovery of infinite Treasure* (1656), pp. 64–5.

on retiring from business sold his famous bull 'Comet' for 1,000 guineas.[34]

Such figures show that specialist breeding could be profitable, and that there were farmers who set great store on the improvement of their stock. It seems likely, however, that as in arable farming, the gap in standards between the wealthy, progressive fatstock farmer and his poorer, less-enlightened colleague tended to widen, at least through the first half of the nineteenth century. In time, however, the old unsatisfactory breeds gradually disappeared or were revitalized by crossing with new strains. In sheep the Dishley longwools and the improved Southdown closewools were the greatest influence on new breeds. The Dishley made an important contribution to the development of other longwools, such as the Border Leicester and the Wensleydale, and abroad the Rambouillet and the Australian Corriedale. The new Southdowns of Ellman and Webb have remained pre-eminent among British sheep, and from them have derived the Hampshire, Oxford Downs, and Suffolks—the last originating from crosses between Southdowns and the old horned Norfolks, largely the result of experiments carried out by Arthur Young himself. Much of the later improvement of the shorthorn cattle, which early replaced Bakewell's longhorns in favour, went on in Scotland, associated with men like the Booths, Cruikshank of Sittyton, Barclay of Urry, and others. The shorthorns tended to divide into milk and beef types, though some have been good for both purposes. Native milk breeds were supplemented by Holsteins imported into Scotland, and by Guernseys (first miscalled Alderneys) brought into the south-west of England, where they were crossed with Devons. The Aberdeen-Angus, bred around Angus and Speyside, became world-famous as a great beef animal, and the Herefords developed in the nineteenth century as 'the best ranch cattle in the world through their hardihood, prepotency, and high economy in fodder; they swarm in their thousands over the plains of South America and South Africa'.[35]

[34]Pawson, *op. cit.*, p. 73; Robert Trow-Smith, *English Husbandry* (1951), pp. 157, 165.
[35]Trow-Smith, *op. cit.*, pp. 154, 158-9, 164-7.

## 4. THE PROBLEM OF FERTILITY

Jethro Tull's theorizing about the sources of plant food led him to discount the importance of manure, and his view may have been influenced by the peculiar mineral content of his land. For the generality of farmers the supply of manure remained a critical factor in maintaining the fertility of the soil and producing remunerative yields. The main source of manure was, and remained, the dung of horses, cattle, and sheep—hence the significance of the new roots and legumes and the various systems of convertible husbandry which made it possible to keep more animals and obtain a more favourable ratio of livestock to arable. Efficient collection and utilization of farmyard manure was a point of considerable interest among agricultural experts, though one still neglected by many farmers in the middle nineteenth century. Edward Laurence, writing in 1727, urged landlords to prevent their tenants from drying and burning their cow-dung as fuel; and he warned also that their 'using hog's dung instead of soap to wash their linen' should not be indulged to excess. William Marshall, too, was one of the later authorities who suggested methods of avoiding waste of valuable farmyard manure.[36] In the old common-field husbandry manuring was often effected by means of systematic folding of the village flocks on the arable, each section of the field receiving in turn an intensive dunging from closely-packed beasts.

To supplement the farm's own supply of dung many other materials were brought in. One widely used source of manure was the contents of privies and cesspools and the street and stable sweepings of the towns, and farmers within easy distance relied heavily on loads of 'town muck'. Human ordure was particularly recommended by Laurence for 'hot, dry, burning lands' where it made 'a great improvement'. It was said to be widely used in Kent, especially for pastures, and about 1830 a wagon-load of 90 bushels could be purchased in London for 15s. Farmers in Essex had it brought out by the Thames or canal, at a total cost, including spreading, of £2 13s to £3 3s per acre; and it was

---

[36] E. Laurence, *The Duty and Office of a Land Steward* (2nd ed. 1731), p. 45; W. Marshall, *On the Landed Property of England* (1804), pp. 165–8.

shipped to farmers farther afield as ballast in vessels sailing home
from London without sufficient cargo. It was often mixed with
other dungs or ditch earth 'to make it commodious for carriage',
and there was at one period a large concern in London which
processed it with lime and exported it in powder form to the
colonies, where market-gardeners applied it as a top-dressing.[37]
Young relates how the potato-growers of Lewisham bought their
supplies of London muck from the barges at Deptford. He found
it surprising that farmers near towns sometimes neglected this
source of manure, although some enterprising cultivators made
special arrangements for the muck to be brought out by the carts
and barges of night-soil contractors. Caird noted an instance of
the purchase of as much as 2,000 tons of town manure for a farm
of 156 acres situated near Manchester, while the Duke of Portland
watered his meadows in Clipstone Park with a stream 'charged
with the whole sewerage' of the town of Mansfield.[38]

Farmers also made use of industrial waste materials—
pulverized slag from ironworks, soot, coal ashes (thought to be
valuable for encouraging wild trefoil), soap ashes from the soap
boilers, waste brine from salt pans, waste bark from tanneries,
horn and bone left over by cutlers, fellmongers' poake or waste,
and the shoddy of the textile centres. Rags, cut up small and
spread at 24 bushels to the acre, were considered good for chalky
soils, and were bought by the cart-load in London at 2s or 2s 6d a
hundredweight, together with shreds of leather, old shoes, hats,
and stockings.[39] Farmers near the coast carted sand from the
seashore to lay on unyielding clays, and ploughed in seaweed
thrown up by gales, either raw or burnt and composted. Worlidge, writing in the later seventeenth century, mentioned all these
aids to cultivation, and also 'fish garbage', pigeons' dung, cows'
urine, hair, 'wool-nappings', fruit pulp, slurry or waste from coal
mines, blood, sawdust, and 'snail-cod or snag-greet'—mud
obtained from rivers 'full of eyes and wrinkles and little shells',
and so rich that one load went as far as three of the best horse or

---

[37] Laurence, *op. cit.*, p. 281; Society for Diffusion of Useful Knowledge,
*British Husbandry; Exhibiting the Farming Practice in Various Parts of the
United Kingdom* (1834), I, pp. 268–9.

[38] A. Young, *Southern Tour* (3rd ed. 1772), p. 94; J. Caird, *English
Agriculture in 1850–51* (1852), pp. 46, 270.

[39] Edward Lisle, *Observations in Husbandry* (2nd ed. 1757), I, p. 51.

cow dung, and farmers sent as far as twenty miles to get it. Not to be forgotten, too, was the 'denshiring' or paring and burning of turf, the burning of stubbles, as also of small wood, bushes, furze, broom, and fern.[40] He did not, however, mention oil-cake, made from the crushed seed of coleseed or rape, a valuable fodder crop which was widely grown from the middle seventeenth century and which could be ploughed in as a soil dressing.

More often used were lime and marl. Both were soil dressings of ancient origin whose popularity increased and waned over the centuries. As coal became more widely available for use in the lime-kilns, farmers in limestone country turned increasingly to lime after 1650.[41] By about 1750 the leases of large farms often required the tenant to lime his land periodically, though this injunction followed what had clearly become established practice; lime continued to be applied to acid soils in the nineteenth century, but its use declined as artificial manures came to be treated as substitutes.[42] Laurence advised it especially for heaths and moors, and in 1850 Caird reported that lime was considered essential for clay soils in Holderness; but at that date marling was said to be almost abandoned in Staffordshire, where it had been commonplace in Young's time.[43] It had, perhaps, been overdone, making light soils too tenacious and awkward to work; and it was certainly expensive, the cost depending on the distance it had to be fetched and the number of loads applied to an acre: in Norfolk about 1768 a dressing of a hundred loads per acre cost between £250 and £300, a great sum at that time.[44] This outlay could only be justified when the effects were clearly beneficial and of long duration, but much of the marling was done by trial and error, and was not always advantageous. There were in fact several different kinds of marl, including stone or slate marls, the clay sort used to give body to thin soils and reduce their porous nature, and the chalk which was applied to clays. In Essex Young remarked on the heavy traffic of wagons bringing home chalk

---

[40] Worlidge, *op. cit.*, pp. 102–21.

[41] Kerridge, *op. cit.*, pp. 248–9.

[42] M. A. Havinden, 'Lime as a Means of Agricultural Improvement: the Devon Example', in C. W. Chalkin and M. A. Havinden (eds.), *Rural Change and Urban Growth* (1974), pp. 127–8.

[43] Laurence, *op. cit.*, pp. 255–6; Caird, *op. cit.*, pp. 229, 303.

[44] A. Young, *Southern Tour* (1st. ed. 1768), p. 23.

from Grays and Purfleet, or shipped across the Thames from north Kent, a traffic which made the road from Tilbury to Billericay almost impassable.[45] Already by the end of the sixteenth century areas of Lancashire and Cheshire had been sated with an excess of marl, showing a consequent loss of fertility. Marling continued where it remained beneficial, especially on sandy soils, but increasingly it gave way to lime and other manures.[46]

Water meadows were widely used in some districts for the purpose of producing an early bite of lush grass, so filling the 'hungry gap' in early spring and enabling more stock to be kept over winter. The idea was to direct a shallow flow of silt-laden water from a stream over the meadow during the winter by a system of specially-constructed sluices and channels. The costs of installation and repair were considerable, however, and the dampness of the meadow might prove conducive to rot in sheep. In due course the adoption of roots in rotations provided a more convenient and cheaper alternative, though water meadows could still be found in the middle nineteenth century; so too could watering with diluted sewage conveyed by pipes, as an American visitor remarked (Document XX).

Guano, the dried droppings of seabirds found in quantity along the coast of Peru and elsewhere, began to be imported in 1835, but the quantities remained small until the 1840's. About the same time bones, for grinding into bonemeal, began to be imported in quantity. Net imports of guano, a very rich, and at first an expensive manure, were between 139,000 and 232,000 tons a year in the 1850's and 1860's but fell sharply from the later 1870's. The advent of cheaper supplies was of little advantage to farmers, since much of the cheaper guano was adulterated and less valuable as a fertilizer. Imports of bones to supplement home supplies rose substantially in the later 1830's and early 1840's, and reached a peak of over 86,000 tons a year in the late 'sixties and early 'seventies, when imports were more than double the amounts available at home. By the 1860's, too, imports of nitrates were rising, and the total supply of superphosphate was over 200,000 tons. Superphosphate, the first 'artificial' or chemical fertilizer, was introduced on a commercial scale in the 1840's, and for some

---

[45] *Ibid.*, p. 72.
[46] Kerridge, *op. cit.*, pp. 247-8.

twenty years was based on the chemical treatment of coprolites, fossilized dung and bones mined in Cambridgeshire and Hertfordshire. From the 1860's the home-produced coprolites were supplemented, and eventually replaced, by imports of cheaper phosphate rock. By 1880 the quantity of bone manure, guano, superphosphate, imported nitrates and other imported manures were sufficient to treat some 17 million acres—an area roughly equivalent to the whole of the arable land or half of the total cultivated acreage.[47]

The development of superphosphate owed much to the work of two men, the Hertfordshire squire, Sir John Bennet Lawes, who inherited his Rothamsted estate in 1834, and his assistant J. H. Gilbert, a student of the eminent chemist, Justus von Liebig. From 1835 Lawes and Gilbert carried out scientific field trials of the effects of fertilizers on various crops, and they also measured the nutritive value of animal foods. Their results brought them to challenge the 'mineral theory' of Liebig, and they showed as erroneous his belief that the supply of minerals alone governed the growth of plants, and his view that mineral fertilizers should be applied in the same ratio as the minerals appeared in the ash of the plant (Document XXI). The English pioneers' first factory for the manufacture of superphosphate was established at Deptford in 1842, and larger works were subsequently developed at Barking Creek and Millwall. The business was sold in 1872 for £300,000.

The revolution in fertilizers solved the age-old problem of inadequacy of farm manure. Nonetheless, the great majority of farmers who did not follow the learned discussions which filled the pages of the *Journal of the Royal Agricultural Society*, had no scientific gauge by which to judge which manures, and in what quantities, were appropriate for their lands. Application of fertilizers was still very largely a matter of trial and error, and the looked-for gains in corn yields and richer pastures did not always materialize. One beneficial effect, however, was that the use of purchased manures led to cleaner farming and a greater concern with effective drainage. Farmers who had paid £10 a ton for fertilizers, as Ernle remarked, were unwilling to waste it on badly-drained land or in growing weeds. In consequence there

---

followed a more extensive adoption of under-drainage, the drill, and the hoe.[48] New manures, new styles of drainage, and new forms of implements and machinery were thus inter-connected, paralleling the combination on pasture land of costly livestock, heavy purchases of imported cattle food, and better housing for stock. The full advantage of one advance could not be gained without a corresponding outlay on complementary improvements. Furthermore, farmers who were spending large sums on pedigree stock, model dairies and bullock pens, fertilizers, feedstuffs, and machinery wanted as skilled and intelligent a labour force as they could get. As a result, those landowners who went in for building model cottages for labourers had as one of their motives the attraction of a superior class of labourer who would satisfy the superior class of farm tenant.

## 5. THE AGE OF MACHINERY

Advances in stock, fertilizers, and drainage emphasized the need for improved farm tools and machinery. Advertising in local newspapers and the salesmanship of agents of the specialist manufacturers brought new designs of machinery to farmers' notice. Also important were the shows of the agricultural societies, in which trials of new machines came to play a prominent part. When the Royal Agricultural Society was founded in 1839 the mechanical department was thought to be of little importance. In the space of a few years, however, this situation was changed out of all recognition. Only 23 implements were exhibited at the Society's first show; but five years later, in 1844, the number rose to 948. At the Gloucester show in 1853 as many as 2,000 implements and machines were on display.

To some extent the need created the supply. But the supply itself was facilitated by the industrial revolution, specifically the production of cheap iron, and subsequently cheap steel, and the introduction of factory methods of production of improved designs, offering cheaper, more efficient, and more durable machines and implements. As long as implements and machines were mainly available only from local craftsmen who used traditional

---

[48] Ernle, *op. cit.*, p. 370.

designs and materials, progress was bound to be slow. Gabriel Plattes showed an appreciation of this difficulty in connection with his new design of drill: 'though the making of this engine be somewhat chargeable and troublesome, yet if skillful men first broke the ice, then it will be common, and the most profitable invention that ever was found out'.[49] Mass production, however, was possible only to a limited extent. Farming conditions differed so greatly as to demand a wide range of implements of varying design; moreover, many farmers were conservative and tended to prefer implements which were based on the traditional models of the area. Thus in 1840 the famous firm of Ransome produced as many as eighty-six different designs of plough to suit local needs.

Before the nineteenth century the changes in implements, other than ploughs, proceeded only slowly. There was already much interest in improved ploughs, and enthusiasm was stimulated by numerous books on the subject, including James Small's *Treatise on Ploughs and Wheeled Carriages* (1784). For the most part, however, traditional designs held sway. The Rotherham plough, based on Dutch designs and patented in England as early as 1730, came into favour only towards the end of the century, and then mainly in the north and east (Document XXII). Various new designs were offered, too, for carts and wagons, and for harrows, rollers, and cultivators. From 1786 Andrew Meikle's threshing machine—the first effective one—began to be adopted. Threshing machines could be operated by hand, by horses, and eventually by steam, and their popularity was enhanced by labour shortages during the Napoleonic Wars. They were most readily adopted in areas of large-scale arable farming and where the competition of industrial employment had driven up farm wages, as in Scotland and the north-east of England (Document XXIII). Other barn machinery included winnowers (often attached to threshing machines), bean-mills, chaff-cutters, root-slicers, and cake-crushers used for preparing cattle food. Experimental horse-drawn reapers, mainly prototypes of various patterns, appeared in the early decades of the nineteenth century. The 1812 design of John Common, a Northumberland millwright, became the basis of the famous McCormick reaper, which after achieving success on the American prairies was exhibited to wide acclaim at the Great

---

[49] Plattes, *op. cit.*, p. 57.

Exhibition of 1851 (Document XXIII). Another design, produced in 1826 by the Reverend Patrick Bell, was improved and reintroduced as the 'Beverley Reaper' in 1853.

Local conditions—the size of the farms, nature of the farming, the cost and availability of labour, and the wealth and outlook of the farmers—might all be influential in the adoption of new implements and machines. The threshing machine was first adopted in Scotland, and by 1815 was commonplace there and in north-eastern England. It was not general in the south, however, until after 1840, when the labourers' revolt of 1830 was fading from memory, and when the large supplies of cheap farm labour were being reduced by migration and the growth of alternative employments. A recent study of Oxfordshire newspaper advertisements of those farm sales listing implements has shown some remarkable differences in the dates when some implements were widely in use in the county. The mention of drills, for instance, rose steadily from the 1820's until by about the 1870's about half of the sales notices included them. Horse-drawn hoes and rakes, however, were not at all numerous in the notices until the 1850's and 1860's, with rakes lagging behind hoes. Reapers and mowing machines do not appear until about 1860, and became common only in the 1870's.[50]

It is not to be expected that these findings for Oxfordshire would necessarily hold for other areas: local conditions varied too widely. Apart from farm sales and labour costs, the date of adoption was determined in part by availability and by the existence of skilled manpower for installation and repair of complicated machinery—a factor which influenced the adoption of threshing machines. However, many of the improved implements were reasonably cheap, and their availability improved as large-scale producers like Ransome and Garrett came into being, and small local manufacturers began to act more as agents for the larger companies. In 1849 ploughs cost about four or five pounds, harrows about the same, horse-rakes and horse-hoes began at a few pounds more, and drills were priced at between £20 and £50.[51] Twelve years earlier, in 1837, W. Drummond & Sons of

---

[50] J. R. Walton, *A Study in the Diffusion of Agricultural Machinery in the Nineteenth Century* (Oxford School of Geography Research Paper No. 5, 1973), pp. 8–10.

[51] *Journal Royal Agricultural Society of England*, X (1849), pp. 535–6.

Stirling offered Bell's reaping machine for £45, and Smith's reaper for £50. More important than price was efficiency and reliability. The early threshing machines had a bad reputation for breaking down, and the small ones were not sufficiently powerful to give a good result or to have winnowers and rakes attached to them. Moreover, it was necessary to build or adapt a suitable shelter for the machine, and farmers who lacked the security of a long lease may have been deterred from making the investment. However, the appearance of portable models overcame this objection, though there were still many smaller grain producers who felt the outlay on a machine unjustified. At mid-century the greater part of the British corn crop was still threshed by the flail. By 1849, however, portable steam engines could be easily attached to the thresher, and after that date, with hiring of machines more popular than purchase, powered threshing spread rapidly. In the late 1850's four-horse portables with an output of 160–180 bushels a day—a rate thirty times greater than a single man with a hand flail—could be bought for as little as £45–50, and the less efficient two-horse portables for only £30.[52]

The cost and availability of labour was probably the prime factor in the early adoption of powered threshing in northern areas and the much more sluggish response evident in the south. The threshing machine offered more advantages than mere economy of labour. It 'may be considered', said Marshall, 'as the most valuable discovery in machines of agriculture which has been made for centuries past'.[53] Powered threshing enabled farmers to catch a sudden upswing in prices, and made it possible to utilize spare labour when bad weather brought other operations to a standstill. On the other hand, the machine was hard on horses, and was a source of numerous accidents to the labourers. As long as male labour was cheap and plentiful, as it was in East Anglia and the south down to about mid-century, the advantages of the thresher were not very great, particularly when it is remembered that the machine itself required several hands for its operation, and the labour that was saved might have to be employed on unremunerative odd jobs. It has also been argued that the lower

---

[52] See E. J. T. Collins, 'The Diffusion of the Threshing Machine in Britain 1790–1880', *Tools and Tillage*, II, 1(1972), pp. 19–21, 25.

[53] Marshall, *On Landed Property*, p. 163n.

value of the machine to southern farmers led them to seek cheaper and less efficient designs, with unsatisfactory consequences in regard to performance and reliability.[54] A further deterrent in the areas of cheap labour was the high poor rates. Threshing with the flail was a major source of winter employment, and if adoption of machinery meant more hands on the parish and higher poor rates, this must have weighed in the scales against the machine. Some farmers deliberately kept to the old methods in order to avoid throwing their regular men upon the mercy of the parish.[55] Another factor was the belief that hand threshing produced a better result, the maltsters preferring hand-threshed barley—as, much later, the hop producers preferred hand-picked hops and resisted the onset of the hop-picking machine.

More generally, field machines like drills, horse-hoes, cultivators, hay-tedders, and reapers could only be used to best advantage on wide stretches of well-drained, unencumbered and fairly level ground. The complex of small fields and closes which had been created in the past by a drawn-out process of piecemeal enclosure had to be modified, if not removed entirely. Farmers who wanted to use machinery set about grubbing up hedgerows, taking down trees, levelling steep banks, filling ditches, diverting streams and drainage cuts, and removing large stones from the soil by dint of gang labour. Such changes were particularly vital for the adoption of steam ploughing, which some mechanically-minded farmers were trying out in the middle nineteenth century. Direct-traction locomotive ploughs were invented but made little headway, those engines having the necessary power being too heavy for cultivated ground. However, by the 1850's the use of traction engines to haul ploughs by means of wire ropes was becoming practicable, and in 1856 John Fowler, the well-known agricultural engineer, patented his system of ploughing with two traction engines, one on each side of the field. The cost of the equipment, at prices beginning at several hundred pounds, meant that most steam cultivation came to be carried out by contractors, and the use of steam power in the fields remained exceptional. In 1866-7 a mere 200,000 acres—under 2 per cent of the arable

---

[54] See Stuart Macdonald, 'The Progress of the Early Threshing Machines', *Agricultural History Review*, XXIII, 1 (1975), p. 75.

[55] Caird, *op. cit.*, p. 84.

acreage—were steam tilled, and at the height of steam cultivation during the First World War there were only about 450 twin-engine hauling sets in England.[56]

The horse-drawn reaper, especially when it was later equipped to bind the sheaves automatically, made greater progress after mid-century, but its adoption was still slow. Again, it required suitably level, unbroken ground and uncluttered fields for efficient operation, and a recent writer has argued that a certain 'threshold size' of corn acreage was necessary for its profitable use. This 'threshold' or minimum acreage varied with the rent paid and with the cost of adapting the fields to machine operations, but had to be sufficient to meet these outlays as well as the interest and amortization costs of introducing a reaper.[57] However, the theory, though expressed in sophisticated calculations, fails to take account of the numerous technical weaknesses of the earlier machines, their inadequacy on wet soils and in dealing with heavy or laid crops, and the obstacle offered by a shortage of skilled men capable of maintaining and repairing the machines. A further and more serious weakness for the theory arises from the possibility that the cost of mechanical reaping might be reduced by the hiring of machines from contractors or borrowing from other farmers, as a contemporary reference suggests was sometimes the case; hiring and borrowing of reapers depended on the crops not ripening all at the same time, but if these practices were so widespread in England as in the middle west of America, they make the threshold concept invalid.[58]

One of the most uncertain influences in the adoption of machinery as a whole is the question of labour substitution. In the first place, it must be remembered that the machines themselves often required a considerable labour force. McCormick's reaper in its earlier designs, for instance, required a dozen hands to follow the

---

[56] Harold Bonnett, *Saga of the Steam Plough* (1965), pp. 38, 142; Clark C. Spence, *God Speed the Plough* (Urbana, 1960), pp. 106, 118–19.

[57] Paul A. David, 'The Landscape and the Machine: technical interrelatedness, land tenure and the mechanization of the corn harvest in Victorian Britain' in Donald N. McCloskey (ed.), *Essays on a Mature Economy: Britain after 1840* (1971), pp. 157, 168–9.

[58] Alan L. Olmstead, 'The Mechanization of Reaping and Mowing in American Agriculture 1833–1870', published in the *Journal of Economic History* XXXV, 2 (1975); Professor Olmstead mentions a reference to the hiring of reapers in the *Journal of the Royal Agricultural Society*, XX (1861), p. 127.

machine and to quickly gather, tie, and stook the cut corn out of
the way of its return path across the field. Compared with the
revolutionary machinery applied to textile production the
advances in farm machinery were not spectacularly labour-saving.
Philip Pusey, writing in the *Journal of the Royal Agricultural
Society* in 1851, recognized this, but pointed out that farm
machinery, nevertheless, was relatively much cheaper and more
easily applied to production[59] (Document XXV). The introduction of the machines, however, involved a substitution of
relatively expensive horsepower for cheap manpower, and horses
required hands to tend and feed them. Furthermore, the use of
machines like drills, horse-hoes, horse-rakes, manure spreaders,
and cultivators may have increased, on balance, the total labour
demands by increasing the number of operations per crop, so that
the main effect of the machinery was to raise the standard of the
crop rather than dispense with labour. The preparations needed
for the efficient use of machinery, including the provision of
special buildings and workshops, and in the fields under-drainage,
levelling, clearing, and hedge-straightening, were all labour-
intensive.

In the southern half of the country labour remained cheap
through the whole of the first half of the nineteenth century, and
wages began to show a significant upward trend only from the
1860's onwards. Indeed, it is arguable whether, for southern
farmers at least, economy of labour was an important motive in
the adoption of machinery. Even in the midlands and the north,
where the competition of non-agricultural employments drove up
farm wages, the rise between the 1820's and the 1860's was
generally quite small, amounting to an addition of only from 9d to
2s 3d a week, or an increase of between 6 and 22 per cent.[60]
Where farm servants were still engaged by the year, as was the
case in northern counties, and in parts of the south, as in Dorset,
they still had to be found work to do when threshing machines,
for instance, reduced winter work with the flail. Since many farm
servants were engaged primarily to look after the livestock, the
increased use of horses may well have helped to maintain or even

---

[59] *J.R.A.S.E.*, XII (1851), pp. 642–3.
[60] C. S. Orwin and B. I. Felton, 'A Century of Wages and Earnings in
Agriculture', *J.R.A.S.E.*, XCII (1931), pp. 3, 17.

increase year-round employment, while the so-called day-labourers were often regularly employed through the year. Caird noted that it was common in areas of surplus labour for the spare hands to be divided among the ratepayers according to the size of their farms, so directly discouraging the use of machinery.[61] Perhaps the main effect of machinery was to reduce somewhat the seasonal demand for the assistance of women and children and gangs of itinerant harvest workers. The national statistics suggest that the number of male workers in agriculture fell only slowly in the thirty years from 1851 to 1881, by 271,000 or 15 per cent; the numbers of females fell much more drastically, by 113,000 or almost 50 per cent. In any event, the fall in the labour force was not due solely to machinery, but much more to the effects of widening horizons among the farmworkers and the impact of railways and steamships on movement to the cities and emigration to new lands. Improved living standards, and the Education Acts after 1870, also tended to reduce the employment of women and children, though this may have been offset to some extent by the expansion of vegetable-growing, market-gardening, and fruit production on a commercial scale, with consequent demands for part-time labour over a large period of the year. In fact farmers may have been induced to resort to machinery more because of a growing difficulty in obtaining labour than because of its cost, though the railways helped the Kentish hop-growers to continue picking by hand with the aid of families from London's East End.

The main advantage of machinery, then, was probably in saving time rather than labour. Field machinery enabled farmers to catch the right weather and soil conditions for cultivating, sowing, and harvesting, while barn machinery enabled them to take advantage of peak prices and sudden market fluctuations. With machinery some of the risks inherent in farming, especially weather losses, could be reduced, and there was a further gain in securing the best economy in seeds and expensive fertilizers.

Also significant was the improvement in the efficiency of hand implements which occurred in the first half of the century, a development recently brought to notice by Dr E. J. T. Collins. Varying greatly from region to region as crop and labour-supply conditions differed, hand implements of improved design and

---

[61] Caird, *op. cit.*, p. 515.

materials were introduced to speed up the heavy work of harvesting. Mowing with the scythe or bagging with the hook
gradually replaced the sickle, and this change in technology,
which began in the later eighteenth century, was most evident
between 1835 and 1870. The development was influenced by the
rise in harvest wages and short-term shortages of harvest labour
which occurred in some areas, and in the long run was encouraged by the slow decline in the permanent farm labour force
after 1850, the reduced supply of female labour, and the decline of
migratory harvesting gangs. Improved hand implements were yet
another factor in the slow progress of mechanical reaping. As late
as 1870 possibly as much as three-fourths of the corn harvest was
still cut by hand.[62]

## 6. THE ADVANCE OF DRAINAGE

Until recent years the importance of drainage in the nineteenth
century has been neglected by historians. Yet it has been suggested that the total sum expended on under-drainage and associated improvements to farm buildings in the thirty years after
1846 (when drainage costs were lowered by improved techniques)
may have amounted to some £24 million;[63] at between £4 and £8
an acre the money poured into drainage was certainly comparable
with that expended on the consolidation and fencing of former
common lands and wastes in the era of parliamentary enclosure.
Unlike enclosure, however, the drainage schemes of the middle
nineteenth century were financed in part by cheap government
loans, those loans provided after 1846 representing some degree of
compensation to the landed interest for the loss of protection.
Drainage was encouraged, too, by the invention of means for
making cheap pipes and tiles right on the farms, and by the
enthusiasm of landlords and their agents and the tenants, who saw
effective drainage as the basic prerequisite for cheaper, efficient,
and more productive cultivation. Yet, unlike enclosure again,
many of the drainage schemes never paid, either because the work

[62] E. J. T. Collins, 'Harvest Technology and Labour Supply in Britain
1790–1870', *Economic History Review* (2nd series), XXII, 3 (1969), pp. 453–73.
[63] J. H. Clapham, *Economic History of Modern Britain*, II (1932), p. 271.

was badly done, or because rents failed to rise sufficiently to compensate for the outlay. This was especially the case where large sums were sunk in improving arable land just before the big fall in grain prices in the 1870's.[64]

The extent to which drainage enabled the claylands to be adapted to more productive farming has been the subject of a recent controversy. On the one hand it is argued that on the heavy clays of the south and east traditional grain rotations persisted, even after enclosure: without adequate drainage fodder crops could not be grown on these soils, while a lengthy period was required for production of a good sward, and farmers were not in a position to bear the costs of creating and stocking grass farms. In the clays of the north and west, however, drainage enabled arable to be converted in the 1850's and 1860's to intensive grassland husbandry, using artificial fertilizers and supplementing hay with oil-cake. Contrary views are urged, on the other hand, to the effect that drainage provided negligible results in improving the claylands, and that all that occurred was a series of adaptations to increased livestock production, encouraged by the current market trends of rising livestock prices.[65] A subsequent intervention in the debate pointed out that the claylands should not be treated as one problem; they varied in adaptability, and the light clays could be more readily converted to grass when drained, especially when supported by a heavy rainfall, as in the north and west.[66] To a considerable extent the dispute has turned on the question of how much land was effectively drained, as well as the effects of drainage on production; and it has been argued that, despite the wide variety of contemporary estimates, it may be concluded that as much as 27–28 per cent of the land worth the cost of draining had been treated by 1880.[67] The precise figure remains uncertain,

---

[64] See F. M. L. Thompson, *English Landed Society in the Nineteenth Century* (1963), pp. 248–53.

[65] See R. W. Sturgess, 'The Agricultural Revolution on the English Clays', *Agricultural History Review*, XIV, 2 (1966), pp. 104–21; 'The Agricultural Revolution on the English Clays: a Rejoinder', *ibid.*, XV, 2 (1967), pp. 82–7; E. J. T. Collins and E. L. Jones, 'Sectoral Advance in English Agriculture 1850–80', *ibid.*, pp. 65–81.

[66] E. H. Wetham, 'Sectoral Advance in English Agriculture, 1850–1880: a Summary', *Agricultural History Review*, XVI, 1 (1968), p. 47.

[67] A. D. M. Phillips, 'Underdraining and the English Claylands, 1850–80: a Review', *ibid.*, XVII, 1 (1969), p. 46.

but at all events large sums were invested in drainage, and contemporary opinion leaves no doubt that it was considered a major, and indeed essential, advance in adapting land use and improving the productivity of ill-drained soils.

Drainage was not, of course, a new problem in the nineteenth century. From time immemorial a degree of surface drainage had been achieved by the ridges and furrows simply created in the course of ploughing with a fixed mouldboard. Ridge and furrow helped sloping land to shed some of its moisture, but on flat and low-lying ground only the ridges might stay dry. There were various attempts at under-drainage, especially in Essex, which was said to be also the home of the earliest drainage ploughs.[68] Eighteenth-century under-drains consisted merely of open trenches on pasture land, or of closed trenches, filled loosely with stones, boughs, bracken and furze with the soil replaced above, on arable land. The Essex drains were 2 feet deep, wedge-shaped, and filled with branches, twisted straw or stones; in Norfolk pits or soakaways were dug at intervals and filled with boughs at a cost of 33s an acre.[69]

Towards the end of the eighteenth century the importance of effective under-drainage was increasingly recognized and discussed. William Marshall devoted eighty pages to the subject in his treatise on landed property, and mentioned mole ploughs making small channels a foot or more below the surface as a recent innovation.[70] Hollow drains, kept free of soil by arches of stone slabs, were expensive to construct, though the replacement of stone by arched clay tiles resting on flat soles reduced the cost as improved machines were produced for making the tiles in quantity. Drainage specialists, each advocating his own peculiar set of practices, began to acquire a wide reputation. Joseph Elkington in 1764 proposed the making of borings or small wells into the lower subsoil so as to enable water to pass through an impervious stratum to a porous one. His method, however, was applicable principally to wetness arising from underground springs, while the larger problem was that of leading off an excess of rainwater. This became the special province of an enterprising

---

[68] G. E. Fussell, *The Farmer's Tools* (1952), pp. 29–30.
[69] W. Marshall, *Rural Economy of Norfolk*, II (1787), pp. 2–3.
[70] Marshall, *On Landed Property*, pp. 30–109.

Scotsman, James Smith of Deanston farm, whose system consisted of constructing parallel hollow field drains 30 inches deep and 21 feet apart. These led the water into receiving drains 6 inches deeper, and so on to the main drains sunk at 4 feet. The cost of his method, using tiles, flagstones or broken stone, varied with differing conditions from £2 8s 6d to £9 10s per acre. He also designed his own plough for breaking up the subsoil and improving the permeability of the land.[71] Josiah Parkes began his career as an agricultural engineer just prior to the appearance of Smith's pamphlet in 1831. His speciality was the drainage of bogs, and his work on the infamous Chat Moss between Manchester and Liverpool led him to propose deep drains at 4 or 5 feet as more effective than Smith's shallower system.

By this time large sums were being expended on drainage, and the precise methods of drainage best adopted had become a highly controversial subject. In addition to the appearance in the 1840's of many improved tile-making machines there were also numerous mole, subsoil, or drainage ploughs of various new designs. In 1845 Thomas Scragg won the Royal Society's award for a mobile pipe-making machine, and six years later Fowler's drainage apparatus, which in one operation laid a string of drain pipes in the hollow made by a mole plough, attracted almost as much attention as did the American reapers of McCormick and Hussey (Document XXVI). The main drawback of the drainage ploughs was the enormous power required to draw them, and though at the 1854 show a portable steam engine was added to wind the capstan of Fowler's mole drain and pipe-laying plough, such expensive implements never caught on. The cost and weight of the apparatus made them more suitable for contractor's operations, and few farmers wished to acquire them.

The fall in prices in the 1870's and the consequent decline of arable farming greatly reduced the progress of drainage. In the last quarter of the century even improved arable farming could seldom be made to pay: landlords were unwilling to throw good money after bad, and in any case neither they nor their tenants had the resources to spare for it. Clays still undrained tumbled down to grass, and frugal dairy farmers were able to make some

---

[71] James Smith, *Remarks on Thorough Draining and Deep Ploughing* (4th ed. 1838).

kind of a living from them after their arable predecessors had
given up, emigrated, or bankrupted. Thus the severe change in
the economic climate brought this 'greatest of all nineteenth-
century improvements' to an end.


## 7. LABOUR

Almost all the farming innovations of the eighteenth century were
labour-intensive, and the subsequent introduction of machinery
was not, as we have seen, greatly effective in economizing in
manpower. As noted above, the agricultural labour force of Great
Britain continued to grow until the 1850's, and at the census of
1851 absorbed 1,788,000 males and 229,000 females.

Farm labour, other than members of the farmer's family, was
generally distinguished by two characteristics: dependence on
wages, and little or no access to land (except for rented cow-
pastures, allotments, potato patches, and cottage gardens). Farmworkers varied considerably, however, in regard to conditions of
employment. The farm servants consisted of the regular hands
required for continuous tasks, such as care of livestock and the
dairy. They were normally hired and paid by the year, and
received their board and lodging gratis. In the later eighteenth
century there was a tendency, especially noticeable in southern
England, for the male farm servants to be replaced by annually-
paid or weekly-paid men housed in cottages instead of in the
farmhouse. In the north, however, they continued to live with the
farmer in the traditional way, and some were still doing so at the
beginning of the present century. The day labourers, the largest
category of farmworkers, were cottagers paid either at day rates or
at piece rates for particular tasks. In southern England in the
early decades of the nineteenth century they tended to be
wretchedly paid, and might be subject to much unemployment in
winter. On the other hand they were not always very insecure, for
though nominally hired by the day they might find regular
employment with one farmer for a period of years. A third
category consisted of highly skilled specialist workers, such as
men experienced in hedging, thatching, and draining, who were
called on by farmers as required; they worked over a considerable
area, often doing a little higgling or dealing on the side. Lastly, a

reserve of casual labour was provided by itinerant harvest gangs, the wives and children of day labourers, and gangs of women and children hired for particular operations such as lifting potatoes, weeding, or clearing ground of stones. The availability of the different types of labour, their rates of pay, and working conditions, all varied considerably from one area to another.

Very little attention was paid in our period to the education and training of farmworkers. The children might pick up the rudiments of education at a village charity or Sunday school, but their skills and knowledge of husbandry were acquired at home or on the farm. Employment began at an early age, and although there was a form of apprenticeship it seems to have been confined to pauper children and involved little formal training or instruction (Document XXVII). Farm labourers were not expected to show intelligence or initiative, and they were widely criticized for their slow pace of work, their prejudice against innovations, and their conservatism on such subjects as the need for huge plough-teams or the necessity of putting wet land into excessively high ridges. Part of their wages was customarily paid in kind, and might include a free or cheap cottage, free fuel, milk, or a potato patch. It also included a daily allowance of beer or cider, and as Marshall observed, the quantities of drink consumed were sometimes such as to stupefy the men and make heavy inroads into the supply of malting barley (Document XXVIII). The leisurely movement and low productivity of many labourers may have owed something to inadequate diet, especially in the south where wages were lower and fuel dearer.[72] If so, this was a point that seems to have escaped most contemporary observers, and indeed, farmworkers were generally regarded as having much better health and a stronger physique than their urban counterparts. Investigations into poverty carried out near the end of the eighteenth century by Sir Frederic Morton Eden emphasized the labourers' heavy reliance on bread, and also noted important differences in the diet as between north and south, the northern labourers enjoying in particular the advantages of cheap fuel and more hot food (Document XXIX).

In the first half of the nineteenth century wages in the south

---

[72] See E. H. Hunt, 'Labour Productivity in English Agriculture 1850–1914', *Economic History Review* (2nd series), XX, 2 (1967), pp. 280–92.

were often abysmally low, even when allowance is made for the
higher income possible on piece rates, extra harvest earnings,
payments in kind, and the additional earnings of the women and
children.[73] It was in southern England that wages were frequently
supplemented from the poor rates in accordance with a minimum
scale of subsistence based on the price of bread, a method of relief
familiarly known as the Speenhamland system, though it did not
in fact originate with the celebrated meeting of the Berkshire
magistrates in 1795. At the core of the persistent problem of
southern labourers' poverty was a surplus of hands created by
population increase in areas where the growth of employment
failed to keep pace with the growth of numbers, and where
migration or emigration was insufficient to relieve the over-supply
of labour. Local conditions of employment, the growth or decline
of alternative occupations, certainly influenced the situation, as
did the nature of the farming. Dairy farms, market gardens,
woodlands offered scope for smallholdings and additional sources
of income, food, and fuel. The extreme poverty of the labourers
on Salisbury Plain owed much to the bare, arable landscape, the
huge size of the farms, and the monopsonistic character of the
farmers, as Caird noted in 1850 (Document XXX). The labourer's enormous ignorance, his dullness and inertia, together
with his lack of means, help to explain why the limited degree of
migration abroad or to the industrial towns was insufficient to
have much effect on the conditions. Even the daily allowance of
beer might become a strong motive for staying put, as an
American visitor observed (Document XXXI). Though some
allowance must be made for the prejudices of those who contributed to the Poor Law Report of 1834, it must be accepted that
continuous reliance on the parish had degraded and demoralized
the labourers as it reduced the incomes of the farmers and
hardened their attitudes (Document XXXII). The workhouse
regime sanctioned by the new Poor Law, though harsh and
insensitive, may have contributed with other factors, such as
increased industrial and railway employment, to the gradual
reduction in the rural surplus, and hence to the slow improvement in wages from about mid-century.

---

[73] See G. E. Mingay, 'The Transformation in Agriculture', in A. Seldon
(ed.), *The Long Debate on Poverty* (1972), pp. 39–44.

However, Caird's analysis in 1851 of the causes of the differing wage levels in the country still gave considerable emphasis to the adverse effects of continuing labour surplus, the ill consequences of attempts to keep down the poor rates, and the unfortunate effects of the settlement law (Document XXXIII). Over the rest of the century little was done directly to improve labourers' conditions, as distinct from the relief provided by private charity and the minimal maintenance offered by the poor law. Some great proprietors, however, followed the lead of the Duke of Bedford in gracing their estates with clusters of new model cottages. This interest in cottage building arose from the antiquated and inadequate nature of many of the old cottages which were replaced, the desire to set new standards of accommodation and so to attract more and better labourers for the estate farms, and also from a concern with improving the morals and habits of the labouring population (Document XXXIV). Some gentleman-farmers, too, like Mr Sotheron, M.P. of Bowden Park, near Chippenham, attempted to revive the boarding in of farm lads and unmarried labourers, a practice

> driven out in the southern counties partly by the encourage-
> ment given to early marriages under the old Poor Law, and
> partly by the refinement of modern habits, which have
> banished the labourer from the society of his master, whereas
> he would derive great advantage from it, and be made a more
> useful servant. (Document XXXV).

Though labourers' conditions slowly improved in the second half of the century there still remained much poverty, severe hardship, and deplorable housing. While some great landlords and wealthy farmers took steps towards reform, the general standards remained low, as they were to do for many years to come. The agricultural revolution, like its industrial counterpart, was based on the poorly remunerated toil of a generally ill-educated and informally trained labour force, whose lot it was to benefit last from the advances that changed their lives.

## 8. CAPITAL

By the middle eighteenth century a generally clear (if locally variable) distinction could be drawn between the farming capital provided by the landlord and that supplied by the tenant. By that time the majority of landlords had ceased to participate in farming except to the extent of running a home farm near the mansion or occasionally an experimental farm which might produce marketable surpluses of grain, wool, or livestock. (Landlords generally retained their woodlands in their own hands, however, and sales of timber and bark might form an important source of profit to the estate.) The greater part of the farmland was usually rented out to tenant farmers who were expected to provide their own working stock: plough teams, implements, carts and wagons, livestock, seed, manures, and all the other items necessary for working the farm. Tenant's capital varied with the nature of the farm and increased with the acreage, and on large farms might amount to a considerable sum. Contemporary experts advised such figures as £5 or £7 per acre as necessary working capital, but it seems from complaints about tenants taking on farms larger than they could properly stock that the normal figure was generally much lower. A capital equal to four times the rent of the farm (i.e. capital of between £1 and £4 per acre in the eighteenth century) was a common rule of thumb. Early in the nineteenth century William Marshall stated that farms of £100 to £500 a year required a capital of between £500 and £1,000 for every £100 of rent, while thirty years later, in 1834, it was held that an appropriate farm capital was between £7 and £10 per acre, and yielded a profit of from 10–15 per cent.[74] At all events it is clear from landlords' estate correspondence that tenants commanding the capital necessary for stocking large farms were scarce, and indeed it was sometimes necessary to break up a large holding into smaller units in order to find tenants.

The landowner's farm capital consisted of the land itself, the farm buildings, fences and gates, and other more or less permanent improvements such as private access roads, drainage works,

---

[74] See G. E. Mingay, 'The Size of Farms in the Eighteenth Century', *Economic History Review* (2nd series), XIV, 3 (1961–2), pp. 478–9; Marshall, *On Landed Property*, p. 391; *British Husbandry*, I, pp. 43, 49.

and flood embankments. It was frequently the practice for buildings, fences and other fixtures to be put into repair at the beginning of a tenancy, and for the tenant to be expected to keep them in repair thereafter. Sometimes the tenant was allowed wood from the estate, but if times were hard the landlord might agree to undertake the whole cost of repairs. Expensive improvements, such as under-drainage, were usually undertaken by the landlord, though the interest on the capital expenditure involved, at a rate of perhaps 5 per cent, was often added to the tenant's rent. Sometimes the landlord provided the materials, such as drainage pipes, and the tenant the labour. The expenditure by landlords on repairs and improvements varied considerably according to many influences: these might include the proprietor's financial circumstances, his interest in improvements, the frequency of his visits to his estates, the enthusiasm of his agent, neglect on the part of previous owners, and the general economic climate. Figures collected by Dr Holderness show that on estates in East Anglia the proportion of gross rental devoted to repairs and improvements between 1750 and 1870 did not fall below 7 per cent, but as he remarks, it appears from other figures that 'an average in excess of 7 per cent was very high by the standards of all but the greatest and most dynamic estates'.[75]

Although many farms might be run down through the neglect of proprietors and the negligence of tenants, nevertheless the fact remains that the sharing of the capital costs, and hence of the risks, under the English landlord-tenant system offered important advantages. The system allowed the tenant to concentrate his resources in working capital, enabling him to stock the farm adequately and cultivate it efficiently: he escaped all or most of the burden of providing the land itself and its permanent assets. The attraction of the system to the landlord was that his share of the risk was much reduced, and he escaped the expense and trouble of detailed farm management. The tenant, who took the larger share of risk, received appropriately the larger share of the profits: farmer's profit was generally reckoned to amount to 10 per cent of his capital, and this is probably on the low side;[76]

---

[75] B. A. Holderness, 'Landlord's Capital Formation in East Anglia, 1750–1870', *Economic History Review* (2nd series), XXV, 3 (1972), p. 442.

[76] See W. Marshall, *Review of Reports to the Board of Agriculture* (York, 1811–18), III, p. 422.

while the landlord rarely earned more in rent than a net return of
about 3–4 per cent on the capital value of the land. The landlord-
tenant system had the further advantage of maintaining stability
and ensuring at least a minimum level of efficiency in farming. It
was in the landlord's interest to see that his tenants had the
necessary means of farming well, and also that they had no good
cause for giving up their tenancies; and in bad times landlords
reduced rents and offered other inducements to tenants in order
to encourage them to remain on their farms. On the tenant's part
it was worth his while to make sure of retaining a farm let at a
moderate rent, by making repairs and keeping the land in good
order, and by adopting a mode of cultivation that was at least as
good as the general standard of the district.

How did the farmers acquire their capital? This important
subject has been little explored until recent years, and much work
remains to be done. It is evident, however that there existed in the
countryside an active local market for loans which goes back to the
middle ages.[77] We now know from inventories that farmers might
be either lenders or borrowers, and sometimes both at once.
Contemporary references indicate that farmers holding land on
leases under which occasional large fines had to be paid frequently
borrowed the sums required. Most of this local lending and
borrowing was simply arranged on the basis of a personal bond,
but owners of land could also borrow on mortgage: a flourishing
market in mortgages developed from the later seventeenth century
as legal decisions made this form of borrowing more attractive. In
addition to borrowing on personal bond or mortgage, it is likely
that many farmers built up their capital by ploughing back profits,
using their thrift gradually to climb up the farming ladder. There
is evidence that successful farmers could make very high profits,
as some did in Lindsey in the first half of the nineteenth
century,[78] and it was not uncommon for such farmers to have
several farms under their control at one time. These farms might
be used to put sons into the business, and inheritance was
undoubtedly a factor in enabling young farmers to get a start. The

---

[77] See the discussion of this subject by Dr B. A. Holderness, 'Credit in
English Rural Society before the Nineteenth Century, with special reference to
the period 1650–1720', *Agricultural History Review*, XXIV, 2 (1976).

[78] See J. A. Perkins, 'The Prosperity of Farming on the Lindsey Uplands,
1813–1837', *Agricultural History Review*, XXIV, 2 (1976).

unforeseeable accidents of death might also mean that a struggling
younger son would come into the family farm, as happened, for
instance, to Arthur Young. Little is known at present about the
use made by farmers of banks, though there are indications as
early as the post-Napoleonic Wars depression that bank failures
and restrictions on lending caused liquidity problems. In 1816
farmers in some badly depressed counties complained of retrench-
ment caused by shortage of money, of being forced by lack of
credit to send their grain to market as soon as it was threshed, and
of being obliged to sell off stock because of the calling in of bank
loans[79] (Document XXXVI). The records of the Banbury bank of
Gilletts show that the numbers of farmer-customers, mainly the
wealthier farmers of the district, increased considerably in the
1820's and 1830's; they were badly affected by the depression
conditions of the years 1842–3.[80] Such isolated pieces of information suggest that there is great scope for further investigation
of the role of banks in the rural capital and credit market.

In the minds of contemporary experts the question of farmers'
capital and their investment in improvements such as costly
manures, preparation of fields for machine cultivation, and drainage, was linked with the provision of adequate security of tenure.
It was widely held that if landlords did not grant leases they could
not expect tenants to invest in their farms. In practice, however,
tenant farmers seem to have enjoyed considerable security without having any kind of lease. They had confidence that the
landlord would not turn them out without good cause, and indeed
there is evidence that families holding farms merely on annual
tenancies or 'at will' often stayed on the same land for generations. In the eighteenth century leases were largely confined to
the bigger farms, and were generally as much concerned perhaps
with protecting the landlord's property from the tenant's
depredations as with giving the tenant security. There were some
important exceptions, however. In Norfolk leases with mandatory
husbandry covenants were features of the leading estates, and

---

[79] See the replies given by numbers of leading farmers to the enquiry launched
by the Board of Agriculture into agricultural depression, *The Agricultural
State of the Kingdom, 1816* (1816, new ed. Bath 1970), pp. 38, 42, 153–4, 156,
158, 194–5, 201, 208–9, 211–13, 224, 309, 364, 370.

[80] Audrey M. Taylor, *Gilletts: Bankers at Banbury and Oxford* (Oxford,
1964), pp. 52–8.

were regarded as an essential ingredient of the 'Norfolk system' of great farms, capitalist farmers, and heavy outlays on marl and manures. In other parts of the country antiquated forms of tenure existed, some of which gave the tenant a perpetual right of tenure and, therefore, virtually a freehold interest in the land; others, such as leases for three lives, were uncertain as to duration, and especially when they were brought to an end resulted in run-down farms—in neglected buildings and land exploited without regard to the future (Document XXXVII). Progressive landlords gradually converted such tenures, where they could, to annual agreements or leases for fixed terms of years, as a necessary step in the slow process of rooting out destructive practices and inefficient farmers.

The tremendous price swings of the war years between 1793 and 1815 and the post-war aftermath seem to have made both sides wary of leases. Tenants who secured a twenty-one-year lease in the early 1790's experienced two decades of high prices and exceptional profits, while their landlords fretted at having their rents fixed when other landlords saw their revenues doubled. But tenants who took a new lease towards the end of the wartime boom met very different conditions of low prices, high costs, and uncertain markets; and their landlords found that leases did little to keep rents up: they had to offer abatements or risk untenanted farms. In the nineteenth century neither landlord nor tenant showed much enthusiasm for leases, despite the heavy outlays incurred in drainage, buildings, machinery, fertilizers, and other improvements.[81] What became more significant than the long lease was the efficacy of 'tenant right'—the compensation of an outgoing tenant for his unexhausted improvements. (Document XXXVIII.) Indeed, it can be argued that the flexibility of tenancy at will, allowing tenants readily to adjust their farming to changing market and cost conditions, consorted better with high tenant investment than did the restrictions of a lease—provided there was an effective system of tenant right.[82]

The importance of the efficient use of landlord's and tenant's

---

[81] For a brief general survey of leases see Chambers and Mingay, *op. cit.*, pp. 46–8, 164–6.

[82] See the discussion by J. A. Perkins, 'Tenure, Tenant Right and Agricultural Progress in Lindsey, 1780–1850', *Agricultural History Review*, XXIII, 1 (1975).

capital is demonstrated by the estimates which suggest that between 1798 and 1835 land represented as much as 54-55 per cent of the capital of the United Kingdom, while farm capital accounted for another 8-9 per cent, amounting together to more than three-fifths of the total. As late as 1865, when the importance of land was declining, farm capital (according to further estimates) represented 16 per cent of total reproducible capital.[83] The landlord-tenant system, by encouraging enterprise, providing flexibility, and promoting stability, played a major role in the efficient exploitation of this huge proportion of the national assets.

## 9. THE ENVIRONMENT OF IMPROVED FARMING

As we have seen, the role of conscientious landlords was to provide their tenants with the means of farming the land efficiently. There was more to this, however, than providing adequate buildings, fences, and drainage, and offering suitable terms of tenure, important though all these were. Access to markets was of even greater significance, and hence landlords (and sometimes farmers, too) interested themselves in river improvements, canal construction, port developments, and the formation of turnpike trusts.[84] It is worth noting that landlords involved themselves in such projects, and in the early railways, not merely because they would improve market access for their farm tenants but also because they were often even more valuable for the marketing of minerals, building materials, iron, and other non-agricultural products of their estates.[85] English farming had always been commercially oriented to a considerable degree; it became more so as transport improvements opened the way to reaching more distant and profitable markets. And markets them-

[83] Deane and Cole, *op. cit.*, pp. 271, 274.
[84] See G. E. Mingay, *English Landed Society in the Eighteenth Century* (1963), ch. VIII; William Albert, *The Turnpike Road System in England 1663-1840* (Cambridge, 1972), pp. 98, 101-6, 110-13, 116-19; J. R. Ward, *The Finance of Canal Building in Eighteenth Century England* (1974), pp. 74-6, 143-60.
[85] See, for example, T. J. Raybould, *The Economic Emergence of the Black Country* (Newton Abbot, 1973); J. T. Ward and R. G. Wilson (eds.), *Land and Industry: the Landed Estate and the Industrial Revolution* (Newton Abbot, 1971).

selves were increasing. The old pull of the London market, which had long affected farmers in the home counties and East Anglia, as well as specialist producers farther afield, was supplemented in the eighteenth and nineteenth centuries by the new influence of expanding ports and centres of commerce and industry in the midlands and north.

At the same time, farming necessarily became more closely influenced by market fluctuations, trends in imports, and movements in prices. In the long term the gradual shift towards higher consumption of meat and dairy produce influenced the expansion of livestock production and dairying, while the growth of large urban markets also encouraged more specialist production of market-garden produce, poultry, hops, and eventually fruit. The overall balance between demand and total supply (including imports) was also subject to long-term change. Before 1750 output tended to run ahead of the market, and there were periods of low prices and some considerable exports of grain. Between the 1750's and about 1815, however, the situation was reversed as a larger proportion of poor harvests and bad seasons for livestock kept the rise in output behind the growing demand emanating from a rising population. At the end of the Napoleonic Wars, and broadly for the next sixty years or so, a new situation emerged: output, greatly expanded by the big increase in acreage under cultivation and increasingly supplemented by imports, maintained a rough balance with the growth in the market. At first prices fell sharply from the extraordinarily high pre-1815 peaks, soon to subside and level out on an irregular plateau still somewhat higher than that which ruled before 1793. In due course, as the market trend towards meat and dairy products became more pronounced, livestock production moved upwards while the price and output of grain, increasingly influenced by imports, tended slowly to decline.

There were, therefore, many necessary adjustments which farmers had to make in order to meet the changing conditions of the times, and it is not surprising that the questions of heavy burdens on farming and increasing imports of grain became subjects of political discussion in the difficult years between 1813 and 1852. The first question was resolved by the lifting of the malt duty and by legislation aimed at reducing the weight of the poor rates and achieving the commutation of tithes. The second made the issue of protection highly controversial in a society that was becoming increasingly industrial and urbanized: in the result the struggle between the landed and industrial interests came to a head in the 1840's in the charged atmosphere of the severe depression of 1839–42, the Chartist agitation, and the propaganda of the Anti-Corn Law League.

The best farming of the period was necessarily that most highly adaptable to changing market conditions. Within the limitations imposed by acreage and capital, soils and climate, techniques and transport facilities, the successful farmers moved in the appropriate directions, converting suitable land to grass for dairying and fattening, and on arable shifting between varying courses of crops, inclining more towards a higher proportion of green crops for fattening bullocks and a reduced acreage of grain for the market. The widening range of fodder crops which could be sown as breaks in corn rotations, and the application of chemical fertilizers, helped many farmers to use land more flexibly, and to depart farther and farther from the strict four-course prescription. It was Caird, the most respected authority of the middle nineteenth century, who advocated farming 'high', i.e. farming intensively, investing heavy inputs in order to obtain the greatest yields. But, he pointed out, the compositiion of the output was to be determined by market trends, and these were away from corn and in favour of livestock:

> With the great mass of consumers, bread still forms the chief article of consumption. But in the manufacturing districts where wages are good, the use of butcher's meat and cheese is enormously on the increase; and even in the agricultural districts the labourer does now occasionally indulge himself in a meat dinner, or seasons his dry bread with a morsel of cheese . . . It is reasonable to conclude that the great mass of the consumers, as their circumstances improve, will follow the same rule . . .
>
> Every intelligent farmer ought to keep this steadily in view. Let him produce as much as he can of the articles which have shown a gradual tendency to increase in value . . .[86]

---

[86]Caird, *English Agriculture*, pp. 484–5.

As Caird saw it, high farming, with more green crops for dairying and fattening, was the answer to the loss of protection against foreign corn (Document XXXIX). And, he argued, this change in husbandry would create no risk of the country being starved out in time of war: in well-manured lands would reside 'a store of fertiility which might be called into action in a single season'. Nor would the labourer be injured: 'green crops require more manual labour than corn; and even an increase of grass combined with green crops would probably not diminish the demand for labour. It is in the strictly corn districts of the south and east that the labourer's condition is most depressed'.[87] The progressive farmers followed Caird's advice, and when in 1871 George H. Cook, Professor of Agriculture in Rutgers College, New Jersey, spoke in New York of his recent visit to England, he argued that 'heavy stocking and high feeding' formed the secret of the English farmers' success.[88]

The flexibility and productivity of high farming was facilitated by drainage, improved buildings, machinery, and the new fertilizers. But basic to these investments was the prior existence of compact, consolidated farm units operated under the sole managerial control of the farmer. In many areas of progressive farming, as for instance in Kent, Norfolk, and East Lothian, these conditions had long pertained. The creation of them in other areas, as in much of the midlands, was the long-term result of efficient estate management and the achievement of the much-discussed enclosure movement of the later eighteenth and early nineteenth centuries. Through enclosure the dispersed and fragmented holdings in open fields, subject to common grazing rights and certain communal rules of husbandry, were replaced by holdings which were individually controlled and highly consolidated, much easier to work, and more flexible in the use of the soil. Land was enclosed by private agreement among the owners as well as by private Act, and together between 1760 and 1844 both forms of enclosure affected a large amount of the total farmland, probably some 6–7 million acres (of which perhaps 2 million acres was former waste)—about a third of the earlier

---

[87] *Ibid.*, pp. 486–7.
[88] Thomas L. Bushell, 'English Agricultural Methods and the American Institute, 1871–1872', *Agricultural History*, XXXI (1957), p. 25.

cultivated acreage. The investment involved was very substantial. The direct costs of the parliamentary enclosure of some $4\frac{1}{2}$ million acres have been estimated at nearly £7 million, and the addition of private expenditure on fencing, and the construction of new farm building and drainage works (where undertaken) would greatly increase this figure.[89]

Enclosure was highly important both in improving the efficiency and flexibility of former open-field land and in bringing valuable waste lands, marshes, heaths, and hill grazings, into full cultivation. But it also produced some significant side-advantages. Frequently, the opportunity was taken of rearranging not only the open fields and commons but also the inconvenient jumble of old closes which had accumulated over the centuries. The tithes, an unpopular levy, widely regarded as damaging to improvements and particularly burdensome when taken in kind, were often abolished as part of the enclosure arrangements; usually the titheholder was compensated by an allotment of land given him by the other proprietors, or less often by a corn-rent. At enclosure the road system of the village might well be improved, with the old winding and narrow lanes replaced by new, wide avenues, running along straight lines. Watercourses might be diverted into more convenient channels, and some drainage works or flood embankments executed. Farmhouses were rebuilt on the site of the new allotments, with new barns and byres. Finally, the new hedgerows broke up the old expanse of fields into convenient units and provided windbreaks and shelter for stock (though often creating obstacles to machine cultivation at a later date) (Document XL).

Not all of these changes followed upon every enclosure: quite often the old closes remained as before; the titheholder would not always agree to reasonable terms of compensation; expenditure on roads and bridges was minimized to save money; compactness of the new farms was sometimes sacrificed in order to suit proprietors' wishes in regard to situations and soils; long delays might occur before the new homesteads were built; and sometimes even the hedgerows were omitted in order to reduce the expenses. Most important, the limitations of soils (and a great

[89]B. A. Holderness in J. P. P. Higgins and Sidney Pollard (eds.), *Aspects of Capital Investment in Great Britain 1750–1850,* (1971), p. 166.

many enclosures occurred on the heavy midland clays) meant that the farming system itself could only be modified as cheaper drainage techniques evolved and suitable fodder crops were introduced. Nevertheless, the abolition of common rights and tithes, and the reorganization of holdings, were valuable long-term gains for which farmers were willing to see their rents doubled, even if their husbandry remained much as before. Where large improvements in output and efficiency followed enclosure the increase in rents was much greater, especially on former hill grazings and other areas of old 'waste' land. It is true, as an American historian, Professor McCloskey, has commented, that English historians have tended to be far more interested in the controversial issue of the effects of enclosure on rural society than in its economic advantages, though these were of very great and more permanent consequence. He points out that the increased efficiency resulting from enclosure must have made a notable contribution to the national product, and has suggested a sophisticated formula for calculating its extent.[90] We await with interest further work along these lines.

How far enclosure contributed to the social changes in the countryside remains uncertain. Among the more evident of these social developments were the predominance of large landowners, the decline of owner-occupiers and of small farmers in general and a corresponding rise of large-scale capitalist farmers, and the growth of poverty and unrest among an enlarged rural proletariat. The causation of these phenomena is complex and in many respects obscure. And though they were related in some degree to the changes in farming with which we have been concerned, other factors were certainly relevant and perhaps preponderant. The rural changes did not occur in a vacuum: one has to look also at the contemporary expansion of industry, towns, transport, and markets; the effects of warfare and of government policy in areas such as taxation, poor laws, and game laws; and the whole changing social milieu, which included the growth of population, increased geographical and social mobility, and the widening of personal horizons—to mention but a few aspects. So involved a

---

[90] Donald N. McCloskey, 'The Enclosure of Open Fields: Preface to a Study of Its Impact on the Efficiency of English Agriculture in the Eighteenth Century', *Journal of Economic History*, XXXII (1972), pp. 15–35.

set of problems defies simple summary, and we do not command the space to examine these matters in the depth that they deserve: indeed, they require a volume of their own.

## 10. CONCLUSION

The era of high farming had its weaknesses. Not all farmers were efficient or up to date, and remarkable differences in techniques could be seen even across the hedge between neighbouring farms. Caird referred to this phenomenon and to other examples of backwardness in his famous tour of 1850–1 (Document XLI). But in his conclusion to this work he was able to present data showing how far agriculture had progressed since the time of Arthur Young. Productivity, rent, and the labourer's real wages had all risen (Document XLII). Nevertheless, much remained to be done, and not only by farmers. Landowners and government too, had their part to play. Among the measures advocated by Caird were procedures to cheapen and facilitate the transfer of land, especially of estates neglected by over-burdened proprietors—as a tenant farmer of liberal leanings he was critical of the family trusts which made it difficult for owners of encumbered property to sell. He argued also for the granting by landlords of leases containing liberal husbandry covenants—a predilection which reflected his own experience of large-scale farming in the Lothians. He recommended, too, the alteration of the law of settlement in order to encourage a higher degree of labour mobility, a measure which would tend to reduce poor rates and help farmers to eliminate wasteful hiring of unnecessary hands. And finally, he pointed to the need to obtain more precise information through the collection of agricultural statistics, a failing rectified only in 1866.[91]

Though these and other deficiencies were evident, at the middle of the nineteenth century British farming led the world. In 1824 James Paul Cobbett emulated his celebrated father by embarking upon a rural ride, but on the plains of northern France rather than among the woods and downs of Wessex. At this date the agricultural gap between the two countries was perhaps even

---

[91] Caird, *op. cit.*, p. 526.

more noticeable than when Arthur Young made his celebrated French tours of 1787–90. According to the younger Cobbett, in some districts little progress had been made either in implements or livestock, although in some respects, and especially in diet, the French labourers were better off than their English counterparts (Document XLIII). Thirty years later a French agriculturist, Léonce de Lavergne, repaid the compliment by undertaking a tour of Britain. He emphasized the great importance to British farmers of the urban market—a stimulus to agricultural production which, he said, hardly existed in large areas of France. It was the existence of great and prosperous markets, he argued, which accounted for the British farmer's concern with maximizing output and profits, and for his tendency to concentrate on the production of meat and milk; in France, on the other hand, the absence of markets on anything like the same scale discouraged agricultural progress and justified the self-sufficiency of the peasantry. 'Markets—this is the greatest and most pressing requirement of our agriculture.' (Document XLIV.)

Caird, meanwhile, was concerning himself with the future. He saw that as industry and town populations expanded the land available for farming must shrink. Competition for increasingly scarce farmland must drive up its price, and he advised the 'young and enterprising' to leave for new countries where land was cheaper, 'where they may become the owners of a fertile soil, and profitably contribute to supply the wants of the old country, whose land can no longer meet the demands of her dense population'.[92] To assess the advantages of America for British farmers he crossed the Atlantic and in 1859 published his account of prairie farming. Greatly impressed by the upsurge of the American grain trade, and with it the dramatic rise of Chicago, he made a particular investigation of the prospects for grain production in Illinois. He pointed out that land there was only a thirtieth of its price in England, and he collected figures to show what expenses and potential profits awaited the enterprising British settler (Document XLV).

In the next twenty years the enormous expansion of agricultural production in America and elsewhere gave added weight to Caird's warnings of the danger to British farmers of relying too

---

[92] J. Caird, *Prairie Farming in America* (1859), p. 3.

heavily on corn. Imports of grain were stimulated by the introduction of free trade, and subsequently, as he pointed out in 1878,
corn imports had been supplemented by a growing influx of meat
and dairy produce.[93] The disastrous harvest of 1879 brought to a
close the long era of gradually declining British isolation, when
the home supplies of corn and meat still largely determined the
prices ruling in the market. Caird foresaw what lay ahead. In 1878
wheat production in America already dwarfed that of France and
the United Kingdom put together. A new age of intense foreign
competition was at hand, and the British farmer must brace
himself to meet the shock (Document XLVI). 'We must not
deceive ourselves', he wrote.

> A great change in the agricultural position is impending. The
> older States on the eastern seaboard of America are rapidly
> going out of cultivation by the competition of the richer
> virgin soils of the west. That competition is nearer to our
> doors now, by the cheapening of transport, than it was to
> theirs twenty years ago. The time has come when it must be
> promptly met, if we would avoid the same fate.[94]

The solution was to move away from corn towards meat and
vegetables:

> Bakers' shops are diminishing, and butchers' shops increas-
> ing. Vegetables fresh from our own fields, or brought by fast
> steamers from the ports of the neighbouring continent, are
> more and more displacing bread. That proportion which
> thirty years ago the richer classes in this country alone could
> afford to spend on other articles of household consumption
> than bread, is being rapidly reached by the working class.
> Our agriculture must adapt itself to the change, freely ac-
> cepting the good it brings, and skilfully using the advantages
> which greater proximity to the best market must always
> command.[95]

So, as Caird warned, a new era dawned. Grass and livestock,
market gardens and fruit were the logical response to the sea-

---

[93] J. Caird, *The Landed Interest and the Supply of Food* (4th ed. 1880), p. 2.
[94] *Ibid.*, p. 169.
[95] *Ibid.*, p. 175.

change in the market. In thirty years from 1871 the wheat acreage halved, dropping by 1·7 million acres, while land under permanent grass rose from 11·4 to 15·4 million acres, an increase of over a third. More disappeared in this thirty years than the ancient supremacy of wheat. A remarkably efficient, technically advanced, and highly productive system of mixed farming, the product of more than two centuries of experiment and innovation, yielded to the overwhelming pressure exerted by the combination of rich foreign soils and enormously diminished costs of transport. One kind of agricultural revolution had passed its apogee; another was in course of inception.

# I

This report of the Woburn Sheep-shearing of June 1800 is taken from the *Farmer's Magazine*, I (1800), pp. 328–34.

---

*It is with singular pleasure that we present a particular Account of the truly rational Agricultural Fete lately given by his Grace the Duke of Bedford, at Woburn Abbey, which cannot fail to be attended with the happiest consequences to the husbandry of Great Britain. Compared with this rural entertainment, how contemptible do the innumerable details of balls, routs, etc. given this spring in the metropolis, appear ! His Grace has adopted a line of conduct creditable to himself, and useful to the public; and holds out a pattern which we earnestly hope may be extensively imitated.*

On Monday, 16 June the sheep-shearing and show of cattle commenced; and this truly laudable institution attracted several hundreds of agriculturists and breeders from all parts of this country, among whom were several gentlemen, members of the well-known Society of Breeders from Leicestershire; a Baron from Germany, who is at the head of an agricultural establishment in that country; and four gentlemen from Ireland.

His Grace the Duke of Bedford gave a public breakfast at the Abbey, at nine o'clock.

At about eleven o'clock, His Royal Highness Prince William of Gloucester arrived at the Abbey from the seat of Sir George Osborne at Cheaksands, where he had been on a visit since the review, on Friday, at Hatfield. His Royal Highness was attended by Sir George; and, soon after their arrival, the company proceeded in a grand cavalcade to the New Farm-yard, in the park, for the purpose of inspecting the sheep-shearing, at which five of the best hands that could be procured were employed: They then proceeded to the building lately erected for examining the *ewes* that are to be let for the next season, which were viewed by the hirers of *tups*; but their prices were not fixed, as last year: they were to be shown again on Tuesday, with the prices fixed on them.

The certificates were then opened by his Grace and a Committee, of the different candidates for the prize of fifty guineas, to be given by his Grace (for encouraging the introduction of the Leicester and South Down breed of sheep into Bedfordshire) to the person in Bedfordshire, who should, between June 1799 and Christmas, expend the largest sum of money (not less than sixty guineas, in the purchase of breeding ewes, or theaves of the new Leicester or South Down breed. These were taken into consideration; but the successful candidate was not announced.

About three o'clock the company adjourned to dinner; and his Grace entertained near 200 noblemen, gentlemen, and yeomen, in the large hall in the ancient part of the Abbey where tables were laid which branched out in three directions, but so contrived, as to have but one head, at which his Grace presided. Prince William of Gloucester sat as Croupier.

About six o'clock they left the Abbey and proceeded to the farm-yard again, when a very fine hog, the property of Mr Pickford, wagon-master, in Market-street, was shown, which was supposed to weigh about a hundred stone. During the whole of this time, the men continued shearing the sheep, in a place conveniently adapted for the whole of the meeting to see them. His Grace then conducted the company to a paddock, near the Evergreens, to see some select Devonshire oxen; and from thence they proceeded to the water meadow, near Birchmore House, in Crawley Lane, where there were some very fine Devonshire cows.

The meeting did not break up till near dark, when the Prince returned to Sir George Osborne's.

SECOND DAY

On Tuesday the Duke of Bedford, attended by his company, proceeded from the Abbey on horseback to the New Farm-yard in the park, where they were met by great numbers who had arrived from different parts.

The tups that were shown yesterday, were shown singly again today, and they were described as follows:

Shearhogs, No. 1 to 8 by the Dishley L. Mr Stone's sheep.

No. 9 to 12. Two Shears, by a son of the Dishley L.

No. 14 and 15. Three Shears, by Mr Breedon's L. a son of ditto.

The Sweepstakes of five guineas each, made by the Duke of Bedford, Lord Winchelsea, Lord Somerville, and Mr Bouverie, to produce at this sheep-shearing the best two-year-old heifers of the Devonshire breed: The Duke of Bedford's being dead, and Mr Bouverie not producing one, it rested with Lord Winchelsea and Lord Somerville; and a committee was appointed, consisting of Mr Smith of Tirmarsh, in Northamptonshire, Mr Stone of Loughborough, in Leicestershire, and a Mr Warren, when, after a considerable examination, they declared in favour of Lord Winchelsea.

Mr Garrard the modeller of cattle from London, exhibited the models of the famous show cattle, which were exhibited at Smithfield last Christmas, which were highly approved of: he likewise exhibited a number of other well-known cattle. Several improved implements in husbandry were exhibited, particularly a chaff cutter, ploughs, harrows, etc. At three o'clock, the Duke entertained about two hundred of the company in the great Hall in the Abbey with an elegant dinner, consisting of 160 covers.

About six o'clock the company assembled again at the New Farm-yard, when the tups, shown in the morning, were put up to be let for the ensuing season . . .

### THIRD DAY

Wednesday there was a greater number of people assembled than on the former days; and the weather proving fine, the sight of such a number of opulent men, assembled upon so laudable and rational a purpose, was highly gratifying.

About eleven o'clock the company began to move in a grand cavalcade from the Abbey, and they were met in the park by a great number of others, who had come from different parts, horsemen, and others on foot, of the first respectability, when they proceeded to the New Farm-yard.

Nine South Down two-shears, and one three-shear, were exhibited in the Exhibition Room, and were examined by the hirers of the tups.

Two remarkable fine and fat cows, which had been fatted by poor feed, under certain management, the property of Mr Maxay of Knotting in this county, were exhibited.

A machine for dressing corn in an expeditious way was exhibited in the yard, for which Mr Cooche of Malston, in Northamptonshire, has lately obtained a patent.

As soon as the inspection of the rams and exhibitions were over, the company, headed by the Duke, proceeded to a fallow field, near Birchmore House, where experiments were tried by five different ploughs, namely, a Northumberland, a Surrey, or Duckets, a Bedfordshire, a Norfolk, and a Scottish one, on which experiments were made in sowing turnips, by making the harrows wide apart. The manure was then regularly distributed in them; after which a roller was drawn by an ox, and to the roller was attached a drilling machine, so contrived for the roller to cover the manure with the ridges of earth, and the seeds to fall on the earth which had fallen on the manure; and the machine was so contrived as to cover the seed with earth; so that the seed lay as on a hot-bed. After the inspection of the ploughs, the company proceeded to Ridgemond fields, where experiments were made with Mr Leicester's scuffling harrows; for the improvement of which he has lately obtained a patent. Experiments were also made on Mr Pott's improved harrows.

These experiments were made in consequence of his Grace (with that truly laudable zeal for which he is so eminently distinguished in the encouragement and improvement of agricultural pursuits) having offered a premium of twenty guineas to the person who should produce, at this sheep-shearing, the best and most newly invented implement in agriculture. It is left to a committee to decide which implement produced ought to have the preference; whether any of them merit the reputation that the acquisition of a premium would confer; and which will be made known by the committee on Thursday. About three o'clock his Grace entertained about two hundred gentlemen with an elegant dinner at the Abbey, at which his Grace presided.

A challenge was made by some Hereford gentlemen to produce better cattle than any county in England, which was taken up by Sir Thomas Carr, High Sheriff for the county of Sussex, who undertook to produce as fine from Sussex.

After dinner, the company proceeded to inspect three fat

wedders, two of them belonging to Mr Platt of Lidlington, and one to Mr Cowley of Aspley, as candidates for a silver cup, value ten guineas, for one, and a premium for a second, of a cup, value five, which his Grace has offered. They are to be sheared, weighed alive, killed and weighed when dead; and, after all circumstances are taken into consideration by a committee, they will determine which are the best.

The company then proceeded to the New Farm-yard, when the ten South Down tups were let as follows: No. 1 for 10 guineas; No. 2 for 40 guineas; No. 3 for 30 guineas; No. 4 for 25 guineas; No. 5 for 30 guineas; No. 6 for 80 guineas; No. 7 for 50 guineas; No. 8 for 40 guineas; No. 9 for 120 guineas; No. 10 for 25 guineas.

An experiment was tried on the corn-dressing machine, produced in the morning; when it completely dressed a bushel of wheat in six minutes.

### FOURTH DAY

Thursday morning, his Grace gave another public breakfast at nine o'clock; and, about eleven, his Grace and the company arrived at the New Farm-yard; when the following Leicestershire breed of tups were exhibited in the exhibition-room . . .

Mr Garrard exhibited a model of a piece of the loin of Mr Booth's fat three-shear weather, which won the premium at the sheep-shearing in 1799.—The fat measured seven inches.

Mr Johnson, an eminent farmer near Northampton, exhibited twelve fine ewes, and sold them all.

After three o'clock, they adjourned to the Abbey to dinner; but on account of some engagements of his Grace, it was not served up till five o'clock.

After dinner, the following toasts and sentiments were drank: The King—Success to Agriculture—The Threshing Mill—Small in Size, and great in value—A good Crop of Wheat—Drilling—Bleeding in all its branches—Success to Experiments—The Fleece—The Plough—Grazing—The Tup Trade—To the Memory of Mr Bakewell—Mr Coke—Lord Winchelsea—Sir Charles Davers—Lord Lauderdale.

When the cloth was removed, the cups to be given by his Grace as premiums were put on the table; and his Grace informed the company in an address of the determinations of the committee which had been appointed to investigate the different claims. He began with the premiums offered for the discovery of implements of husbandry; and stated that the committee had examined the corn-dressing machine belonging to Mr Coochie, and the scuffling harrow belonging to Mr Lester, both of which they highly approved; but as they had obtained patents, they did not think them entitled to premiums; and they were of opinion that none of the other implements exhibited were deserving of the prize.

The next premiums were for encouraging the introduction of the New Leicester and South Down bred sheep in Bedfordshire.

No. 1. To the person in Bedfordshire who should, between June 1799 and Christmas following, expend the largest sum of money (not less than sixty guineas) in the purchase of breeding ewes, or theaves of the Leicester or South Down breed, a premium of fifty guineas.

No. 2. A premium of twenty guineas to the person who should expend the next largest sum in the same object, and on the same conditions.

His Grace stated that the candidates were Mr Parkins of Dunstable, Mr Bailey of Marston, and Mr Runciman of Woburn: and the committee, on investigating their claims, found that Mr Parkins had expended £168, Mr Bailey £126, and Mr Runciman £104. He was sorry to say, they had not strictly complied with the conditions: however, under all these circumstances, the committee determined that Mr Parkins was entitled to the premium of fifty guineas, and Mr Bailey to the premium of twenty guineas.

### PREMIUMS FOR FAT WETHERS

No. 1. To the person who should breed and produce at Woburn Sheep-shearing, 1800, the best two-shear fat wedder, the premium of a cup, value ten guineas.

No. 2. To the person who should breed in Bedfordshire and produce at Woburn Sheep-shearing, 1800, the second best two-shear fat wedder, a cup, value five guineas.—The same person not to have both premiums.

The former the committee adjudged to Mr Cowley of Aspley, and the second to Mr Platt of Lidington.

PREMIUMS FOR THEAVES BRED IN BEDFORDSHIRE

No. 1. To the person who should breed in Bedfordshire and produce at Woburn Sheep-shearing, 1800, the best theave, a cup, value ten guineas.

No. 2. To the person who should breed in Bedfordshire and produce at Woburn Sheep-shearing, 1800, the second best theave, a cup, value five guineas.

The former was adjudged to Mr Butfield of Postgrave, and the latter to Mr Bennet of Temsford.

His Grace then concluded by congratulating the company upon the progress in agricultural improvement which had been made, and by exhorting them to persevere in their laudable exertions.

# II

The following account of the proceedings of the Smithfield Club in December 1807 is taken from the *Farmer's Magazine*, IX (1808), pp. 82–5.

---

Sir,

Allow me to present your readers with a brief account of the late proceedings of the Smithfield Club, an association of noblemen, gentlemen, and practical farmers, for the laudable purposes, by a public exhibition and premiums, of encouraging the effectual, early, and economic feeding of animals for the London market, and whose desire it is to give every possible degree of publicity to all such authentic documents as they may be able to obtain which are calculated to increase our knowledge of the comparative merits of different breeds of animals, and the best modes of treating each. On Wednesday evening the 9th of December, the cattle, sheep and pigs began to arrive at Mr David Sadler's repository yard in Goswell Street, near Smithfield Market, from different parts of the country, the stewards being in attendance to open and examine the regularity of the certificates as the animals arrived that evening and early next morning; when the five following gentlemen, who had been appointed as judges for examining the animals, and awarding the premiums, viz. Charles Gordon Gray, Esq., of Tracey Park, near Bath; Mr Thomas Barker, grazier, of Willsborough, Kent; Mr John Ellman, grazier, of Glynde, Sussex; Mr John Hand, butcher, of Carnaby Market, London; Mr Thomas Ellard, butcher, of Leadenhall Market, London; proceeded to compare the certificates and examine the animals, and, before they parted, drew up and signed their award of the prizes, as the same are mentioned in the accounts of the animals, for which dead-weight returns have been made . . .

The show continued during Friday, Saturday, and Monday,

and was, as usual, visited by a great concourse of noblemen, gentlemen, and practical men, engaged in agriculture and its attendant arts; and much interesting discussion took place on the merits and defects of the animals shown. Mr Thomas Pickford produced some very fine turnips, from his newly enclosed farm in Hertfordshire; and many prospectuses and notices interesting to agriculturists were stuck up or distributed . . .

In the afternoon of the first day of the show, about thirty of the members of the Club dined together at the Freemason's Tavern; and, on the last day, the annual dinner of the Club was held at the same place; of which upwards of 130 of the principal agriculturists of the kingdom partook, his Grace the Duke of Bedford, the president, being in the chair, who, after dinner, publicly adjudged the premiums as below, noticed the alterations made in the premiums proposed for next year, and gave, as toasts, a number of names and sentiments ever held dear by enlightened British agriculturists. Lord Somerville, on this occasion, called the attention of the landowners present to the expediency which may perhaps occur, his Lordship said, of relinquishing the restrictions in their leases against the growing of hemp on their farms in case the interruptions of our trade with the Baltic should continue, and the expected quantity of *sun* hemp from the East Indies should prove inadequate to supply the navy with cordage.

I am, Sir, your obedient servant,

JOHN FAREY, Secretary

12 Upper Crown Street, Westminster, 22 January 1808

# III

William Marshall's discussion of the enlightened condition of the large 'capital' farmers, and his proposals for advancing agricultural research and education are taken from his *Rural Economy of the Midland Counties*, I (1790), pp. 115–30.

Every district has its leading men, its 'capital farmers': their proportionate number varying, in some degree at least, with the size of farms prevalent within it, and the state of husbandry at which it has arrived.

These men consist either of tenants, whose fathers, having profited by their good management have left their sons sufficient capitals and knowledge to increase them; or of the superior class of yeomanry, cultivating in continuation their paternal estates.

This class of occupiers have many advantages over the lower orders of husbandmen. They travel much; especially those whose principal object is livestock. They are led to distant markets, and perhaps to the metropolis. They see, of course, various modes of management, and mix in various companies: consisting not merely of men of their own profession: men of fortune and science have, of late years, admitted them into their company, and to their mutual advantage. Thus their prejudices are worn off, their knowledge enlarged, and their dispositions rendered liberal and communicative, in a degree which those who have not mixed and conversed freely with them are not aware of.

The midland district may boast of a greater number of this description of men than any other I have yet been over; and we may, I apprehend, venture to add without risk, than any district of equal extent in the kingdom. It is not only a large-farm and grazing country, but the spirit of breeding, which has gone forth of late years, has infused an ardour and exertion among them unobservable in other districts. Except in Yorkshire, I have found the spirit of improvement nowhere so high.

Besides these, many of the midland farmers have had other two great advantages, of which farmers in general are in want.

Formerly, and still in many districts, yeomen and farmers who were able and willing to educate their sons did it solely with a view to fit them for trade, or enable them to follow one or other of what are emphatically termed the *professions*. Being educated, they were of course incapacitated for farmers!

Not so, however, in this country. There are men, now at the middle age of life, who have had a regular school education; and who, instead of being sent out of the country to a trade or a 'profession', have been placed as pupils with superior farmers at some distance from their fathers' residences: thus not only improving their knowledge by a double tuition, but breaking off in their tender state those attachments to customs, right or wrong, which those who have seen only one mode of management are too liable to form.

Hence we find this description of men not only adopting such improvements as have gained a degree of establishment, but striking out others by experiment, and still further enlarging their ideas by reading: and this with little danger of being misled. Their judgements are in a degree formed. They have a basis to build on.

Among the rising generation, and in a very few years, we may expect to find numbers of this class of occupiers. Almost every substantial farmer now educates his sons, and brings up one or more to *his own profession*.

If ever agriculture be brought near to perfection, this is the class of men who must raise it. Men of fortune may, and ought for their own interest, to *encourage* and *promote*, for with them, eventually, center the profits of improvement. But the superior class of professional men must *suggest* and *execute*.

With respect to the lower classes of husbandmen, who form the main body of occupiers, their business is to *follow*: and, if the men, whom they are in the habit of looking up to, lead the way, though it may be slowly, they are sure to follow.

Thus improvements struck out and effected by the superior class of professional occupiers, are introduced into common practice; while those of unprofessional men, if they merit adoption, die for want of being properly matured; or if raised into individual practice seldom become serviceable to the community at large.

The great bulk of occupiers consider every man who has not been bred up in the habits of husbandry, or enured to them by long practice, as a visionary; and are more inclined to sneer at his plans than adopt them, though ever so excellent.

Hence, probably, the inefficacy of the numerous societies of agriculture, which have been formed, in various parts of the kingdom. There is only one, that of Bath, which, from all the information that has come within my knowledge, has been in any considerable degree successful; and the success of this, probably, has been, in some degree at least owing to the professional men who belong to it.

Societies formed of professional men, *encouraged* and *assisted* by the landed interest, could not fail of being beneficial in promoting the rural affairs of these kingdoms; and the midland counties, whether from centrality of situation, or from the number of superior managers in it, are singularly eligible for such a society.

But societies on the plan which has hitherto been adopted, though they were to be formed of professional men under the patronage of the landed interest, would still be in their nature little more than *theoretical*. Mere societies want the *subject* before them. Their most probable good effect could be that of assimilating by frequent meetings the sentiments of the proprietors and the occupiers of lands, thereby increasing the necessary confidence between them; and thus far, of course, becoming essentially serviceable to their common interest. But they fall far short of being the most eligible institutions for the advancement of rural knowledge.

In the Digest of the minutes of agriculture, on the subject public agriculture, I proposed an establishment of agricultural colleges, to be distributed in different districts as seminaries of rural knowledge. It is now more than twelve years since that proposal was written, during which time my attention has been bent, unremittingly, on rural subjects; and the result is that I now see, still more evidently, the want of rural seminaries.

The seminaries there proposed are, however, on too large a scale for anything less than national establishment; and commerce, rather than agriculture, appears to engage at present the more immediate attention of government: and this notwithstanding the present scarcity of corn is such that we are asking even the Americans for a supply; and notwithstanding a very considerable part of the cattle, which now come to market, are the produce of Ireland.

I have already said in the course of this work that it is not my intention to obtrude my sentiments, unseemingly, on national concerns; but possessed of the mass of information, which, in the nature of my pursuit, I must necessarily have accumulated—no man, perhaps, having had a similar opportunity—I think it a duty I owe to society, and an inseparable part of my present undertaking, to register such ideas, whether national or professional, as result aptly and fairly out of the subject before me: and, in this place, I think it right to intimate the probable advantage which might arise from a board of agriculture—or, more generally, of rural affairs—to take cognizance, not of the state and promotion of agriculture, merely; but also of the cultivation of wastes and the propagation of timber: bases on which not commerce only, but the political existence of the nation is founded. And when may this country expect a more favourable opportunity than the present of laying a broad and firm basis of its future prosperity?

The establishments I am now about to propose might be formed by individuals, in various parts of the kingdom; and might readily be raised into practice.

The situation of an establishment of this nature ought to be (though not necessarily) upon a considerable landed estate; as five thousand acres of tolerable soil. The immediate site might consist of five hundred acres, more or less, laid out into two farms, or general divisions:—the one economical, the other experimental.

The economical division to be established, in the outset, on the best practice of the district it may lie in; and to be conducted on the most rigid principles of pecuniary advantage.

The experimental part to be appropriated, chiefly, to husbandry, with a compartment for planting, and another for botany.

The part appropriated to planting to consist of a nursery ground and such corner or screen plantations as may be wanted for the use of the estate: the intention being that of making experiments on the propagation of woodlands and hedges, as well as that of raising new varieties of trees and hedgewoods.

The botanic garden to receive a collection of native plants, as well as of the several varieties of cultivated plants, whether native or exotic: its intended use being that of a school of botany; as well as that of raising new varieties of the agricultural plants already cultivated; and of endeavouring to discover, among the uncultivated species fresh plants fit for the purpose of cultivation.

The rest to be appropriated to experiments in husbandry, on the several departments of the arable and the grassland management as well as on livestock—a most interesting subject of experiment, as will appear fully under that head at the close of this volume.

The use of this compartment requires not to be explained. It may, however, be proper to say that the general intention proposes, as the main purport of the establishment, that as an operation, a process, or a general principle, shall be fully proved by experiment (but not before, however plausible it may be in theory), it shall be transferred to the part purely economical, and be there registered as an improvement of the established practice.

The buildings of the two farms to be distinct: those of the economical, the ordinary farm buildings which may be supposed to be on the premises; those of the experimental to consist of:

A farmery or regular suite of farm buildings on the best plan, and in the best style of rural architecture at present known; endeavouring to unite, as far as situation and materials will permit, simplicity and conveniency with cheapness and durability.

A repository of implements, and models of farm buildings, fences, gates, etc. Not the ingenious fabrics of theory, but such as are admitted into the established practice of the different districts of the island; or such as have been otherwise *fully proved* by a continued course of practice, in order that by bringing the whole under the eye, regularly arranged and duly classed, their comparative merit may be more readily ascertained; and the judgement be, of course, assisted in selecting such as may be best adapted to a given soil and situation. With a manufactory of implements, for the more easy dissemination of those which are already proved to be superiorly useful as well as for the construction of such new implements as invention may suggest. And with a trial ground adjoining for the purpose of testing new implements (when no other ground may be at leisure), and for regulating and setting to work those to be transferred to distant districts, that less impediment may arise when they reach the intended places of practice.

An experimentery, for analysing soils and manures, and investigating the vegetable and animal economy; and, generally, for the study of the more abstruse branches of the science.

A library for the reception of books on rural subjects; as well as of those on every other subject which may serve to elucidate rural knowledge.

A lecture room for the purpose of instructing pupils in the principles of the rural science, whether they arise out of natural or scientific knowledge.

The professors requisite to such an establishment would be a principal to form and conduct with such assistants, as circumstances would readily point out, when the scale and the departments were determined.

But who would wish to have such an incumbrance upon his estate? and what individual would be at the expense of such an establishment?

Such questions would be futile. Rather let it be asked, who would not wish to have the rural knowledge of the island collected upon his estate? and what liberal mind, especially if bent to agricultural pursuits, would not be gratified in seeing improvements in the first art and science the human mind can be employed upon growing daily under his eye? and what man, who regards the interest of his family, would not wish to see the best cultivated farm in the kingdom upon his estate; and, of course, in due time, to be in possession of the best cultivated estate in the kingdom?

This alone might be a sufficient recompense for the original expense; which would in all probability be repaid with still greater interest by the pupils which such an establishment would, with a degree of moral certainty, draw together.

The present premium given with a farm pupil to an individual varies with the ability or character of the tutor, and with the treatment the pupil expects to receive. The usual term is four years, and the premium forty to two hundred pounds. With the first, they are treated as a superior kind of servants; with the latter as assistants.

What man, whether of the superior class of yeomanry or tenants, or of the superior class of tradesmen or others, who are now bringing up their sons to husbandry, would not, after his son had gone through a course of private tuition and received the rudiments of instruction from himself or some professional friend, wish to perfect his education in a public seminary; where he would have, not only an opportunity of seeing practice in its highest state of improvement and of conversing with professional men of the most enlightened understanding, but where he would be duly initiated in the theory of rural knowledge, in the method of making, registering, and observing the result of experiments, of ascertaining the natural qualities of soils and manures, of improving the varieties of cultivated crops, as well as of ascertaining the inherent qualities and improving the various breeds of livestock; where he would see order and subordination, and learn the proper treatment of servants; and among a variety of other branches of useful knowledge, the form and method of keeping farm accounts, and of ascertaining with accuracy the profit or loss upon the whole and every part of his business; consequently, of bringing it as nearly, as in its nature it is capable of being brought, to a degree of certainty.

And what possessor of landed property would not wish to have the heir of his estate initiated, at least, not in the management of estates only, but in the proper management of farms, without a knowledge of which, no man can be a judge of the proper management of an estate: a part of education, as essentially requisite to an heir of landed property as the acquirements of political knowledge are to the heir of a kingdom. Indeed, the more immediate happiness of a principal part of every nation depends rather on the possessors of estates than on the possessor of the crown. And it is a fact incontrovertible that, in either case, the respectability and personal happiness of the possessor will ever be reciprocal with those of the people, on which alone they can be built with firmness and full security. Surely, then, a branch of knowledge which naturally leads the possessor of a landed estate to live in the hearts of his tenants can be no mean acquirement.

# IV

Arthur Young's reputation was such that he attracted a great many foreign visitors to his home at Bradfield in Suffolk. Of the few whose record of their visit has come down to us was François de la Rochefoucauld, who with his brother and a prominent French agriculturist, M. de Lazowski, was at Bradfield in 1784. In the summer of that year Young and the three Frenchmen set out on a brief tour of Suffolk farming, and de la Rochefoucauld's memoir provides an interesting discussion from a stranger's viewpoint of some of the factors underlying the country's farming progress as well as of the valuable role played by a travelling investigator such as Young. This extract is from Jean Marchand (ed.), *A Frenchman in England, 1784* (Cambridge, 1933), pp. 157, 172–3, 194–7.

---

Mr Young, whom I have already mentioned and who had become one of our best friends, suggested that he should accompany us on a tour of five or six days which we were due to make in the county in which we were living. This suggestion was so pleasing to us that we accepted with one voice and with deep gratification. We prepared to start in two days' time on the 21st of July.

M. de Lazowski and Mr Young hired a cabriolet and my brother and I went on horseback. We had no servants with us; we travelled as farmers and as people who wanted to learn something. We went first to Sudbury, on the London road. The road as far as this town is quite pleasant, especially when one gets near to it, passing through a very long and beautiful village called Melford . . .

A little time afterwards we met a stout farmer, mounted on quite a good horse, who had been inspecting his crops. He had an air of prosperity about him and, although dressed like a farmer, had something in his manner which suggested a man of substance.

Mr Young stopped him and asked him several questions, a good many of which I remember, though some points have escaped my memory.

Nearly all the farmers in this district own their farms, which they manage to do only after they have acquired some little wealth; these farms are not very extensive, being usually worth not more than £300 or £400 sterling; they get their manure from London and mix it with a kind of chalk which comes from Kent; they arrange for the manure to be brought from London on the return journey of those vessels which have carried the produce of the district to London. This return transport costs them little, as otherwise the vessels would come back empty, and it must take considerable skill and far-sighted calculations to enrich the land, and make money on it, with manure brought from a distance of a hundred miles. The farmer told us, further, that the land never lies fallow and that they divide the crops in a four-year rotation: in the first year, turnips; in the second, barley sown with clover; in the third, clover by itself; in the fourth, wheat.

What astonished me profoundly was the way in which not only the farmer, but all those whom Mr Young questioned on the way replied to his questions, all with more intelligence than one would expect from peasants.

I forgot to say that about a mile back we had passed this man's own farm. It was a large house surrounded by a decorative little flower-garden, very well kept and containing several trees purely for the owner's gratification . . .

Agriculture is the foundation and, by an opposite process of reasoning, the product, of a prosperous and well-populated state. These two propositions, which prove each other, also prove the fact and the reason of England's good cultivation. It must not be thought that my motive in putting forward such a proposition is simply admiration for the country which I am visiting—an admiration which makes me see things in too favourable a light. It is only necessary to glance for a moment at the form of government and at the kind of life led by the great landowners to realize that agriculture, as a fundamental principle, tends to a wide-spread equality. The facts of the case entirely support this and there is no difference between the great landowner and the farmer except in the matter of wealth. I am not speaking of the lords who sit in the Upper House; it is easy to see that the esteem in which they are held and the reputation which they enjoy in their own county depend simply and solely on the way in which they treat the smaller country gentlemen and the farmers.

The method by which the taxes are imposed serves to encourage the farmers. It is true that the taxes they pay are heavy, but as they raise the prices of their produce proportionately, their rate of profit is maintained. The tax to which they are liable is calculated on their land; if they discover a means of increasing the produce of their land, they do not pay any more. A second tax which they pay is on behalf of the poor. This is based on the value of the lease, but the leases are for twenty years and in the course of twenty years they may make considerable improvements in respect of which they pay no tax.

Most of the gentlemen who live on their estates for eight months of the year have some portion of land under their own care, sufficient to keep them occupied and also to guard them against disaster in the event of losses being incurred as the result of bad farming. Some of them have a better grasp of the business than others, and immediately proceed to take over more and to farm on a larger scale. Thus does agriculture, which is the very life-blood of the state, come into good repute and the farmers enjoy a considerable respect.

This circulation, so to speak, of people who spend two months in London, then about the same length of time at a spa or with their friends and then return for eight months to their county seats is, in my view, the second foundation of England's splendid agriculture. Certainly, the form of government is the first. But why are the farmers well off and why do they invest immense sums in their farms? Because it is generally regarded as an honourable thing to be a 'substantial' farmer, that is, a rich man with a large farm and a widely extended trade in cattle. The reason why farming is regarded as an honourable estate is that the highest in the land engage in it, and although they may do so as a pastime, they endeavour to make any profit they can. This is also the reason of the great and continual progress made in agriculture. Experiments are made on a big scale by these amateurs and they are promptly taken up by the farmers. It is incredible how intelligent these farmers are, even the small farmers. In the course of our little tour in Suffolk and round about Bury I have seen a hundred of them talking with Mr Young on the principles of their calling, making suggestions and recounting their experiences for three-quarters of an hour or an hour; they never failed to win Mr Young's admiration, though he was well used to it.

# V

Arthur Young's account of Mr Dann's farm at Gillingham, Kent,
was published in the *Annals of Agriculture*, XX (1793), pp. 231–8.
This extract brings out well the concern of Young and progressive
farmers like Dann with calculating the costs and profits of new
and experimental modes of husbandry, and is a good example of
the kind of precise observation of leading farms which filled
Young's tours.

---

To Gillingham, near Chatham, Mr Dann's, whose very valuable communications, in this work, rank among the most practical
and useful I have been able at any time to insert in it. His highly
cultivated farm afforded me ample pleasure, even at this season.
In addition to what he has favoured me with on potatoes, the
following notes are interesting. I found the land intended for next
year's crop ploughed once, having been a wheat stubble. Before
the second earth in the spring two horse-loads of dung are spread,
choosing long dung, fresh from the fatting stalls of the preceding
winter; value charged 1s 6d a load, including carriage. Then
plough three horses at length, *walking on the land* and plant at
same time, in every other furrow; sets nine or ten inches from set
to set, and the rows twenty inches. 133 sacks of seed planted, last
year, sixteen acres, or thirty bushels an acre; this large quantity of
seed is owing to his always having two eyes to each set, which he
thinks beneficial. Cutting the sets 6d a sack. The time of planting
which he prefers is April. Befor they come up he rolls, which he
prefers to harrowing, that the long dung may not be drawn out;
in July hand-hoes and weeds at 5s an acre; horse-hoes twice or
thrice, the chief object of which is, earthing up, which he
considers as very important towards gaining a crop—the more
they are earthed up the greater the produce. The horse-hoe used
the second time is narrower than that used first. He finds that
thus managed potatoes will smother and kill the couchgrass, and

leave the ground perfectly clean. The taking up he puts out by the
sack; for digging and cleaning 3d to 6d a sack—this year 3d and
some at 2½d. The sort all the pheasant-eye. Crop 450 bushels per
acre on an average of twenty-three acres. This produce is extraordinarily great, and demands that I should remark the soil, being a
dry gravelly loam on a chalk bottom and certainly is fertile; for
though the management is very good yet it does not indicate 450
bushels: in one of the potato fields, we dug down nine inches and
found the colour unchanged—and even at twelve it scented well.
His selling price, for all demanded, is 1s a bushel; but the major
part given raw to fatting beasts: he has now twenty-nine bullocks
thus feeding on them, having nothing but raw potatoes and
barley-straw; six fine large Sussex beasts have eaten today
twenty-one bushels: they are kept quite clean and curried, one
man looking after and feeding sixteen of them. These beasts were
bought in October, were a month in sainfoin rouen (after-grass),
then put to potatoes, and will be sold, as heretofore, in March or
April. Each bullock is allowed five feet ten inches of stall, and has
a small box fixed on a post out of which he eats the potatoes; a
rule is never to leave any before them at night for fear of their
choking when no assistance is at hand. In one yard Mr Dann has
very economically taken advantage of an earth bank, against
which he has built a shed, and by that means saved a wall;
thirteen beasts in it at present eat fifteen bushels of potatoes per
diem. After potatoes he sows spring-corn, having found the land
left in too loose a state for wheat. Last year 11½ acres yielded
1,029 sacks, which sold at 3s a sack, £154—expenses £104—profit
£50. Seven acres, the same year, 525 sacks, £78—expenses £58—
profit £20. He began in 1788 with ¼ acre which yielded 45 sacks.
In 1789—1¼ acre, 233 sacks. In 1790—9¾ acres 3,700 bushels. In
1791—20 acres, 4,928 bushels, expense 8½d per bushel. In 1792—
23 acres, 10,700 bushels. And in 1793, will have 28 acres . . .

In 1790, he procured from London the finely sifted coal ashes
which are sold there, and spread them, forty-five bushels per
acre, on clover and sainfoin, the benefit very trifling; but the
ashes from Chatham barracks (not kept under cover), and not
finely sifted, have improved those crops to the amount of a load of
hay superiority per acre; the cinder therefore, says Mr Dann, is
better than the ash . . .

Mr Dann's farm is well arranged:

450 acres.

£. 500 labour. He answered me, with good sense, the more the better.

12 horses.

30 fatting beasts.

300 sheep.

60 hogs.

He keeps a distinct account for every field; and separates corn in the barns with this view. In treasuring experience this is an excellent practice; a man has it in his power at the end of every year to review his practice in various lights, and to draw conclusions which must be valuable.

# VI

Sir Richard Weston spent much of his life in improving his estates at Sutton in Surrey, an undertaking which included making the River Wey navigable and irrigating his meadows. He was most renowned, however, for his championing of the field cultivation of roots and clover. Driven into exile during the Civil War, Weston studied Flemish husbandry and embodied his observations in his *Discours*, probably written in 1645. First published in 1650 by Samuel Hartlib, the following extract is taken from the second corrected edition: Sir Richard Weston, *A Discours of Husbandrie used in Brabant and Flanders* (2nd ed., 1652), pp. 5–8.

---

It is a certain thing that the chiefest and fundamentallest point in husbandry is to understand the nature and condition of the land that one would till, and to sow it with such seeds as it will produce either naturally or by art that which may turn to a man's greatest profit and advantage. I did think I had understood that point when I went out of England after thirty years' experience in husbandry and having improved my land as much as any man in this kingdom hath done, both by water and fire. But after I had been a while in Brabant and Flanders I found I was to learn a new lesson in point of husbandry for that the barrenest, heathy and sandy lands in those countries did produce richer commodities by an ordinary way of husbandry there in practice than the strongest and richest grounds in both these countries.

When I first arrived at Dunkirk and went to Bruges (which was near forty miles) I saw as rich a country as ever my eyes beheld, stacked with goodly wheat and barley, and excellent meadows and pastures. The soil began to alter into worse midway between Bruges and Ghent, which were twenty-four English miles asunder; and so soon as I was past Ghent in my journey towards Antwerp I did see such land for about twenty miles together that I cannot compare to any ground more than the land by Sandy

Chapel, three miles distant from Kingston upon Thames . . . The soil did not much amend until I came within two miles of Antwerp, which was thirty English miles from Ghent . . .

A few days after my return I fell into a discourse with a Dutch merchant, then living at Ghent but had lived some years in England, and told him that I did not think that all Flanders had yielded so much barren ground as I had seen between Ghent and Antwerp. He answered me that that land was the richest part of all Flanders. I smiled to hear him say so, thinking at first he had jested, and I replied that I believed that one acre of land between Bruges and Dunkirk was worth ten acres of any land I saw there between Ghent and Antwerp . . . , for the one did bear goodly wheat, barley and peas, and was in many places naturally excellent meadow and pasture; and the other would carry no other corn but rye, French wheat [buckwheat] and oats, and would never bear any considerable grass but turned presently after it was laid down to heath and broom. The merchant told me again that the best commodities were pulled and cut before I went that way; but he could prove that that land did yield more profit yearly than the best land in Flanders, and that the bores (for so they term their farmers) were richer there than in any part of the country.

I must confess at first I thought his discourse to be some kind of riddle, but seeing him earnest in offering that which seemed strange to me, I desired him to explain himself, how it was possible that that land should yield more profit than the other. I will tell you (said he) the reason why it yieldeth more profit, because that land is natural to bear *flax*, which is called the *wealth* of Flanders; and one acre of good flax is worth four or five acres of the best corn which groweth between Dunkirk and Bruges; and after the flax is pulled it will presently bear a crop of turnips; which may be better worth, acre for acre, than the best corn in the country. After that crop is off, about April following, you may sow the same land with oats; and upon the clover-grass seed, only harrowing it with bushes, which will come up after the oats are mowed, and that year yield you a very good pasture till Christmas; and the next year following you may cut that grass three times, and it will every time bear such a burden, and so good to feed all sorts of cattle as the best meadows in the country do not yield the like, and will continue good four or five years together without sowing it.

After this we parted. At first I wondered much at his discourse; but much more at the ignorance and slothfulness of our country, which being near to Flanders, and many merchants and gentlemen travelling thither daily, none should understand, or at least put in practice their husbandry, there being so much barren and heathy land in England of very little value, which might, by following their example in this husbandry, be much more profitable than the best land in this kingdom. I after pondered what the merchant said all that day and the next, and then began to imagine with myself what a huge improvement I might make of my own estate if these things were true which he had told me, and if God almighty pleased to permit me quietly to enjoy it.

# VII

In this account of a short tour of Norfolk Young gives some details of the methods in use in the north-west of the county, the area which he considered the home of the 'Norfolk system'. After visiting the celebrated Coke of Holkham Young goes on to comment upon the drilling of wheat, manuring with oil-cake, and the amounts of capital and profit which were usual in this district of large-scale farm enterprises: *Annals of Agriculture*, XIX (1793), pp. 441, 451–60.

---

## A WEEK IN NORFOLK
### *By the Editor*
### 29 October 1792

The reader will not expect more than some scattered notes from an excursion into a county whose husbandry I have so repeatedly registered. At Wretham, the seat of Mr Colhoun, I met Mr Bevan, and next day had the pleasure of accompanying them to Holkham.

We passed by Swaffham, Raynham, and Fakenham; and I must remark, with great pain, that from Wretham to Swaffham, the quantity of land in cultivation is not near equal to the boundless heaths and sheep-walks, covered with ling, furze, and fern, which spread everywhere in all directions, and which are left under the idea either of their being unprofitable to cultivate and necessary for sheep, or that the marl found under them is not of that clayey quality which is found best adapted to improving such land. The Chinese principle of improvement, that of adapting plants to the state of the land, rather than improving land for adapting it to plants cultivated on better soils, is as much unknown and unpractised in Norfolk as among the Hurons . . .

## FARM BUILDINGS

Mr Coke, since I was last at Holkham, has built several barns in such a style as can be effected only by men of the first fortune in the kingdom. He has raised on his own farm one which is 120 feet long by 30 broad and 30 high, and surrounded with sheds for sixty cows; it is capitally executed in white brick, and covered with fine blue slate; it is therefore an object for the surrounding grounds, and for that purpose is very advantageously placed.

At Syderstone also he has built another enormous barn, with stables, cattle-sheds, hogs-sties, and shepherds' and bailiffs' houses, surrounding a large quadrangular yard, likewise in a style of perfection and expense rarely met with. The spirit that instigates a man of great fortune to make such exertions in husbandry cannot be too much commended so far as he is personally concerned; but I cannot approve of the rage all Norfolk farmers have for barns; if a landlord was to gratify them fully, I believe half the land would be covered with barns to receive the corn from the other half. In discourse with the men threshing in this barn of Mr Savary's, they informed us, that to one man who *unpitched* the wagon at harvest, seven others were necessary on the *goff*, to receive and dispose of the corn after it was raised to some height; an enormous expense at a time of the year when labour is the dearest. The farmers are, however, very generally advocates not only for barns, but for *great* barns. Another inconvenience is their not daring to *tread*, except lightly, in large barns; and the men complained, that the corn threshed the worse for want of more treading. 140 acres were now in this barn of Mr Savary's. Floor 11 yards; barn 9 wide.

## OIL CAKE

This manure Mr Coke uses in common with most of the farmers in the country; it is £5 5s a ton, and 10s for breaking. Lay half a ton an acre, at, all expenses included, £3 3s an acre . . .

## A FARM

Particulars of a farm in this vicinity.

1,000 acres
 £450 rent

50 acres wheat

150 acres spring corn

120 acres turnips

240 acres layer

40 acres sundries

400 acres grass sheep walk

10 harvest men, each £5 5s for the harvest, in general five
weeks, but this year six

500 sheep

14 farm horses

40 young cattle, including a few cows

The course pursued; (1) turnips, (2) barley, (3) layer two years,
(4) wheat, peas, etc. Of wheat, sow three bushels of seed per acre;
oats four to five, and barley three. Of grasses, 12 lb clover, and
half a bushel of rye-grass. In tillage each pair of horses ploughs an
acre each journey; the man in the two journeys does therefore two
acres a day. To each stable of five horses nine bushels of oats a
week, from the beginning of wheat sowing to the end of barley
sowing; no hay: until Christmas give cut chaff, which is paid for
4s a last, running measure, they earn 2s to 3s a day doing it.
Threshing wheat, £1 1s a last; ditto barley, 9s. Thatching stacks,
1s a yard, running measure of length of stack, all widths on an
average.

## NORFOLK FARMS

I took the opportunity of Mr Coke's conversation to inquire
whether I had been accurate in reporting many years ago, that the
late Mr Mallet of Dunton made a fortune of £70,000 in two leases
of a farm under 2,000 acres, and having nothing to begin with but
the stock of the farm, which might be about £4,000. He explained
the fact: the original stock was valued at £7,000 but he made his
fortune in thirty-four years, for there were eight unexpired of the
second lease. The original fortune being £7,000 takes off much
from the reputed greatness of the profit; for give the forty-two
years to £7,000 at compound interest, and it doubles thrice, that
is, it becomes, at only 5 per cent, £56,000 deducting which from
£70,000 there remains only £14,000 to be made by what is
properly called farming, which, for so many years, on the *profit* of
£7,000 originally is a trifle, and even much less than he ought to
have made. And I believe this will be found a general fact, that

there are no fortunes made, except in extraordinary situations and circumstances, that have nothing in them which bear upon general life. It shows that the common adage, that there are more fortunes saved than got, is not only strictly true but that the fact goes much further; and we may truly assert that there are few things more extraordinary than a fortune made beyond the operations of compound interest. They are all saved: whoever begins with £5,000 and saves steadily for fifty-six years, becomes worth £80,000 with only common interest; what, therefore, may he not do with a trade that gives him 10 or 12 on all the capital invested in it? But there is another circumstance which will make a cruel deduction from Mr Mallet's farming profits, and that is his rent of favour. I am clearly of opinion that if this question is well examined it will be found that Mr Mallet did not make one shilling by farming; and that his £14,000 I just now allowed, will be swallowed up three times over by the beneficial terms on which he had his farm, and the compound interest chargeable on those terms. And I take it, that the whole limit and extent of Norfolk profit goes no further than this—that a man will, on a capital of £5,000, make from 10 to 12 per cent; that, if he is a worthy character, and something of an *honest fellow* in him, that he will nearly spend it; but that if he saves what his neighbours spend he will grow rich; not one jot by his farming, but by the silent and imperceptible progress of an operation whose effects are as sure even as those of the plough.

It gave me pleasure to hear that this district, which is the real field of Norfolk husbandry, and by no means those to the east, has yet men whose wealth give a reputation to the good cause; and that it possesses a Collisson of Tittishall; a Raby of Raynham; and a Dersgate of Swaffham, of whom the farming world speaks.

The following detail of the live stock on Mr Coke's farm will show the scale of his business:

HOLKHAM: CATTLE ON THE FARM, 1 NOVEMBER 1792

| | |
|---|---:|
| Twenty-one cows and one bull | 22 |
| Young cattle, of various ages | 48 |
| Draft oxen | 22 |
| Fatting cattle | 73 |
| | 165 |

Horses for the farming business, gardens, brick-kilns, and
   sundry other employments     50
Cart colts and foals     7
Hunters, hacks, coach horses, keeper's horses, colts and
   foals     <u>84</u>
                                  <u>141</u>

2 November—Left Holkham, where I had been highly gratified
with that steady attention Mr Coke is in the habit of paying to the
plough. He truly loves husbandry, practices it with equal intelligence and success, and is always most liberally ready to make
any experiments that promise to be of public benefit. He had the
goodness to accompany me to Burnham Deepdale to view the
farm of Mr Overman, a farmer remarkable for the neatness of his
husbandry in general and the success with which he practises the
drill culture. Called in the way on Sir Mordaunt Martin, who we
found in a field of mangel wurzel, which were taking up and
storing for winter; they were laid against a hedge bank in the
field, and then covered with earth; a good thought enough for
disposing of them easily in safety against frost. Sir Mordaunt is a
great advocate for the culture of this plant, both in respect of
quantity of produce and utility in feeding cows. He accompanies
us to Burnham; Mr Overman, unfortunately, was absent, but the
bailiff showed us the farm and gave such explanations as were to
be had in a ride over it. The first feature is a general air of
neatness and good husbandry, which is satisfactory to any eye
accustomed to the best culture of Norfolk, found more generally
there than in other counties, arising from several circumstances,
as soil, which is universally in this country a dry loamy sand;
large modern enclosures; it is the hedges, ditches, banks, and
borders, old and crooked in richer countries, with dirty roads and
lanes, that give an air of slovenliness everywhere in wet soils, very
difficult to remedy without expenses that will not pay a due
percentage on the capital employed, with views of mere neatness.
But examining Mr Overman's stubbles you soon find unequivocal
marks of good husbandry. His wheat is most of it drilled with Mr
Cook's machine, and it is executed with great regularity, straight,
and the stubble *perfectly* clean after this wet summer, so productive everywhere of weeds. He is now in his third year of drilling;
the experiments of the first encouraged him; the second his

drilled peas yielded 12½ coombs per acre, the dibbled 10, and the broadcast 8. This year all his peas, and the greatest part of his wheat, were drilled, and superior to what he had broadcast; he has attempted more than once to drill barley and oats, but is convinced it will not do, and does not intend to try it any more. He drills six pecks an acre of wheat and sows two bushels; he horse-hoes once, doing an acre an hour if the furrows are long; hand-hoes twice, each time 20d per acre. These prices, and this ease of cleaning land, shows what the soil is—perfectly dry, good loamy sand in the vale and on slopes of the hills; thinner and poorer on the heights. These dry and loose soils, which admit of being laid quite flat, which consequently demand neither ridges nor water furrows, and on which, whatever the weather, all sorts of operations can go on at all times, are obviously much better adapted to drilling than any other land.

The machine was at work drilling wheat, and we passed a *bout* beside it. The marker is a suspended log which drags along and marks the surface on sand sufficiently. The boy who guides the horse does not lead but rides on him, and goes straight by regarding the mark. The man that holds directs the plough by the wheel-mark; and as he holds for that purpose only one handle, the pressure is counteracted by a leaden weight hung on the other handle. Some crops of wheat thus drilled were above ground, and we had consequently here as well as in the stubble an opportunity of seeing the straightness of the work.

Mr Overman's arable amounts to 523 acres, and he keeps twenty-one horses.

# VIII

Here Marshall describes the convertible husbandry, or ley farming, system of the midland counties, emphasizing its unusual character, and noting as extraordinary the practice of preserving the turf in the soil during the cropping cycle in preparation for the following ley: W. Marshall, *Rural Economy of the Midland Counties* (1790), I, pp. 186–8, II, pp. 40–3.

---

No circumstance belonging to the provincial practice of this kingdom has been to me a matter of more surprise, than the succession of crops in the prevailing practice of this district.

The general principle of management is that upon which every middlesoiled district ought to form its practice: namely, that of changing the produce, from grass to arable crops, and from grain to herbage.

But whether the minutiae of practice, established in the district under survey be eligible in every other middlesoiled district, I mean not here to say. I will endeavour to give a faithful register of the practice, and leave the reader to adopt the whole or such part of it as may be found eligible in his own situation.

In the prevailing practice of the district—a practice whose origin I have not been able to trace, having been prevalent in the inclosed townships, I understand, time immemorial—the course of management is this:

The land having lain six or seven years in a state of sward—provincially 'turf'—it is broken up, by a single ploughing, for oats; the oat stubble ploughed two or three times for wheat; and the wheat stubble winterfallowed for barley and grass seeds—letting the land die during another period of six or seven years in herbage; and then, again, breaking it up for the same singular succession of arable crops.

There are men, however, who object to this practice, arguing that the soil cannot be kept sufficiently clean under this course of management; and on the lighter lands, on the forest side of the district, it is become prevalent to clean the soil for barley and grass seeds by a turnip fallow: a practice which has spread itself, more or less, over the whole district. But the turnip crop, as will be shown under the head turnips, is losing ground on the stronger soils; on which, nine acres of ten are kept as regularly under the course of:

> Turf
> Oats
> Wheat
> Barley
> Turf

as the lands of Norfolk are under the Norfolk system of management . . .

Mighty turf being the midlander's idol, no wonder he is so tenacious of it as to preserve it with reverential care by pinfallowing; lest, by a turnip or a summer fallow, he should destroy his turf and therein destroy his hope.

From what I can understand, however—by land's having turf in it is not meant literally, at least not altogether, the unbroken sod or roots of grass which remain undissolved in the soil; but is more or less a figurative expression, meaning that land which has lain some time in grass will bear better or heavier corn than that which has been under the plough time immemorial; an idea perfectly well understood throughout the kingdom: and it is an opinion as universally received that land which has been long under the plough, more particularly commonfield land, is prone to grass. And I never had before today any idea that commonfield lands were longer in acquiring a turf than other lands which had been under the plough, because I had never, till lately, known grassland broken up and laid down again to grass, without having during the time it was in tillage received a turnip or a summer fallow.

What an endless labyrinth is husbandry! I have, till now, considered it as an unerring rule to cleanse land thoroughly from every thing vegetable before it be laid down to grass. But, I confess, I now begin to be of opinion that there may be cases in which even this rule may be erroneous; and the practice of this district, founded on long experience, strengthens my opinion.

I have frequently been struck with the rapidity with which the lands of this district acquire a *natural* sward: three or four years after they have been laid down they begin to wear the face of old grasslands: yet it never struck me till now that this new turf is raised out of the *ruins* of the old. For although a midland farmer turns over his old turf and takes a crop of oats; re-turns it and crops it with wheat: which being harvested he repeats the operation of turning over the old turf twice, or perhaps thrice, pulling it about with the harrows, and disengaging it from some of its foulness—yet it is still the old turf in ruins. The roots and seeds of the grasses which formed it are still there: for although the farmer has had two crops of corn he has, at the same time, had two crops of grass; the roots of which a winter fallow of two or three ploughings is wholly inadequate to *destroy*; though no doubt it gives them a considerable *check*: and this accounts for the received opinion here that the 'second year's seeds' are the worst grass, because the clover is then gone off, and the natural grasses, having been checked by the pinfallow and kept under by the barley and the clover, have not yet recovered themselves: but, the third year, having nothing to struggle with they *rise again*, resuming the appearance, and, in a considerable degree, the profitableness of old grasslands!

What a new system of husbandry is this! at first sight slovenly in the extreme; yet it is possible that before I have been twelve months longer in this district I may conceive it to be, for lands which are equally productive of grass and corn, an eligible system of management.

A turnip or a summer fallow delays the laying down to grass a year extra, and the hoe or the ploughing and the exposure through the summer, do more towards the extirpation of the turf than all the five ploughings of the pinfallow system.

Extirpating the roots of twitch and other root weeds without destroying those of the better grasses is the leading principle of this plan of management: and if, by a winter fallow judiciously conducted, the former can be kept so much under as not to prevent a profitable turf from forming, the practice is least plausible.

The labour and expense attending this plan of management is small. Five ploughings in ten years, and a crop every year.

# IX

Young's account of the achievements of Turnip Townshend (who died three years before Young was born) appears to have been based on contemporary works and personal knowledge of the Townshend estates. It is taken from the *Annals of Agriculture*, V (1786), pp. 120–6.

---

Charles Lord Viscount Townshend was ambassador extraordinary to the States General in 1709; a Lord of the Regency on the death of Queen Anne; Knight of the Garter; Lord Lieutenant of Ireland; twice Secretary of State, and Lord President of the Council. He resigned the seals in May 1730; and, as he died in 1738, it is probable that this period of eight years was that of his improvements round Raynham. The growth of the hedges and trees of his planting agrees with this epoch. It is not known when Pope's sixth imitation of Horace was first published, but they all came out between 1730 and 1740, whence it appears that this noble improver's turnip-culture very soon became famous.

> Why of two brothers, rich and restless, one
> Ploughs, burns, manures, and toils from sun to sun;
> The other slights for women, sports, and wines,
> All Townshend's turnips, and all Grosvenor's mines.

It is at present not unamusive to remark in a great variety of foreign publications, not only in French and Italian, but as I am informed, in Spanish and German, and probably in every other language of Europe, that the name of this Lord Townshend is repeated with an increase of applause and eulogy for his agriculture, by writers; and relished by whole nations of readers who scarcely know an iota of his political life; or if any particulars of it are dwelt on, they amount to no more than the contrast of his quitting a court for his farm. The importance of embassies, garters, vice royalties and seals is as transitory as that of personal beauty; and the memory of this lord, though a man of great abilities, will in a few ages be lost as a minister and a statesman, and preserved only as a farmer. What is this but the triumph of good sense and of that gradual refinement of the human mind which the universal culture of experimental philosophy has effected? The period will perhaps arrive when this spirit will be matured, and politicians and military heroes registered in colours which have not yet been assigned them.

There is reason to believe that Lord Townshend actually introduced turnips in Norfolk; but the idea that he was the first who marled there is probably erroneous. That branch of husbandry is much more ancient all over the kingdom; and the account given by a French author that Mr Allen of Lynghouse preceded him in marling, is, I believe, just.

But to be the father of the present great foundation of Norfolk husbandry, which has quadrupled the value of all the dry lands in the county, is an honour that merits the amplest eulogy. He certainly practised the turnip culture on such an extent, and with such success, that he was copied by all his neighbours. That he had admirable notions of rural economy is evident from what yet remains of his works. For many hundred acres of land around Raynham, enclosed and planted by him, nothing could be more judiciously planned, nor more correctly executed. The fields are of a proper size for farms of from 300 to 800 acres; they are square; well disposed in relation to the homestall, to roads and to soil; all admirably fenced, in as great perfection as any hedges of the present time. They are single rows of white thorn, so well preserved while young that a gap is rare. Trees are planted at equal distances which were put in among the quick; many are oaks, but they have not thriven proportionably to the quick. It is indeed the worst way of planting.

It is not easy to imagine a greater improvement than that lord must have effected. The extent of new enclosures, shows what the former state of the country must have been: to have divided, built, planted, marled; and covered this great tract with luxuriant crops of a vegetable new in the county, but so perfectly well adapted to it as soon to become the basis of one of the finest systems of husbandry in England. All this was great; and deserves the warmest praise from that posterity who now must feel themselves so much indebted to his labours.

Their effect, indeed, was so great as to leave little more to his successors than to encourage their tenantry to continue in his footsteps. The present lord has had this object constantly and successfully in view. His system is to give twenty-one year leases to his tenants in order to encourage them in that renovation of marling which is periodically necessary on many of the farms. In these leases a rotation of crops which experience has proved salutary is adhered to, admitting such variations as do not counteract the intention of keeping the land clean and in heart . . .

Where else shall we find such a course as this: (1) turnips, (2) barley, (3) turnips, (4) barley, (5) clover, (6) clover, (7) barley? Upon the first of these farms the proportion of turnips to the other crops is as 15 to 66, or about a fourth. On the other it is $15\frac{1}{2}$ to 56, or considerably above a fourth: when to this is added that the quantity of layer is nearly double to that of turnips, it will be apparent that a great stock of sheep and cattle is the object of their husbandry as the truest foundation for corn.

By means of this husbandry and these principles in the landlord's management of his property, the estate is tenanted as well as any in the kingdom; for upon a rental of £12,000 a year, in this county only, the arrears are too insignificant to mention, and not a shilling of them the receipt of which is uncertain; nor does this arise by any means from rents of favour, for the estate is let near its value, having been raised above £3,000 a year by the present lord.

# X

Arthur Young was a frequent visitor to Holkham and had described the husbandry of that part of Norfolk in his first book of farming travels, the well-known *Southern Tour* of 1768. This more particular account of the farming innovations of the famous Coke himself was published in the *Annals of Agriculture*, II (1784), pp. 353–82.

---

It is not a difficult undertaking for a gentleman of very large property to make a great figure in husbandry when seated in a country generally ill cultivated; the smallest exertions make a figure in such a situation; and modes of culture appear as efforts of improvement which, in a better district, would pass for nothing more than common management. This is a sort of advantage totally unknown in the vicinity of Holkham: Mr Coke resides in the midst of the best husbandry in Norfolk, where the fields of every tenant are cultivated like gardens; a landlord makes an ill figure who comes short of them in that race in which he has voluntarily engaged . . .

The scale of his agriculture will appear from the particulars of his farm:

3,000 acres
£2,000 rent
400 acres plantation
400 acres sainfoin
500 acres turnips
300 acres barley
130 acres oats
30 acres wheat
40 acres peas
800 Norfolk ewes ⎱ besides lambs
100 of Bakewell's breed ⎰

600 wethers
120 fat oxen
12 working ditto
30 cows
8 carters, servants
40 labourers.

Mr Coke had three objects in his husbandry which he has more particularly attended to:

I. To discover the means of securing food for sheep in the spring when turnips fail.

II. To discover the best substitute for common clover upon lands surfeited by too repeated sowing.

III. To make certain experiments on objects not sufficiently attended to, but inferior to the preceding in importance.

One of the principal points in the Norfolk husbandry is the flock: upon this depends every thing else; corn is the production of the fold, so that to subsist as large a number of sheep as is consistent with their well-being is the aim of every intelligent farmer. The dryness of the soil co-operates exceedingly with this view: it is thin, loose, and would be poor under the least impropriety of management. This renders it necessary to keep a large proportion of it in *leys* of two, three, and even four years, the longer the better, as the soil recovers itself while at rest; and would after a very long period be broken up again with marl, with the same great profit which attended the first introduction of good husbandry into the western region of this country. This point, of the advantage of leaving the land many years in ley, is admitted by everyone. The dryness of the soil which makes turnips so eligible a crop is another connection with sheep sufficiently obvious, not only for the health of the animal but for its winter support. Thus artificial grasses for the summer and turnips for the winter are the dependence of the flocks. But that root, admirably as it is calculated to clean land and feed sheep, is subject to failures and accidents which place the farmer with a large flock of sheep, in some seasons, in a most lamentable situation. Successive frosts and thaws sometimes rot the turnips before the season of the greatest necessity (the spring) arrives. The fly will, by eating off the first sowings, make the crop so light that it must be husbanded with great care; not to speak of the black canker which now and then utterly destroys a field. The expectation of a frost that may rot them entails another evil almost as bad; which is, the farmer's making so large a reserve to meet such accidents that if they do not happen he has pinched his flock in order to have a surplus on his hands which he does not know what to do with: this is the cause of what I have often seen, neighbours borrowing each others cattle to feed off turnips in April that have thrown out stems a yard long; and, three or four years ago, numbers of acres were carted away to rot into manure.

Last winter the frost destroyed the crop, and the best, as well as the worst farmers, saw their sheep die by scores without the power to help them. One with a very fine flock declared that he would willingly give up all his lambs to preserve his ewes in their usual heart. I viewed a flock at Stanhow that out of 400 ewes lost sixty. The evils attending this insecurity of the turnip crop extend themselves to the barley; for it must be obvious, at the first mention, that leaving a root on the ground through April, a common management when they are good, that shoots very early in the spring and begins immediately to extract considerable nourishment from the soil, must tend every hour to impoverish the barley. What, therefore, must be the state of a man's land who suffers them to rise perhaps a yard high in April, and then either carts them away or feeds them so incompletely as to leave not half the manure on the land, which is the result of a more deliberate conduct? The fact and its consequences are admitted on every hand.

All these circumstances prove beyond a shadow of doubt that they have no real dependence on their turnips for the season when they are most wanted. The large scale upon which Mr Coke practised his husbandry convinced him of this fact, and he no sooner felt its consequences than he determined a remedy. He had observed that in every pinching season the farmers that had any hay on their hands preserved their flocks: but in a country utterly destitute of natural meadows, where artificial grasses yield the only hay, it is no easy matter to procure a sufficiency for the teams and dairies, and very little possible to be spared for the flocks. Mr Coke, who was well acquainted with the culture of sainfoin in other counties, was convinced that the thin, loose, dry, sandy loams of this neighbourhood, situated very generally upon a marl or chalk, would do exceedingly well for that useful grass. It has never been his custom to try any thing by a small experiment when a large one would ascertain the question better. He began with forty acres, and he every year increased the quantity till he arrived at his present breadth of this admirable grass—FOUR HUNDRED ACRES . . .

The advantages of introducing sainfoin do not merely connect with sheep; in a country where every farmer cries, *our lands wear out, they want to be at rest a hundred years again*, surely it is an object of no small consequence to adopt a grass that will last twenty years, and pay the farmer, during that period, as well as the best corn crops of his farm . . .

That Mr Coke's sheep system is in the most perfect style, may be collected from more facts than one. He sent his bailiff (a most sensible and intelligent person, thoroughly fraught with the requisite knowledge) to examine some celebrated flocks in another county, in order to increase his own by the purchase of the best lambs to be procured; none were to be got equal to his own, and his man returned without fulfilling his commission. Let me also add that Mr Coke sold, last April twelve-month, sixty Norfolk wethers, shearling sheep, at Smithfield for 35s each. He has killed them at two years old of 30 lb a quarter: proof, not unsatisfactory, that his sheep system is not deficient.

The advantages of sainfoin being thus obvious, it may be asked whether the neighbouring farmers have copied the excellent example set them by their landlord? The reply is not that entire blank which often occurs in such cases. It was with pleasure I found several of Mr Coke's tenants were in the practice of this husbandry. The Rev Mr Waller, who occupies £500 a year under him, and is a most intelligent husbandman, has a field of it; and others were likewise convinced enough of its value to sow it, though not in a quantity proportioned to its merit. In fact the difficulty of introducing a new article in Norfolk is perhaps greater than in a worse cultivated country: the farmers know that their management is famous, and consequently they have a little of that pride which does not stoop readily to receive instruction . . .

II. The next object of Mr Coke's husbandry is scarcely less important than the preceding, that of discovering a substitute for common clover. Those who have been conversant in the husbandry of the old improved counties know that a very common complaint is the failure of red clover. It has been sown so repeatedly that the land is said to be surfeited with it. In the same district it comes to nothing on the old improved lands, yet yields immense crops on any accidental spot where never or rarely sown before. The observation is so common that no doubt can remain of the fact, however it may be attributed to certain methods in management pursued in this county. To introduce a new system that should have all the advantages of the old one, and, at the same time, demand no peculiar change in the practice or opinion of the farmers, was certainly an object of the first magnitude. Substitutes had been tried and failed: peas and tares are tillage crops, and what these thin soils harassed with the plough want is rest; much tillage, though necessary perhaps for turnips, acceler- ates the subsidence of the clay or marl that has been spread upon the land, which is preserved by rest. Mr Coke turned his views to a different and better quarter, to other artificial grasses which would answer the same purposes as clover and rye-grass. I had recommended to him trefoil (*medicago lupulina*), white clover (*trifol. repens*) cow-grass (*trifol. alpestre*), rib-grass (*plantage lan- ceolata*), and burnet (*poterium sanguisorba*) for laying land to grass upon a former occasion. Mr Coke applied them with no incon- siderable sagacity to the present purpose, and that the experiment might not be delusive tried them spiritedly upon thirty acres in the middle of a large piece laid with clover and rye-grass. The quantities of seed he has found will vary according to circum- stances, but in general,

of cow-grass from 8 to 10 lb,
of white clover from 5 to 8 lb,
of trefoil from 5 to 8 lb,
of rib-grass from 5 to 8 lb,
of burnet from 5 to 12 lb,

according to the price and also the intended duration of the ley: raised upon the farm burnet is very cheap; but bought it is very dear.

The success of the first trial induced him to lay down a yet larger space the second year. And the third (that is with the barley of last spring) no fewer than 221 acres. This is in truth doing justice to a new husbandry, by practising it with a spirit formed to establish it on the unerring dictates of experience . . .

Mr Coke knows from experience that common clover, on his land, would not last two years, and not in any perfection even one: but he has found that these seeds fill the land completely with plants which are abiding two and even three years; and how much longer they may last is more than he can pronounce, as their appearance is yet as good as ever. I rode over all the pieces, and never saw a finer or more regular plant than they exhibit in every spot. This year's crop of barley, with which the 221 acres were sown, was most of it very great, some not less than 6 qrs an acre, yet the grass was uninjured and spread to the eye a perfect carpeting of verdure. Mr Coke is so well convinced that the light lands of Norfolk want rest that he intends leaving some of these fields for experiment unploughed as long as they will remain good, and to break up others at the end of two or three years, according to circumstances.

One of these plants, burnet, made so much noise in the world that he formed an experiment to see expressly what was its merit, and with the noble spirit that characterises his husbandry sowed forty acres, mixing a small quantity of white-clover and rib-grass with it. The result was as decisive as can possibly be imagined; the field has been fully and incessantly stocked with all sorts of cattle, especially sheep, and is constantly pared as close to the ground as a favourite spot in a pasture is by horses. This proves in the clearest manner the value of burnet, and confirms the opinion of my friend Mr Leblanc that it is one of the best grasses for sheep.

The preference which sheep give to these plants, in comparison with common clover and rye-grass, is remarkable. The thirty acres first laid down in the midst of a large field, sown in the common manner, afford a constant opportunity to remark this. The flock kept almost constantly upon that piece, if they were driven into the clover and rye-grass they presently returned; it is within sight of the house, and we remarked them during three days to be regularly on those thirty acres. Mr Coke assured us, he had rarely failed to make the same observation . . .

III. The third object of Mr Coke's husbandry, that of forming various experiments not so much connected with any general system as the preceding articles, branches into many heads, from which I shall select a few that appear to be the most useful . . .

### THE BLACK CANKER

Mr Coke, having heard that ducks had been used in small patches of turnips in gardens to eat the caterpillar called the black canker, determined, on a field of thirty-three acres of turnips being attacked by that pernicious animal, to try how far they might be depended on for a large scale. He ordered his bailiff to buy all the ducks he could get, who presently collected 400; on 16 July they were turned into the thirty-three acres, having water at one corner of the field, and in five days they cleared the whole most completely, marching at last through the field on the hunt, eyeing the leaves on both sides with great care to devour every one they could see, and filling their crops several times in the day. The ducks having saved about £60 worth of turnips were sent to the poultry yards. I should imagine ducks might be allowed fifteen days for doing this work, in which case 400 ducks would secure 100 acres. Upon such a proportion twenty or thirty might be employed on a small farm to great effect.

### OIL-CAKE

Oil-cake has long been used as a manure in Norfolk, but the price was much lower than at present, so that the quantity now is but inconsiderable; the price is £5 per ton. Mr Coke bought a quantity at that rate in order to ascertain the prices at which it will and will not answer. The experiments upon this point are not yet complete. He informed me in general, that it is more forcing to a crop than either dung or the fold: uses it only for wheat, ploughed in with the seed; but the turnips after the wheat will not be so good as after dung spread for that crop.

Refuse salt may be had in London for £3 10s per ton (and if the quantity demanded was large certainly much cheaper): re-shipping 2s; freight to Wells I know not, suppose 15s; carriage to the farm 3s; the whole £4 10s a ton. This is much cheaper than oil-cake. Would it not answer better? Query, if it should not be sown and harrowed in March or April on land intended for turnips? but certainly never with the seed as oil-cake is. There can be no doubt of the propriety of throwing salt into all dunghills when they are turned over or when the yard-dung is shovelled on to heaps. Suppose ten loads the quantity of dung for an acre, five, with a quarter of a ton of salt, would probably be better; but great art and attention would be necessary in mixing and spreading.

## BAKEWELL'S SHEEP

With one of the finest flocks in Norfolk, Mr Coke is not so devoted to the black face and leg as to hesitate at any experiment calculated to compare it with another breed. On the contrary, the fame of Mr Bakewell's sheep made him desirous of giving them a trial. He purchased a number of Leicester ewes of Mr Walker's breed, to whom he put one of Mr Bakewell's tups. He is perfectly well satisfied of the advantage and profit attending this breed, but equally convinced that the Norfolk mutton, for his own table, is the nicer meat of the two. This is a result which I should apprehend must always be the case: for there are two circumstances injurious to the *flavour* of mutton which decide this matter, a great deal of fat and much wool. I speak, however, in a merely luxurious view; for as to *profit*, the great object, I have not a doubt but Mr Bakewell's breed is without any exception the first in the world. The comparison Mr Coke is making will afford much useful knowledge; but it is not complete, and therefore I do no more than touch on it at present.

## WORK ON SUNDAYS

To name Mr Coke's management in this respect in harvest will, I hope, be sufficient to excite a general imitation. His men go to church in the morning, and then immediately to the field, where their useful and honest industry will, I trust, be found as acceptable in the sight of God as the more common dissipation in an ale-house kitchen, to say nothing of the drunkenness, broils, and gaming which usually take place. I could show by a very plain calculation that a day's husbandry-labour in England amounts, in the pay only, to near £50,000. Suppose harvest to last six weeks, as it does upon an average, six Sundays amount to near £300,000 a year; but as they would not work the whole day, let us suppose it only £200,000. We are then to take into account the effect of that labour upon the considerable value which passes under it in harvest: the difference between corn carted on a dry Sunday or a wet Monday. A man, whose pay is 3 or 4s will (in union with his fellows and the assistance of horses) convey from the field to the barn two acres of corn, which may be worth £10. Upon such a value, it is not extravagant to say that we ought, in the national account, to treble the pay of the men, and assert that six Sundays after morning-service are worth in the kingdom £600,000 a year. I leave it to my lords the bishops to form the enlarged comparison of national advantage and good morals on one hand with the common practice on the other.

I cannot quit the management of this spirited improver without relating an anecdote not less to his honour than any of the preceding circumstances. Upon a journey made into Gloucestershire, finding that a tenant of his brother Lord Sherborn, Mr Pacey of Northleach, was an active and intelligent farmer that stepped much beyond the common herd in that ill-cultivated county, he could not see him using six horses in a plough upon a soil and for work which two would stir in Norfolk, without remonstrating against such an expensive waste of strength; he, however, did more than give advice: for on his return to Holkham he singled out an active ploughman that could also hoe turnips, and sent him to Mr Pacey with a pair of horses and a Norfolk plough, desiring him to keep both man and horses as long as he pleased. A man ploughing with a pair in that country, and without a driver, was a phenomenon rare enough to collect the whole neighbourhood; he did the work well, ploughed the land clean and in a husband-like manner, at one-third of the common strength and expense. Mr Pacey was completely convinced that the project was feasible, dismissed his supernumerary horses and bullocks and practised the Norfolk tillage; and, when Mr Coke went again to see him, returned him the warmest thanks with assurances that the experiment had saved him £150 a year, and in memory of the transaction had the original Norfolk plough painted and hung up on his barn, as the instrument of his conversion from prejudice and custom. It hung there a sign of his own merit and his neighbours' stupidity; for, strange to say, the practice has scarcely travelled beyond his own hedges.

There is one article of real utiilty and true magnificence in the environ of a great residence, with which Mr Coke is distinguishing his celebrated seat that I should be unpardonable to omit noticing: it is new-built farmhouses, with barns and offices substantially of brick and tile, in as complete a style as can be imagined. There is no article that ornaments a country more than this; nor did Mr [Capability] Brown ever plan an approach to a great mansion that marks so much real splendour, equally pleasing to the eye and to the heart, as well-built farms and cottages. This is the diffusion of happiness, an overflow of wealth that gilds the whole country and tells the traveller, in a language too expressive to be misunderstood, *we approach the residence of a man, who feels for others as well as for himself.*

# XI

Tull's book describing his ideas and methods, *The Horse-Hoeing Husbandry*, was first published in 1731, nine years before his death. An early and unique contribution to the contemporary debate on farming techniques and the mystery of plant nutrition, his work made a considerable impression. After a lapse of more than eighty years Tull's work was edited and republished in 1822 by one of his best-known admirers, William Cobbett, and the following excerpts are taken from Cobbett's second edition of 1829, pp. 88–9, 100–4.

---

## OF HOEING

Hoeing is the breaking or dividing the soil by tillage, whilst the corn or other plants are growing thereon.

It differs from common tillage (which is always performed before the corn or plants are sown or planted) in the times of performing it; it is much more beneficial, and it is performed by different instruments.

Land that is before sowing tilled never so much (though the more it is tilled the more it will produce) will have some weeds, and they will come in along with the crop for a share of the benefit of the tillage, greater or less, according to their number and what species they are of.

But what is most to be regarded is that as soon as the ploughman has done his work of ploughing and harrowing the soil begins to undo it, inclining towards, and endeavouring to regain its natural specific gravity; the broken parts by little and little coalesce, unite, and lose some of their surfaces, many of the pores or interstices close up during the seed's incubation and hatching in the ground; and as the plants grow up they require an increase of food, proportionable to their increasing bulk; but on the contrary, instead thereof, that internal superficies, which is their artificial pasture, gradually decreases.

The earth is so unjust to plants, her own offspring, as to shut up her stores in proportion to their wants; that is, to give them less nourishment when they have need of more; therefore man, for whose use they are chiefly designed, ought to bring in his reasonable aid for their relief and force open her magazines with the hoe, which will thence procure them at all times provisions in abundance, and also free them from intruders; I mean their spurious kindred, the weeds, that robbed them of their too scanty allowance.

There is no doubt but that one-third part of the nourishment raised by dung and tillage given to plants or corn at many proper seasons, and apportioned to the different times of their exigencies, will be of more benefit to a crop than the whole applied as it commonly is, only at the time of sowing. This old method is almost as unreasonable as if treble the full stock of leaves, necessary to maintain silk-worms until they have finished their spinning, should be given them before they are hatched, and no more afterwards.

Nature, by what she does in the animal economy, seems to point out to us something like hoeing; for when teeth as ploughs have tilled that soil or mass (which is earth altered), and when the saliva and ferment of the stomach have served for stercoration to it, then, as a thing of greatest benefit, the bile and pancreas are employed to further divide and open, and as it were to hoe it, at the very time when it is ready to be exhausted by the greatest numbers of lacteal mouths situate in the intestines.

A plant is almost as imperfectly nourished by tillage without hoeing as an animal body would be without gall and pancreatic juice: for roots pass along the soil, as the soil or mass passes along the guts . . .

In the next place I shall give some general directions, which by experience I have found necessary to be known, in order to the practice of this hoeing-husbandry.

I. Concerning the Depth to plant at.
II. The Quantity of Seed to plant.
III. And the Distance of Rows.

I. It is necessary to know how deep we may plant our seed without danger of burying it; for so it is said to be when laid at a depth below what it is able to come up at.

Different sorts of seeds come up at different depths; some at six inches, or more; some at not more than half an inch. The way to know for certain the depth any sort will come up at is to make gauges in this manner: saw off twelve sticks of about 3 inches diameter; bore a hole in the end of each stick, and drive into it a taper peg: let the first peg be $\frac{1}{2}$ inch long, the next 1 inch, and so on; every peg to be $\frac{1}{2}$ inch longer than the former till the last peg be 6 inches long; then in that sort of ground where you intend to plant make a row of twenty holes with the $\frac{1}{2}$-inch gauge; put therein twenty good seeds, cover them up, and then stick the gauge at the end of that row; then do the like with all the other eleven gauges: this will determine the depth at which the most seeds will come up.

In the common way of sowing it is hard to know the proper depth, because some seeds lying deep and others shallow, it is not easy to discover the depth of those that are buried; but I have found in drilling of black oats that when the drill-plough was set a little deeper for trial, very few came up; therefore it is proper for the driller to use the gauges for all sorts of seeds; for if he drills them too deep he may lose his crop, or if too shallow, in dry weather, he may injure it, especially in summer seeds; but for those planted against winter there is the most damage by planting too deep.

When the depth is known wherein the seed is sure to come up, we may easily discover whether the seed be good or not by observing how many will fail; for in some sorts of seeds the goodness cannot be known by the eye, and there has been often great loss by bad seed, as well as by burying good seed, both which misfortunes might be prevented by this little trouble; besides, it is not convenient to plant some sort of seeds at the utmost depth they will come up at, for it may be so deep as that the wet may rot or chill the first root, as in wheat in moist land.

The nature of the land, the manner how it is laid, either flat or in ridges, and the season of planting, with the experience of the planter acquired by such trials, must determine the proper depths for different sorts of seeds.

II. The proper quantity of seed to be drilled on an acre is much less than must be sown in the common way, not because hoeing will not maintain as many plants as the other; for, on the contrary, experience shows it will always, *ceteris paribus*, maintain more; but the difference is upon many other accounts: as that it is impossible to sow it so even by hand as the drill will do, for let the hand spread it never so exactly (which is difficult to do some seeds, especially in windy weather) yet the unevenness of the ground will alter the situation of the seed, the greatest part rebounding into the holes, and lowest places, or else the harrows in covering, draw it down thither; and though these low places may have ten times too much, the high places may have little or none of it: this inequality lessens in effect the quantity of the seed, because fifty seeds in room of one will not produce so much as one will do, and where they are too thick, they cannot be well nourished, their roots not spreading to near their natural extent for want of hoeing to open the earth. Some seed is buried (by which is meant the laying them so deep that they are never able to come up, as Columella cautions, *Ut absque ulla resurrectionis spe sepeliantur*). Some lies naked above the ground which, with more uncovered by the first rain, feeds the birds and vermin.

Farmers know not the depth that is enough to bury their seed, neither do they make much difference in the quantity they sow on a rough or a fine acre; though the same that is too little for the one is too much for the other; it is all mere chance-work, and they put their whole trust in good ground and much dung to cover their errors . . .

III. The distances of the rows is one of the most material points wherein we shall find many apparent objections against the truth; which, though full experience be the most infallible proof of it, yet the world is by false notions so prejudiced against wide spaces between rows, that unless these common (and I wish I could say, only vulgar) objections be first answered perhaps nobody will venture so far out of the old road as is necessary to gain the experience, without it be such as have seen it.

I formerly was at much pains and some charge in improving my drills for planting the rows at very near distances, and had brought them to such perfection that one horse would draw a drill with eleven shares, making the rows at 3½ inches distance from one another; and at the same time sow in them three very different sorts of seeds which did not mix, and these, too, at different depths; as the barley rows were 7 inches asunder, the barley lay 4 inches deep; a little more than 3 inches above that, in the same channels, was clover; betwixt every two of these rows was a row of sainfoin, covered $\frac{1}{2}$ inch deep.

I had a good crop of barley the first year; the next year, two crops of broad clover, where that was sown; and where hop clover was sown, a mixed crop of that and sainfoin, and every year afterwards a crop of sainfoin; but I am since, by experience, so fully convinced of the folly of these or any other such mixed crops, and more especially of narrow spaces that I have demolished these instruments (in their full perfection) as a vain curiosity, the drift and use of them being contrary to the true principles and practice of horse-hoeing.

# XII

In agriculture as in industry there was often a long time-lag between the appearance of a new machine or practice and its widespread adoption. Here Arthur Young gives some reasons for the slow acceptance by farmers of the drilling of seeds: A. Young, *Rural Oeconomy: or Essays on the Practical Parts of Husbandry* (1770), pp. 314–34.

It is so many years since the first notion of sowing corn, etc. in rows was first started that writers do not even pretend to decide who was the inventor; but certain it is that the use of the drill plough never made any progress worth mentioning till Mr Tull, perhaps *originally* (though not very likely in a man of his reading) *again invented it*. He practised it upon an extent of ground far beyond that of any person preceding him. His success, unhappily, is not so clearly to be determined even in the minuteness of a voluminous work. That he was a prejudiced writer, no one can deny; for, from his work, one would be almost led to imagine the old husbandry totally inadequate to the wants of mankind; and that the human species, notwithstanding all the attention given to cultivating the soil, must be in perpetual danger of starving.

The spirit of drilling died with Mr Tull, and was not again put in motion till within a few years; perhaps the dispute between the value of the old and new methods never occasioned half the enquiry it has done within these ten years. Several courses of experiments have been published, and some of them very ingeniously conducted; but yet the point remains absolutely in dispute. If this mode of sowing be really superior to that in common use why is it not more spiritedly promoted? What are the circumstances that impede its progress? These questions, though of importance, are not easily decided. Another which is of equal consequence is, the effect of the drill culture *in general*?

A very little attention will discover the causes of the drill husbandry making so slow a progress, even under the supposition of all the merit which the most sanguine of its pursuers assert it to possess. In the first place, the principal reason of all others is the insufficiency, real or imaginary, of all the drill ploughs hitherto invented in performing the complex offices which are requisite in such a machine ...

The common plough varies prodigiously in different countries; but yet it everywhere agrees in the great points which farmers expect from it. There is some degree of complexity in the operations which it performs; and yet such a simplicity as to be with great ease familiar to the stupidest country clown. It is everywhere strong enough to bear the hardest usage, firm and compact in all its parts, and everywhere to be repaired without trouble. The variations in the merit of ploughs are found in none of these points; only in deviations from mathematical principles in the construction respecting the strength of the draught. If horses or oxen enough are put to them all ploughs answer their purposes; and hence the grand difference found in them lies in the number of draught cattle used, which varies in almost every county.

Suppose, on the contrary, that the common plough was so complex in its powers as to render simplicity extremely difficult to be preserved in its construction; that the variety of its parts was so great, and had so little firmness and connection in them, as to render the whole machine unavoidably weak; that the same objections which rendered it so complex and so weak made it likewise difficult and expensive to repair; without multiplying these suppositions to a tenth of the extent to which they might be carried, we may venture to determine that husbandry would be at once reduced to infancy if the common plough remained under these three disadvantages.

Now the drill plough is attended with many other disadvantages, for it is of a high price, very difficult to procure, and, notwithstanding the variety invented, not one of such particular excellency as to be allowed to exceed the rest. In such a situation is it possible that drilling can flourish? Let us consider the powers which a drill must possess, or the cultivator have more than one.

There is no reason to limit the number of rows sown at a time; the experiments on this point by no means decide that two rows with intervals are better than four. I have myself found that three are better than two in many instances; and, if drilling in equally distant rows be practised, the more sown at a time the cheaper and better it is. However, we will suppose the number to be three, and the distances from each to vary from 6 inches to 2 feet.

Various seeds require various depths of sowing: turnip seed, lucerne, sainfoin, etc., must not be thrown as deep into the earth as beans. Hence the necessity of the drill's shedding the seed to various depths, from $\frac{1}{2}$ inch to 5 inches.

The mention of the above seeds reminds us of their size. The apparatus for sowing turnips must be very different from that which drops beans, so that there must be varieties in the parts answerable to such effects.

A coulter to each share is requisite to all drill ploughs; for, however fine the soil may be, yet little obstructions will happen which should be thrown aside and not suffered to choke up the shares. It is also necessary to have a harrow or harrows, or teeth, or some contrivance for covering the seeds, which should also act in proportion to the depth at which the seed is to be laid into the ground.

Thus a drill plough must be able to sow any kind of seed, from lucerne and turnips to beans. It must sow one row; two rows at 6 inches asunder; two rows at 1 foot asunder; two rows at 18 inches asunder; two rows at 2 feet asunder; three rows at 6 inches; three rows at 12 inches; three rows at 18 inches. It must shed the seed in these varieties from $\frac{1}{2}$ inch to 5 inches deep. And the coulters and harrows must be contrived to vary with the distance and depth of the rows.

I will not say such a machine *cannot* be invented which is strong enough for the countrymen's use, but I firmly believe the impossibility without rendering it so heavy as to require several horses to draw it; which in a hurrying seed-time is a very great objection. All the drill ploughs I have seen are so weak that I am confident they would not live a week in constant use to take the chance of the servants' and labourers' roughness like the other machines of a farm. Common ploughs and harrows the fellows tumble about in so violent a manner that, if they were not strength itself, they would be perpetually dropping in pieces. In drawing such instruments into the field the men generally mount their horses and drag the things after them. In passing gateways they seldom think of what is behind them, which twenty to one but they draw against the gate-post. It is, however, of little consequence, for the implements are strong enough to bear such usage: but suppose a drill plough treated in the same manner! where is one to be found with half the powers that I have described that would not be shattered in pieces?

In a word, if a drill be not strong enough to bear all such rough handling it may at once be pronounced good for nothing. Whenever one is offered for examination the first trial I should make of it would be to whirl it against the ground with all the force I was master of. If it did not stand this, perfectly sound, I should at once pronounce it not worth a groat ...

Now there appears to be a difficulty in drilling, which, though I never practised it to near such an extent, I think is an objection of no trifling consequence. Suppose a man sows annually two or three hundred acres of barley and oats, and that he is situated either in a clay soil or a stiff or moist loam. Now those who are the least acquainted with the nature of such soils must know that the best common husbandry hitherto discovered for them is to sow the spring corn upon a summer fallow on one earth; by which means they are able to take the advantage of the first dry season in the spring to get their seed into the ground: this ensures an early sowing, which is almost sufficient to counterbalance every other advantage. The success met with in this conduct proves the justness of the practice; for in many districts where this method is pursued they gain, at an average, six and even seven quarters per acre of barley and oats.

Now let us consider the application of the drill culture to such a point. The soil, notwithstanding the preceding summer fallow, is by no means in a state for drilling upon one earth: it must be stirred three times, consequently three dry seasons are requisite instead of one. As far as reason can carry a man in matters of agriculture, this alone condemns the practice without one further consideration. He who gives his barley land three spring ploughings must sow late, and upon wet soils *very* late; which is the most pernicious of all evils. But further: the land, notwithstanding the ploughings, must be well harrowed to prepare it for the drill; so that the mere sowing requires a horse, or perhaps two or three extraordinary, that is, it stops a plough when a good farmer would not let a pair of horses at a guinea a day; and this only with one drill plough: but how many are requisite for sowing one or two hundred acres? The land must first receive its tillage and then be drilled. Now, in many millions of acres, a very heavy shower of rain between those operations, would render another ploughing and harrowing necessary, with time to dry. By midsummer the seed would be in the ground . . .

This criticalness of season is a new proof of the necessity of excellent machines: if a drill plough was to fail or break in the midst of a dry barley sowing, what delay and vexation!

I apprehend these ideas will appear improper only to those who have no experience of the nature of wet soils. Such are absolutely improper for drilling those vegetables that require an early spring sowing. However well such land may have been summer fallowed, however dry it may have been laid up during the winter, yet in the spring it is found sodden and beaten down with winter rains; when ploughed up (unless after a long and dry season that has mellowed it as deep as the plough goes) it rises in such an unpulverised state that however fit it may be for harrowing in broadcast corn, either is not in a condition for a drill to work, or all the authors who have wrote on the New Husbandry require a much greater fineness of soil than is really necessary. I could never, in the little experience I have had of drilling, find these unkindly soils fit for the drill plough with only one stirring. I have often fallowed land for barley during a year and half and yet found that three spring ploughings were necessary to gain any degree of fineness, even a sufficiency to make common farmers allow the soil was in order for clover seed. Nor could I ever get three earths given and proper harrowings, etc. and sow in April, unless some other part of the business was neglected. It will always be May before the barley is sown. But I here speak only of these cold, flat, wet soils. All this may appear very strange to those who have only farmed light, dry, sound soils that will admit ploughing all winter.

The utter impropriety of drilling such wet soils in the spring brings on the necessity of never drilling them with anything but wheat, as they are too stiff and wet for the midsummer crop, turnips. And this necessity is open to many objections. In the first place, many of the later writers on the New Husbandry assert that this constant drilling with wheat is not so profitable as a change of crops; but whether it is or not, we certainly may pronounce it bad husbandry to have all the corn of a farm to sow at one season; for although the autumn sowing is by no means so ticklish as that of spring, yet it would be extremely dangerous to have a great breadth of ground to drill at once; and the number of draught cattle must be extravagantly great, as nine-tenths of their year's work would be to execute in a month's time. It does not require much reasoning to prove that such a system cannot possibly be equal to a variety of broadcast crops.

Another circumstance not to be overlooked respecting the practice of the New Husbandry is the constant attention it requires: a farmer that sows one hundred acres of broadcast wheat, as soon as the land is water-furrowed locks up the fields, and has nothing more to do with them till harvest; his attention is then employed about something else without being called back perpetually to crops which are never done with. The operations of sowing and covering the feed in the broadcast method are very compendious, much land is finished in a little time, and no unusual attention required; whereas in the drill method the farmer should attend particularly to the drill plough to see that nothing is out of order (I am supposing an excellent plough invented); that no more or less seed be shed than is requisite, and that the plough does not move on after it is empty. Whatever perfection the drill plough is carried to he is an imprudent farmer that does not himself attend it constantly.

# XIII

Here Léonce de Lavergne, a leading French writer, summarizes his impressions of farming in the Scottish Lothians, which at the time of his visit in the middle nineteenth century was among the most advanced in the country: Léonce de Lavergne, *The Rural Economy of England, Scotland, and Ireland* (1855), pp. 305–12.

A great part of the wheat produced in Scotland is grown in the Lothians, which are particularly famous for cereal crops. The soil at one time was reckoned incapable of bearing even rye; only barley and oats were cultivated, and these are still the cereals generally grown in the rest of the country. It is mentioned that in 1727 a field of wheat, of eight acres, about a mile from Edinburgh, was the object of universal curiosity. Now, one-fifth of the land, or about 250,000 acres, is in wheat, and in good seasons this crop yields from thirty to forty-five bushels per acre. Here again it is the Norfolk rotation more or less modified according to local circumstances, but still maintaining the general character of that system, which produces this large return. Turnip cultivation, the basis of the rotation, is nowhere better understood than in the Lowlands. Indeed, we find in the Lothians, more than in England, the realization of all agricultural improvements. A complete system of drainage has existed for a long time past. Every farm, or nearly so, has its steam-engine. Stabulation of cattle has been long in common practice. The threshing-machine was invented, at the end of last century, by a Scotsman of the name of Meikle, and was in use in Scotland before it reached England. It was also a Scotsman (Bell) who invented the reaping-machine and who claims priority over the Americans. The most successful and extensive experiments in the application of steam to cultivation which have yet been made in the three kingdoms were carried out at the Marquess of Tweeddale's, near Haddington.

In the county of Haddington alone, which contains not quite

200,000 acres, or scarcely the extent of one of our smallest French arrondissements, there were, in 1853 185 steam-engines employed for agricultural purposes of an average power of six horses each, being nearly one for every 1,000 acres—besides eighty-one water-mills.

In former times the lands of a farm in the Lothians, as well as other parts of Scotland, used to be divided into what were called in-field and out-field. The out-field portion remained quite in a state of nature and was used as pasture; the in-field, on the other hand, produced corn crops uninterruptedly, barley and oats in succession. A worse system can scarcely be imagined. Fallows are an improvement on this barbarous practice and were introduced simultaneously with wheat cultivation in 1725-50. The principal merit of their introduction is attributed to the sixth Earl of Haddington, who had seen their good effects in England. Thus we see how much has been done in a short space of time. If the point now reached is the highest that at present exists, the starting point was certainly the lowest of any.

All the Lothian farms are worth visiting; but I will take only one as an example—that of Mr John Dickson, a few miles out of Edinburgh, composed of what was formerly three farms. It contains 500 Scottish acres [equal to 635 Imperial acres], and is let at £5 per acre, or £2,500. In size this farm is an exception, there being few such in this part of the Lowlands. Those around it are in general not so large, but the methods practised are the same on all; and some of them are let even higher. Notwithstanding these enormous rents, the Lothian farmers make a good business of it. They have almost all excellent houses; and whatever may be the national character for frugality, they live at least as well as many of our proprietors, even of the higher class. Wages, as usual, profit by the general state of prosperity; they are paid half in money and the rest in kind, amounting together to from 1s 8d to 2s per day.

In order to make up 1,200,000 acres, I include, with the Lothians proper, all the low country along the coast from Berwick to Dundee, not only on the south, but also on the north of the Firth of Forth, and also the Carse of Gowrie near Perth. This is about one-fifteenth of the whole area of Scotland, and less than one-seventh of the Lowlands. We have already observed that an equal extent is covered by the Border mountains. The remaining 7 million acres of the Lowlands form the intermediate region, which is neither so rich as the Lothians nor as rugged as the Borders. Their average rent is about 8s per acre; and cattle rearing is the chief purpose to which they are devoted.

Of these, in the first place, a portion is occupied by that distinct district which has received the name of Galloway—the way of the Gauls or Celts—because forming, as it does, a peninsula on the south-west of Scotland, it stretches forward, as it were, towards Wales and Ireland, in anticipation of the migrations of Celts which have been always coming over from these quarters. Galloway includes the whole of the counties of Wigtown and Kirkcudbright, and a portion of those of Ayr and Dumfries. The surface is broken by what the English call hills—that is to say, something between mountainous and undulating country. The climate is extremely wet, like that of Cumberland, which is only separated from Galloway by a firth. The soil produces an abundant natural grass, which is superior to that of the mountains in the neighbourhood. There are a few grain farms; but farming, properly speaking, is rather on the decline, on account of the preference given to cattle. Roots and forage crops are cultivated for the winter food of these animals; during summer they are turned out upon the pastures.

The primitive race of Galloway cattle is small, without horns, very hardy, and affording meat of the best description. An export of these excellent cattle began at the time of the union of the two kingdoms, and this has been increasing for the last 150 years; but a change, similar to that already noticed in districts of the same kind in England, has been going on for some time. The Galloway farmers had confined themselves to the rearing of stock, which they sold at two or three years old, and which were sent chiefly to Norfolk to be fattened. But since railroads have established more direct communication with the markets of consumption, the pastures, by drainage and other means, have been improved, and winter food has been increased by means of special crops, so that cattle are now fattened on the spot. The short-horned breed, which almost never fails where skill and the means of fattening are combined with care in the breeding, is being rapidly propagated, and tends to take the place of, or at least seriously to interfere with, the native breed. The quality of the meat will not be improved, but the quantity, to which more importance is attached, will be considerably increased. Another occupation, that of dairy farming, is on the increase in Galloway, where hitherto, notwithstanding the proximity of Ayrshire, it was little known. The farm of Baldoon, under Mr Caird, author of the *Letters upon English Agriculture*, is especially worthy of notice, and offers one of the best models of a well-managed dairy of 100 cows.

At the end of the last century, Ayrshire, which borders on Galloway, was still in a most deplorable condition. 'There was scarcely a road which was passable in the whole country,' says a local writer; 'everywhere the cottages were built of mud and thatched with straw, the fire in the centre, with an opening in the roof to serve as a chimney, and surrounded with a dunghill, while the land was covered with all sorts of weeds. No green crops nor sown grasses, nor even carts, were to be seen. The only vegetable cultivated consisted of a few Scottish cabbages, which, with milk and oatmeal, formed all the food of the population. Successive crops of oats were taken off the same field as long as it continued to produce anything beyond the seed sown, after which it remained in a state of absolute sterility until it was again fit for producing another miserable crop. *The rent was usually paid in kind, under the name of half-fruits.* The cattle were famished in winter; and when spring arrived could scarcely rise without assistance. There was not a farmer with money sufficient to improve this state of things, and proprietors had not the means either.' Might we not almost fancy we were reading a description of one of our poorest and most remote provinces, where a bad state of *métayage* still reigned, and where escape from the common wretchedness seemed impossible?

The Ayrshire country now ranks among the most flourishing districts of Great Britain. It is there where that grand innovation in English agriculture—the distribution of liquid manure by means of subterranean pipes—was originally tried upon a large scale, and where we find the small farm of Cunning Park, the present wonder of the United Kingdom. This radical change has all been effected in the space of sixty years. To be sure, the district is close to Glasgow; this is the great secret of it all. Like the English, the Scots consume a great deal of milk in all its forms. The increasing demand for dairy produce has created the fine breed of Ayrshire cows—probably just our Brittany race improved—and has changed those ancient heaths into profitable pastures. Dunlop cheese—almost the only kind of Scottish cheese which has any reputation—is made from the Ayrshire milk. In the space of a century the rent of land in the county has increased tenfold. One will cease to wonder at this when it is stated that milk in Glasgow is sold at 3d per quart, and butter at 1s 2d per lb.

The upper part of the Clyde Valley—or, as it is called Clydesdale—is remarkable for another production, which also owes its origin to the commerce and industry of Glasgow—namely, a breed of very powerful draught-horses, well adapted for heavy loads, such as are required for the traffic from the collieries in the district, and for the trade of the port, which, after London and Liverpool, is the most active in Great Britain.

Finally, the north part of the Lowlands, comprising the low grounds of the counties of Forfar, Kincardine, Aberdeen, Banff, Elgin, Nairn, and Caithness, and which remained for a long time very backward because of the unfavourable nature of the climate and greater distance from markets, is in its turn making great progress since railways have reached it and now unite Aberdeen to London by way of Edinburgh. The two principal towns in the district, Aberdeen and Dundee, have each a population of about 70,000, and carry on several prosperous trades. Salmon fishing in the rivers, and the North Sea herring fishery, are great sources of profit to them. The two most southern counties, Forfar and Kincardine, are the furthest advanced in agriculture, and almost rival the county of Ayr. Their prosperity is due, in a great measure, to the Angus breed of polled black cattle, which has been skilfully improved by the native breeders upon the Bakewell principles, and has as great a name for its beef as the Ayrshire for milk; nor does it in this respect bear an unfavourable comparison with the best of the English breeds—the Durham not excepted.

# XIV

Dairying was widely carried on throughout the British Isles, but
was the specialist activity of some areas noted for their cheeses. In
the west country Gloucestershire and North Wiltshire enjoyed
particular renown, and here William Marshall describes with
unusual detail the processes of the latter district: W. Marshall,
*The Rural Economy of Gloucestershire* (1789), II, pp. 155–82.

---

I had an opportunity of seeing the entire processes of six
different dairies, from forty to a hundred cows each, and saw a
sufficiency of others to gain a general idea of their management.

### DAIRYROOM

The '*dey*houses' of this district are spacious and commodious, set
round with presses and whey leads; no shelves; the area being left
free for the cowls, churns, etc., the floors of stone.

Cleanliness is seen in every dairy: a degree of neatness is
observable in some. Everything is conducted in a superior style.
There are men of independency and spirit who set the example.
Mr Iles's dairyroom and 'cheeselofts' form an exhibition worth
going some miles to see.

The North Wiltshire dairyrooms, in general, have outer doors,
frequently opening under a penthouse or open lean-to shed, a
good conveniency affording shade and shelter, and giving a degree
of coolness to the dairyroom. In one instance I observed two
doors: a common close-boarded door on the inside; and an
open-paled gate-like door on the outside, giving a free admission
of air in close warm weather, and, at the same time, being a guard
against dogs and poultry: a conveniency which would be an
improvement to any dairyroom in the summer season.

## UTENSILS

Similar to those of Gloucestershire. The weight of the press is a box filled with sand, or gravel. The dimensions of one, filled with sand, was 18 inches square by 2 feet 2 inches long on the inside (measuring the depth of sand only). A cubical inch of the sand, when dry, weighs 368 grains; consequently, the whole weight of sand is not quite 4 cwt.

The 'broad' vats the same dimension as those of Gloucestershire, namely $15\frac{1}{2}$ diameter; the 'loaf' vats 10 to 12 inches diameter, by 4 to 6 inches deep. The vats are mostly without holes in their bottoms that they may retain the brine the longer.

It is observable that the pail of the Avon quarter is the large one-handled pail of Gloucestershire; while about Swindon the common pail of the southern counties (iron hooped, with an iron bow) is universally in use, carried on yokes, in the London manner.

The cowl is proportioned to the size of the dairy. I measured one near 4 feet diameter: yet this is sometimes too small to contain the milk of the dairy. In this case, two cowls are used: and, when part of the whey is laded off, the two parcels of curd are mixed and broken together.

## MILKING

The hours of milking are very early. In the morning, the cows are generally in the yards by four o'clock; in the afternoon by three. In some dairies in the middle of summer the cows are in the yard and the whole family up by three o'clock in the morning! thus dividing the two meals equally. The number of milkers are proportioned to the number of cows—ten cows to a milker is the general allowance. In large dairies the principal part of the milkers are labourers, or their wives or daughters. The cows are milked promiscuously, and only once over at a meal; not stroked or drawn a second time as they are in many districts: a practice which I have not observed either in Gloucestershire or Wiltshire.

The objects of the dairy which in this case will be required to be noticed, are

Calves

Cheese.

I. CALVES. The calves which are not reared are fatted by suckling for the London market. Mostly sent up dead, cut up in quarters, and packed in hampers with damp cloths. The common age of butchering six, seven, or eight weeks.

Here, instead of calf pens, or stages, calf stalls are in use. Each calf has its separate stall, about 2 feet wide and 4 feet long, just room enough to lie down on a platform of boards or laths with a range of troughs before their heads; with which, in this case, they stand towards the wall, tied up short, as aged cattle: a plan which might well be adopted by the suckling farmers about the metropolis. It has many advantages over the pens there in use.

II. CHEESE. The species of cheese made here are various. Early in spring, soft thin cheeses are made and sent up weekly to the London market. Some dairies, it seems, put the whole or a principal part of their make in nets. But the common make of the district consists of

> Thin cheese,
> Broad-thick, and
> Loaf cheeses.

The thin and the broad-thick sorts are similar to those of the vale of Berkeley; and are, I understand, sold in London as double and single Gloucester. It is the narrow loaf cheese which goes under the name of North Wiltshire cheese; and which has of late years become so high in fashion as to fetch 15s to 20s a hundred-weight more at market than thin cheese—of perhaps a superior specific quality! . . .

The management now requires to be particularized.

1. SEASON OF MAKING. In large dairies cheesemaking is continued *throughout the year !* Not only cheese for the *family*; but *factor's* cheese also is made through the winter season. In one dairy I saw a very considerable parcel of broad-thick cheese which was literally made in *winter*. Many tons of factor's cheese is every year made in this district entirely from *hay*; which, if good, is said to afford not only closer but richer cheese than grass. Winter-made cheese, however, is long in ripening, and is liable to be scurfy and white-coated. But time overcomes one of these disadvantages, and a coat of red paint the other.

2. MILK. The specific quality of the milk is not here debased. The milk is run neat, or nearly neat, from the cow. The Gloucestershire practice of 'keeping a little out' for milk butter is not here in use. It is not, at least, the common practice of the country, for the cheesemakers to *sell* milk butter. In one or two instances which I attended to more closely not a drop was added to the new milk neat from the cow.

3. COLOURING. The colouring of cheese has been long a practice in this district. The oldest dairywoman I conversed with (sixty or seventy years of age) does not recollect to have seen cheese made with its natural colour. She remembers very well the introduction of the 'stone colouring', the preparation of anatto now in use, and has herself made use of the 'powder colouring', saunders, which, she says, was usually boiled among a little milk previous to its being put into the cowl.

At present the material and the method of using it is the same as in Gloucestershire, except that a new species has lately made its appearance, giving the milk and the curd a beautiful yellow hue very different from the redness communicated by a superfluity of the common colouring. The base appears to be anatto, the difference being in the preparation.

The colour preferred by the cheese factors of this district is that of well coloured bees-wax. Cheese of this colour will fetch more, by some shillings a hundredweight, than pale under-coloured cheese or that which is too highly reddened.

4. RENNET. I met with nothing new in this district respecting rennets except in one dairy in which a peculiar mode of preparation is made use of. The usual method is to make as much at once as will last several days, perhaps weeks or the whole season. But in this instance it is *made fresh every day*: that is, fresh brine is added every day; and never more than two vells—here provincially 'rades'—are suffered to lie in the jar at once. The older of them is marked with a skewer, and as soon as it grows stale is taken out and a fresh one added.

This method of preparing rennet has been now continued through two or three generations. All I can say further of it is that the dairy in which it is used produces (if any one dairy has a decided preference) the best cheese of the district: but whether from the rennet, the ground, or the management, or from the three jointly, is by no means evident.

5. RUNNING. The milk is universally run as it comes from the cow or as it happens to be lowered by the little skimmed milk which is put into it. Its degree of heat I never saw tried, not even with the hand! It is said that in very close weather the first milking is sometimes kept in separate vessels or spread thin in a whey lead; but in general, I apprehend, its degree of heat during the summer season is never attended to! A fact which I could not have believed, had not my own observation, strengthened by the thermometer, convinced me of it. I had conceived that the superior excellency of the Gloucestershire management consisted very much in running the milk cool, and expected to have found it run still cooler in Wiltshire. But the following memorandums, accurately taken, are a convincing proof of the contrary:

*Swindon, Monday evening* (21 July 1788). Heat of the air in the dairyroom 60°: milk 87½°: uncovered: came in one hour and ten minutes: whey 85°: curd of a middle quality.
*Deyhouse—Tuesday evening.* Air 63°: milk 88°: not covered: came in half an hour: 'too much rennet': whey 86°: the curd untender but far from being of a bad texture.
*Westleycot—Wednesday morning.* Air 60°: milk 86°: uncovered: came in three-quarters of an hour: whey 84°: the curd of a good quality . . .

6. CURD. The management of the curd depends in some measure on the species of cheese. Thin cheese requires the least care and labour, and thick cheese less than loaves which require the best skill and industry of the manager.

In this department of the cheese manufactury the north Wiltshire dairywomen excel. It appears to be their *forte*. In it they seem to think the principal art consists. It will therefore be proper to descend to its minutiae.

1. *Breaking.* This is done entirely with the hand and the dish: no knife in use here as in Gloucestershire. In some dairies great caution is observed in the first fracture of the curd, which is done either with the hand or the dish moved gently in the centre of the cowl, dividing the curd into large fragments so as to let out the whey leisurely, to prevent its carrying off with it the 'fat' of the curd. When the curd has sunk a little way down in the whey it is broken more freely; and, having stood again to subside, and the clear whey on the top being laded off, it is reduced to a degree

of fineness proportioned to the species of cheese. For thin cheese it is broken as fine as curd generally is in Gloucestershire; for thick cheese, still finer; and for loaves it is reduced, as it were, to atoms.

In some dairies, it is violently agitated among the whey with the hands, throwing it up from the bottom of the cowl, making it *boil* up at the top, like a strong spring gushing out from below the surface. This is called 'beating' it, a practice which is objected to by judicious dairymen; though I see most dairywomen do it, more or less, in the last breaking in the whey.

2. *Gathering.* The ordinary practice is to lade off the whey as it rises, pressing down the curd with the bottom of the lading dish, to sink it the faster and render it the firmer.

In one instance, and this in a dairy whose practice is entitled to the first degree of attention, the curd, instead of being pressed with the back of the dish, is while yet suspended in the whey gathered, with the bowl of it to one side of the cowl; first carrying it gently round the cowl to collect the curd more effectually. The whey, by this means, is got off much clearer—'greener'—than it is when the curd is pressed in a soft pappy state; a practice which undoubtedly impoverishes the cheese.

Most of the whey being got off the cowl is heeled (in the common practice) to get the curd into a mass on one side of it. The cowl is then replaced upright; the skirts of the mass cut off and piled upon the rest; the mass gashed with a long knife; and the whey laded off, sopping it up dry with a cloth.

The mass of curd is now pared down slice after slice (about an inch thick) and piled on the opposite side of the cowl; at intervals pressing it close with the hands and gashing it with the knife, to let out the whey more effectually. The whole being thus gone over, the whey, which has been by this means extracted, is laded off and sopped up with a cloth as before; and the curd piled a *third* time, and, in some dairies, a *fourth* time—slicing, gashing, and pressing it with the hands; making it, by this means, in a manner perfectly free from whey. A practice, which was new to me, and which is perhaps peculiar to North Wiltshire.

In one instance, and that in the practice of a most intelligent and experienced dairywoman, I observed an improvement of this method of freeing the curd from the whey. Instead of pressing the pile at intervals with the hands (a power which, when the quality of curd is large, has but little effect) a vat was put upon it and loaded with cheese weights, a cloth being spread over the bottom of the vat to prevent their sliding. As the pile was carried up or gashed, the vat was moved from part to part so as to give an even pressure to the whole. By this means the whey is in a manner wholly extracted.

Some few dairies, it seems, 'double press' the cheeses: that is, put the curd in the press before it be scalded, agreeably to the Berkeley practice. But it is considered as an inferior method. It certainly reduces the richness of the cheese more than the practice which is here described, and which alone fell under my observation in Wiltshire.

3. *Scalding*. The ordinary method of scalding here is similar to that which has been described in the Gloucestershire practice. The mass of curd is broken to different degrees of fineness, proportioned not to the species of cheese altogether, but according to the skill of the dairywoman. In a first-rate dairy making loaf cheeses, I saw it broken very roughly.

The *quality* of the scalding liquor, too, varies here as in Gloucestershire. Some scald with whey: some with water: others with water lowered with whey.

The heat of the scalding liquor likewise varies even in the ordinary practice of the district very considerably: not, however, as in Gloucestershire, according to the quality of the given curd but according to the custom of the given dairy! Custom, however, which may have been founded on long experience, and may be peculiarly adapted to the ground, from which the curd is produced.

In the ordinary practice of the district the North Wiltshire dairywomen may be said to scald highly. Five out of the six dairies whose scalding liquor I tried with the thermometer, heated the liquor from 102° to 140°, the heat of the mixture of the liquor and curd being from 92° to 110°. So that in the ordinary practice of the country the milk is not only run, but the curd is scalded, much higher than in the vale of Berkeley: a circumstance which I did not expect to find in North Wiltshire whose cheese is characterized by a soft saponaceous texture; diametrically opposite to that hardness—toughness—which scalding appears to give to the curd in the first instance.

But if a degree of surprise arises from the ordinary practice of the district, an eccentric practice which I was favoured with the inspection of must be a matter of some astonishment. What renders this instance of practice the more interesting is its being struck out and pursued by one of the oldest, best-experienced, and most intelligent dairywomen I have anywhere conversed with. In this instance the curd is literally scalded with almost boiling water!—namely with boiling water qualified by a dash of cold water before it be thrown into the cowl, to prevent its 'catching the curd': the actual heat 192°.

It is proper to be understood, however, that in this case the curd is not crumbled or broken in the usual manner before the scalding liquor be thrown among it; but is *cut* into checkers, or dies, of about a cubical inch each with the same knife used in nearly the same manner as in slicing it.

Another peculiarity of this practice is that the curd is salted before it is scalded—a handfull of salt to every cheese being strewed over the checkers, spread regularly on the bottom of the cowl and worked in evenly among them.

This is done in conformity with the general principle of this practice: namely, 'to keep the fat in the cheese', the salt being thought to harden and close the outsides of the cubes thereby preventing the butyraceous [buttery] particles from being extracted by the scalding liquor. The fact is, the water, instead of being made as rich and thick as buttermilk, is left in the cowl after the curd is taken from it thinner than the clearest whey, and without a speck of oil on its surface. . . .

4. *Vatting.* Nor is scalding with boiling water, cutting the curd, and salting it before scalding the only peculiarities of that singular dairy. The dies of curd having been stirred among the scalding liquor, and lain a minute or two to be thoroughly heated, are taken out of the 'scald', which yet retains a heat of 130°, with dishes and immediately put into the vats, as hot as the hands can possibly bear! They press into the vats like beeswax, that has been very much softened by heat, or as cheese which is slightly toasted. Two or three vats being filled, they are set in a shallow tub placed on the dairy floor and a loaded vat put upon them to close the curd while warm: in my opinion an admirable stroke of practice; it had long struck me in theory as being likely to be eligible but was among the last things I expected to meet with in actual practice.

Thus, not only richness and a closeness of texture are probably obtained by this course of treatment but the farm on which it is used is considered as being difficult to make cheese from; and it is believed that the method of treatment which is here described is the means of preventing the cheeses from heaving. The fact is, the cheese (thin cheese) appears to be, with this treatment, above par as to quality . . .

What can we infer from the aggregate of these circumstances? There appears to be but one alternative. Either different grounds require very different management: or the art of cheesemaking is less mysterious than has hitherto been imagined. To make good cheese *sometimes* from *some grounds* is, I believe, a very easy matter; but to make good cheese at *all times*, and from *all grounds* on a certainty, is what no person has yet been able to perform. Nevertheless, I am more and more clearly of opinion that with leisure and perseverance, assisted by a degree of chemical knowledge and a proper apparatus, this object, difficult and desirable as it may be, is attainable.

7. THE CHEESE. 1. The management of the cheeses in the press is here much the same as in Gloucestershire. They are generally salted twice (only one instance of the contrary), and remain in the press a time proportioned to the given thickness: thin cheese three or four meals: thick cheese four or five meals: loaves five or six meals.

2. The cheeses on the shelves. From the press they are carried into rooms fitted up with shelves, for their reception, some of them very commodiously: an entire lining round the walls and perhaps a stage or two in the middle of the room with only gangways, wide enough to pass conveniently between them.

On these the young cheeses remain until they be cleaned, or until the shelves be full; turning them as often as the weather and their respective ages require . . .

8. MARKET. The cheese of this district, like that of Gloucestershire, is bought up principally by factors who live in and near the district, and who send it mostly to the London market, the younger by land, the older by water carriage. One factor (or co-partnership of factors) is said to send 700 or 800 tons annually.

The small cheeses are generally drawn from the larger dairies once a month, and down perhaps to five or six weeks old. The large cheeses require a much longer time before they be marketable. The winter and early spring make go off in autumn; the latter make the ensuing spring.

Besides what the factors purchase, considerable quantities are still sent, annually, to Reading fair, the distance thirty to forty miles according to the part of the district from which they are sent, hired wagons being employed to carry them.

The price for the last ten years has been for thin cheese from 30s to 35s a hundred; for thick 40s to 45s; for loaves 45s to 50s . . .

9. PRODUCE. The produce of milk I had not sufficient opportunity to attend to accurately. To that of cows by the day I was most attentive. This ran in every instance except one from 2 lb to $2\frac{1}{2}$ lb a cow. The one exception was somewhat below 2 lb—$2\frac{3}{4}$ lb has, I am told, been produced, from cows which came well in together and were in full milk.

The produce of cows by the year is in this district almost incredible: 3–4 cwt a cow is, I was assured on all hands, the common produce; $4\frac{1}{2}$ cwt not unfrequent, and 4 cwt nearly the par produce. There is a well attested instance in which a small dairyman sold 35 cwt from seven cows, besides what was used in his family! But the cows were in their prime and extraordinary milkers.

There are two reasons why the produce of cows in this district exceeds that of cows in Gloucestershire. The cows are larger, and the season of making longer: cheese is here made the year round; whereas in Gloucestershire the season of making lasts little more than seven months of the twelve.

The annual produce of the district has not, perhaps, been calculated: I met with no estimate of it. Supposing one-third of the district to be appropriated to cows, and allow that each acre thus occupied yields 1 cwt of cheese (calculating on four acres and 4 cwt to a cow) the aggregate produce is, at least, 100,000 cwt or 5,000 tons a year.

# XV

Robert Bakewell struck a visiting Frenchman, François de la Rochefoucauld, as a leading example of the capitalistic, well-educated and progressive kind of English farmer, a type uncommon in France. Here is his account of the celebrated breeder whom he met at the home at Bury St Edmunds of a mutual friend, Mr Symonds, Professor of Modern History at Cambridge, and a keen agriculturist and close friend of Arthur Young: Jean Marchand (ed.), *A Frenchman in England, 1784* (Cambridge, 1933), pp. 198–203.

---

It seems to me fully established that the more money a farmer invests in his land with a view to improvements, the more profit he makes. But for this it is essential that he should have a long lease, since in the case of a short lease he would reap only half the fruits of his labours. It is also very true that the more profit he makes, the more likely he is to acquire some scientific knowledge and agriculture benefits in consequence. This, then, is what they have in England and we have not: in our country a man with money—even if it had been made in agriculture—would not be content to remain a farmer; he would go off to a town to play the part of a small gentleman; whereas in this country, when they have grown quite rich, they take pride in the fact that a hundred years ago their great-great-grandfather occupied the same farm and was badly off.

English farmers are so thoroughly convinced that they must put plenty of money into a farm when they take it over, that a farmer never offers himself as a tenant without having in his pocket a guinea to spend on every acre for the first year in the purchase of a good stock of cattle, in marling the land and so forth.

As a very striking example of the wealth of the English farmer, of his eagerness to learn and of the money he is prepared to pay to that end, I shall cite the case of Mr Bakewell, a farmer near Cambridge [? Leicester], who has acquired a great reputation as the result of the way in which he has brought to perfection every species of animal which is serviceable to agriculture. I saw him at Mr Symonds's house just as he was about to return home after a tour of some 300 or 400 miles through the best cultivated districts of England, with the sole object of gaining knowledge about the various methods employed by other cultivators, who are always willing to give the fullest information about them—there is no fear, as there is in France, that when a man is known to be making a profit, a slightly higher tax will be imposed.

This farmer was accompanied by another, one of his friends, who was making the same trip with the same object. They generally spend two or three months of the year in making a tour with a view to gaining fresh knowledge; they travel on horseback, with good mounts, and spend between them a guinea a day.

Having spoken of Mr Bakewell as an example of the trouble which the farmers take to get instruction, I want to say a little more about him, as he is one of the most remarkable men to meet in the whole country. As a farmer he is quite well off; his father bequeathed his farm to him at an early age and he has maintained it ever since; from his early days he set out to perfect every kind of beast that could be useful to him, and he has attained to the greatest possible measure of perfection. He began by buying every kind of animal, the best specimens he could find, and by crossing them he has achieved a breed which preserves all the good qualities and excellences of the progenitors without any of their defects. I cannot quite understand it myself. Presumably he bought the finest cow and the finest bull he could find, and so contrived it that if the bull was of tall build, was strong and had fine legs; the cow had a fine head, a well-made back and so on . . . It is fairly well known what parts of the body the offspring will inherit from father or mother—arrangements are made accordingly. After many and many attempts, perseverance triumphs, and everyone who knows anything of the matter admits that Mr Bakewell has achieved the finest breed of cart-horses, of cows, of sheep, of pigs and so on. His oxen have the faculty of growing fat in a shorter time than those of other farmers because the cows who produced them were half fattened at the time when they calved, and perhaps the bulls were in the same condition. Mr

Bakewell has made a lot of bets on all this kind of thing and has always won. His sheep have the finest wool combined with such a carcass as those which produce fine wool seldom have when destined for the butcher. They have also the advantage of fattening more quickly. Lastly, his pigs are large, with big bellies and very short legs; they fatten very well on potatoes, which other pigs do not. They also get fat in a short time. It is the same with all his breeds. He is now so sure of himself that he will make an offer to anyone to produce an ox for him that will put on fat in the head or the back or even in such parts of the chest or stomach as do not usually grow fat. He even offered to make us a bet that he would have some beasts which put on fat in the tail. All this is astonishing. I do not properly understand it, but I believe it as I believe in my religion—because I have been told what I ought to believe and because everyone believes in it. It often happens that a man who excels in some particular field is highly esteemed by a certain number of people and that others do not regard him in the same light. This is not the case with Mr Bakewell: he is esteemed by the whole of England and his breeds are famous and eagerly hired.

I say 'eagerly hired' because he never sells any of the finest specimens of his breeds, but lets out a horse, a bull, a ram, a hog and so on for a summer, with a view to establishing the breed in the hirer's farm. The charge for hiring these animals is excessive, the usual charge for a ram of the finest breed being 80 or 90 guineas for the summer. One ram can serve as many as 140 ewes. The charge for the other breeds is in proportion. That which I have quoted is only for the very highest breed. The others which do not attain this supreme quality are sold, but even these are immensely superior to any others in England. All this will seem quite astonishing and will not be believed, but it is gospel truth.

Some time ago the clients who had hired animals of the breeds perfected by Mr Bakewell failed to pay properly; none of the Scotsmen whom he supplied had paid him and so forth. The result was that the continual and heavy expense which he necessarily incurred reduced him to a condition of bankruptcy, although he was not in the least to blame himself. In such cases the English are admirable—their charity is prompt and expansive. Mr Bakewell's friends opened a subscription list for voluntary contributions on his behalf and he received without delay £1,000 sterling, which enabled him to resume his experiments. The Duke of Richmond gave 500 guineas himself. It is in this way that, without any government interference, the generosity and enthusiasm of individual people come to the rescue of the industrious who suffer misfortune through no fault of their own. Moreover, at the present time Mr Bakewell is much better off than he was, as he has now been paid the money that was previously owed to him and forced him to go bankrupt.

# XVI

Young made the pilgrimage to Bakewell's farm on a number of occasions and reported extensively on his livestock and other experiments. The two famous agriculturists became friends, exchanging samples of seed, and Bakewell sent Young some of his sheep to try at Bradfield. The following is Young's account of one of his earlier visits to the great breeder's establishment at Dishley in Leicestershire: A. Young, *The Farmer's Tour through the East of England* (1771), I, pp. 110–17.

---

[Mr Bakewell's] breed of cattle is famous throughout the kingdom and he has lately sent many to Ireland. He has in this part of his business many ideas which I believe are perfectly new, or that have hitherto been totally neglected. This principle is to gain the beast, whether sheep or cow, that will weigh most in the most valuable joints: there is a great difference between an ox of 50 stone, carrying 30 in roasting pieces, and 20 in coarse boiling ones—and another carrying 30 in the latter, and 20 in the former. And at the same time that he gains the shape that is of the greatest value in the smallest compass, he asserts, from long experience, that he gains a breed much hardier and easier fed than any others. These ideas he applies equally to sheep and oxen.

In the breed of the latter the old notion was that where you had much and large bones there was plenty of room to lay flesh on; and accordingly the graziers were eager to buy the largest-boned cattle. This whole system Mr Bakewell has proved to be an utter mistake. He asserts the smaller the bones, the truer will be the make of the beast—the quicker she will fat—and her weight, we may easily conceive, will have a larger proportion of valuable meat: *flesh*, not *bone*, is the butcher's object. Mr Bakewell admits that a large-boned beast may be made a large fat beast, and that he may come to a great weight; but justly observes that this is no part of the profitable enquiry, for stating such a simple proposition without at the same time showing the expense of covering those bones with flesh, is offering no satisfactory argument. The only object of real importance is the proportion of *grass* to *value*. I have twenty acres; which will pay me for those acres best, large- or small-boned cattle? The latter fat so much quicker, and more profitably in the joints of value that the query is answered in their favour from long and attentive experience.

Among other breeds of cattle the Lincolnshire and the Holderness are very large, but their size lies in their bones: they may be fattened to great loss to the grazier, nor can they ever return so much for a given quantity of grass as the small-boned, long-horned kind.

The breed which Mr Bakewell has fixed on as the best in England is the Lancashire, and he thinks he has improved it much in bringing the carcass of the beast into a truer mould, and particularly by making them broader over the backs. The shape which should be the criterion of a cow, a bull, or an ox, and also of a sheep, is that of an hogshead or a firkin, truly circular with small and as short legs as possible: upon the plain principle that the value lies in the barrel, not in the legs. All breeds, the backs of which rise in the least ridge, are bad. I measured two or three cows 2 feet 3 inches flat across their backs from hip to hip—and their legs remarkably short.

Mr Bakewell has now a bull of his own breed which he calls Twopenny, which leaps cows at £5 5s a cow. This is carrying the breed of horned cattle to wonderful perfection. He is a very fine bull—most truly made according to the principles laid down above. He has many others got by him, which he lets for the season from 5 guineas to 30 guineas a season, but rarely sells any. He would not take £200 for Twopenny. He has several cows which he keeps for breeding that he would not sell at 30 guineas apiece.

Another particularity is the amazing gentleness in which he brings up these animals. All his bulls stand still in the field to be examined: the way of driving them from one field to another, or home, is by a little swish; he or his men walk by their side and guide him with the stick wherever they please; and they are accustomed to this method from being calves. A lad with a stick 3 feet long and as big as his finger will conduct a bull away from other bulls and his cows from one end of the farm to the other.

All this gentleness is merely the effect of management, and the mischief often done by bulls is undoubtedly owing to practices very contrary—or else to a total neglect.

The general order in which Mr Bakewell keeps his cattle is pleasing; all are fat as bears; and this is a circumstance which he insists is owing to the excellence of the breed. His land is no better than his neighbours, at the same time that it carries a far greater proportion of stock, as I shall show by and by. The small quantity and the inferior quality of food that will keep a beast perfectly well made in good order is surprising: such an animal will grow fat in the same pasture that would starve an ill-made, great-boned one.

In the breed of his sheep Mr Bakewell is as curious, and I think if any difference, with greater success, than in his horned cattle, for better-made animals cannot be seen than his rams and ewes; their bodies are as true barrels as can be seen: round, broad backs; and the legs not above 6 inches long; and a most unusual proof of kindly fattening is their feeling quite fat just within their fore legs on the ribs, a point in which sheep are never examined in common, from common breeds never carrying any fat there.

In his breed of sheep he proceeds exactly on the same principle as with oxen: the fatting in the valuable parts of the body, and the living on much poorer food than other sorts. He has found from various experience in many parts of the kingdom, as well as upon his own farm, that no land is too bad for a *good* breed of cattle, and particularly sheep. It may not be proper for large stock, that is large-boned stock, but undoubtedly more proper for a valuable well-made sheep than the usual wretched sorts found in most parts of England on poor soils—such as the moor sheep, the Welsh ones, and the Norfolk. And he would hazard any moderate stake that his own breed, each sheep of which is worth several of those poor sorts, would do better on those poor soils than the stock generally found on them—a good and true shape having been found the strongest indication of hardiness, and what the graziers call a *kindly* sheep, one that has always an inclination to feed.

He has an experiment to prove the hardiness of his breed which deserves notice. He has five or six ewes that have gone constantly in the highways since May-day and have never been in his fields: the roads are narrow, and the food very bare; they are in excellent order and nearly fat, which proves in the strongest manner the excellence of the breed. And another circumstance of a peculiar nature is his flock of ewes that have reared two lambs being quite fat in the first week of July, an instance hardly to be paralleled.

The breed is originally Lincolnshire, but Mr Bakewell thinks, and very justly, that he has much improved it. The grand profit, as I before observed, is from the same food going so much further in feeding these than any others; not however that Mr Bakewell's breed is small; on the contrary, it is as weighty as nine-tenths of the kingdom, for he sells fat wethers at three years and an half old at £2 a head. Other collateral circumstances of importance are the wool being equal to any other, and the sheep standing the fold better. He sells no tups, but lets them at from 5 guineas to 30 guineas for the season.

# XVII

William Marshall, who lived for a period in the midlands and knew the area well, here points out that Bakewell's achievements with sheep were based on improvements already carried out by Joseph Allom. He goes on to discuss the dissemination of the Dishley breed, and the reasons why it had not become more universally adopted by the farmers of the day: W. Marshall, *Rural Economy of the Midland Counties* (1790), I, pp. 380–405.

---

During the last thirty or forty years the old stock has been giving way to a modern breed—a new variety—which may be said to be a *creation* of the midland counties, in some parts of which it has already obtained a degree of establishment under the name of the 'new Leicestershire' breed.

This being, at present, the most fashionable breed of the island, and to the grazier one of the most profitable, its history is an interesting subject and its merits an object of enquiry.

The origin of this breed appears to have taken place in this neighbourhood. Joseph Allom of Clifton, who had raised himself, by dint of industry from a ploughboy, seems to be acknowledged on all hands as the first who distinguished himself in the midland district for a superior breed of sheep.

He was known to buy his ewes at a distant market; and was, in his neighbourhood, supposed to buy them in Lincolnshire; but, on better information it appears that he had them, principally, of Mr Stone of Godeby, in the Melton quarter of Leicestershire.

In whatever manner he raised his breed, it is certain, that in his day it was the fashion among superior farmers to go to Clifton in the summer season to choose and purchase ram lambs, giving, as I have been informed by contemporaries of Allom, from 2 to 3 guineas apiece.

This seems to be the only man who became *distinguishable* as a breeder of sheep in this part of the island previously to Mr

Bakewell: and, it may be reasonably supposed, the breed, through the means of Allom's stock, had passed the first stage of improvement before Mr Bakewell's day.

We may nevertheless advance, and without risk I think, that to the ability and perseverance of Mr Bakewell the Leicestershire breed of sheep owes the present high state of improvement.

The manner in which Mr Bakewell raised his sheep to the degree of celebrity in which they deservedly stand, is notwithstanding the recentness of the improvement and its being done in the day of thousands now living a thing in dispute, even among men high in the profession, and living in the very district in which the improvement has been carried on!

Some are of opinion that he effected it by a cross with the Wiltshire breed, an improbable idea as their form altogether contradicts it; others that the Ryeland breed were used in this purpose, and with some show of probability. If any cross whatever was used, the Ryeland breed, whether we view the form, the size, the wool, the flesh, or the fatting quality, is the most probable instrument of improvement.

These ideas, however, are registered merely as matters of opinion. It is more than probable that Mr Bakewell, alone, is in possession of the several minutiae of improvement; and the public can only hope that he will, at a proper time, communicate the facts for the government of future improvers.

Whenever this shall take place it will most probably come out that no cross with any *alien* breed whatever has been used; but that the improvement has been effected by selecting individuals from *kindred* breeds—from the several breeds or varieties of long-woolled sheep with which Mr B. was surrounded on almost every side; and by breeding in and in, with this selection, solicitously seizing the superior accidental varieties produced, associating these varieties, and still continuing to select, with judgement, the superior individuals . . .

Let the means of improvement have been what they may, the improvement itself, viewed in its proper light, is evident and great; evincing in a striking manner the genius and perseverance of its promoter. In the improvement of horses and cattle, Mr Bakewell appears to have acted in competition with other enterprising breeders: but the improvement which has been effected in the midland breed of sheep may be said to be all his own.

Mr Bakewell, however (as other great men have had), has his disciples, who have assisted him very efficiently in establishing and disseminating the 'new Leicestershire' breed of sheep; or, as it might well be named, from the place of its origin, the Dishley breed.

To enumerate the whole of Mr Bakewell's followers would be difficult and superfluous: nevertheless, it appears to me necessary to the due execution of this work to register such individuals as come within the limitation of principal ram breeders of the midland district: a task whose only difficulty will be that of avoiding offence by a misclassification. The best title to precedency appears to be the length of time which each has been in what is termed the 'Dishley blood'.

Mr Stubbins of Holm, near Nottingham.
Mr Paget of Ibstock, in this district.
Mr Breedon of Ruddington, Nottinghamshire.
Mr Stone, Quarndon, near Loughborough.
Mr Buckley, Normanton, Nottinghamshire.
Mr Walker, Wolfsthorp, on the borders of Lincolnshire.
Mr Bettison, Holm, near Nottingham.
Mr White, Hoton, Nottinghamshire.
Mr Knowles, Nailston, in this district.
Mr Deverel, Clapton, Nottinghamshire.
Mr Princep, Croxall, in this district.
Mr Burgess, Hucklescot, in this district.
Mr Green, Normanton, in this district.
Mr Robinson, near Welford, Northamptonshire.
Mr Moor, Thorp, in this district.
Mr Astley, Odston, in this district.
Mr Henton, Hoby, Leicestershire.

Beside these leading men, there are many of less repute in the midland district, and many others scattered over almost every part of the island, particularly in Lincolnshire, Yorkshire, and so far north as Northumberland; also in Worcestershire and Gloucestershire.

It is observable, however, and appears to me an extraordinary circumstance, evincing in a remarkable manner the weakness of men's judgements or the strength of their prejudices, that notwithstanding the rapid progress this breed of sheep are making in distant parts of the kingdom, and notwithstanding the decided preference given to them by those who have had experience of them in this district, the majority of the breeders and graziers, not of Warwickshire only, but of Northamptonshire, Rutlandshire, and Leicestershire, even within sight of Dishley, are inveterately against the breed! and this notwithstanding many of their charming grounds at present are stocked with creatures that would disgrace the meanest lands in the kingdom.

This seeming paradox can be explained in no other way, perhaps, than in the improper manner in which the improved breed have been promulgated. Had the Dishley sheep, twenty years ago, been judiciously distributed over the district, and had been on all occasions *permitted to speak for themselves*, it appears to me probable that there would scarcely have been a sheep of any other breed now left in the midland district.

No professional man, whose judgement were not biased or entirely carried away by the spirit of opposition, could hesitate a moment in his choice. But so long as the fire is fanned and the cauldron is kept boiling, so long the advocates of the breed must expect to be in hot water; and, in the nature of men's passions, so long the new Leicestershire breed of sheep must have its powerful opponents.

It now remains to give a description of the superior class of individuals of this breed, especially ewes and wedders, in full condition but not immoderately fat. The rams will require to be distinguished in the next section.

The *head* long, small, and hornless, with ears somewhat long and standing backward, and with the nose shooting forward.

The *neck* thin, and clean towards the head but taking a conical form; standing low, and enlarging every way at the base; the *fore end*, altogether, short.

The *bosom* broad, with the *shoulders*, *ribs*, and *chine* extraordinarily full.

The *loin* broad, and the *back* level.

The *haunches* comparatively full towards the hips, but light downward; being altogether small in proportion to the fore parts.

The *legs*, at present, of a moderate length, with the bone extremely fine.

The *bone*, throughout, remarkably light.

The *carcass*, when fully fat, takes a remarkable form: much wider than it is deep, and almost as broad as it is long; full on the shoulder, widest on the ribs, narrowing with a regular curve towards the tail; approaching the form of the turtle nearer than any other animal I can call to mind.

The *pelt* thin; and the *tail* small.

The *wool* shorter than longwools in general, but much longer than the middle-wools; the ordinary length of staple, 5 to 7 inches: varying much in fineness and weight.

The comparative merit of this breed will best appear by placing it, in its present state, in the several lights in which it may be viewed comparatively with other breeds: thereby, at the same time, ascertaining how far the principles of improvement have in this case been judiciously applied.

In beauty of form the breed under notice surpasses every other breed I have seen ...

Utility of form: the most distinguishing characteristics of this breed—that which might be considered as its specific character—is the fulness and comparative weight of its fore quarters. This, however, seems to be contrary to the general principle of improvement, and affords matter of argument to the advocates of the old stock who contend that this form throws the meat upon the least valuable parts: legs and saddles, not shoulders and breasts, being the favourite joints.

The advocates for the new breed argue, in return, that the majority of the eaters of mutton are of the poorer class, and that the grand object of the improvement is their supply; arguing further that upon a given set of bones, and with a given quantity of other offal, a greater weight of meat may be laid on the fore quarters than on the hind ones.

Offal: another distinguishing character of the modern breed is the smallness of their bone comparatively with that of the old stock and most other breeds; not of the legs only, but of the ribs and other parts. I have seen a rib of a sheep of this breed contrasted with one of a Norfolk sheep: the disparity was striking, the latter nearly twice the size; while the meat which covered the former was three times the thickness: consequently *the proportion of meat to bone* was, in the one, incomparably greater than in the other. Therefore, in this point of view, the improved breed has a decided preference. For, surely, while mankind continues to eat flesh and throw away bone, the former must be, to the consumer at least, the more valuable.

The other offal is also light: the pelt thin, and the head small, and, it is said, the intestines, and even the blood, are small in a similar proportion.

That the last two are comparatively small in proportion to the carcass when this is loaded with fat, in a manner that the carcass of no other breed of sheep, probably, is capable of laying on, will be readily granted. But that they bear a smaller proportion to the carcass in this breed than they do in others of the same natural size, in the same condition, and going in the same pasture, remains, I believe, among a thousand other things relating to livestock to be proved by a series of accurate experiments . . .

The grazier's object, undoubtedly, is to get sheep that will fat *quickly*: for even supposing them to eat more food than sheep which fat more slowly, there is a material advantage accruing from their reaching market a fortnight or three weeks sooner than other sheep; grass mutton, for instance, bears a better price, at its first coming in, than it does a few weeks afterward, when a glut seldom fails of being poured into market. So far, however, from these sheep consuming more food than others, it seems probable at least that sheep which are, in their nature, disposed to a state of fatness, become marketable at a smaller expense of food than sheep which are naturally of a leaner constitution . . .

The degree of fatness to which the individuals of this breed are capable of being raised will, I am afraid, appear incredible, to those who have not had an opportunity of being convinced by their own observation. I have seen wedders of only two shear (two to three years old) so loaded with fat as to be scarcely able to make a run; and whose fat lay so much without the bone it seemed ready to be shook from the ribs on the smallest agitation. It is common for the sheep of this breed to have such a projection of fat upon the ribs immediately behind the shoulder that it may be easily gathered up in the hand, as the flank of a fat bullock. Hence it has gained, in technical language, the name of the foreflank; a point which a modern breeder never fails to touch in judging of the quality of this breed of sheep.

Extraordinary, however, as are these appearances while the animals are living, the facts are still more striking after they are slaughtered. At Litchfield in February 1785 I saw a fore quarter of mutton fattened by Mr Princep of Croxall and which measured upon the ribs *4 inches* of *fat*! But this I saw far exceeded in the mutton whose bone has been mentioned, and which, notwithstanding its extreme fineness, was covered with about an inch of muscular flesh, interlarded, and *5 inches* of *fat*! Since then (1786) several sheep of this breed have laid 6 inches of meat on their ribs.

It is observable that in sheep of this extreme degree of fatness the muscular parts decrease in thickness as the fatness increases, and are so intermingled with fat as to give the whole a fatty appearance, and this most especially in aged sheep; which, as aged cattle, have more fat in proportion to lean than younger carcasses. A loin of mutton of a sheep (ten shear) of 26 lb a quarter weighed, when the fat was taken off, only 2½ lb!

These are certainly interesting facts. But reflection aptly suggests the question, to what stomach can mutton like this be grateful? The answer held out is 'fat mutton is the poor man's mutton: it goes farther than lean; and has, of course, a smaller proportion of bone than lean mutton. A poor man gives 8d a pound for bacon, but only 5d for fat mutton . . .'

Wool: viewing the coat abstractedly from the carcass, the Leicestershire sheep, compared with most other longwoolled sheep, appear to disadvantage; and the Leicestershire breeders, perhaps, may seem liable to a degree of censure. Indeed, the coat, throughout the improvement, appears to have been set at nought; the carcass alone having engrossed the whole attention of the improvers.

But this is conformable with the general principle of improvement. Flesh—*human food*—is the object the improvers have had in view; and it is highly probable that the more sustenance there is expended on the wool, the less there will remain for the carcass; beside a heavy fleece being, at certain seasons, inconvenient, and not unfrequently fatal, to the sheep.

Nevertheless, it appears evidently that a deficiency in the coat has, more than any other circumstance, hurt this breed of sheep in the eyes of the old graziers; and has, beyond dispute, greatly retarded their adoption . . .

The fact is, this breed of sheep, when seen and examined, are *not greatly* deficient in wool. The wedders generally run about 4 to the tod (of 28 lb); the ewes about 4½; the fleece of the former weighing 6 to 8, of the latter 5 to 7 lb each. Indeed, their cooler advocates argue, and with some show of reason on their side, that they not only produce more mutton but more wool, *by the acre*, than any other breed of sheep. This however remains, with the other desiderata relating to livestock to be proved by a series of accurate experiments.

General observations: from this comparative view it evidently appears that the modern breed of Leicestershire are a valuable variety of longwoolled sheep.

In carcass they may be said to be nearly perfect: superior, at least, to any other breed of longwoolled sheep I have seen.

In wool, however, they fall short, I believe, of every other longwoolled breed: owing principally, it should seem, to a false principle of improvement.

Nevertheless, taking them as they are at present, they are to the *grazier*, professionally and distinctly considered, a very profitable breed of sheep.

# XVIII

In the eighteenth century the dissemination of new breeds of livestock largely depended upon their adoption and recommendation by well-known landlords and leading farmers. The Culley brothers were leading farmers in Durham and were primarily responsible for the introduction of the Dishley sheep into that county. Both brothers were early visitors to Dishley, and George Culley, whom this memoir mainly concerns, was the author of a valuable work, 'Observations on Live Stock'. *Farmer's Magazine*, XIV (1814), pp. 271-5.

---

*Lines suggested by the death of the late George Culley, Esq., who died at Fowberry Tower (the seat of his son), after a few days' illness, on 7 May 1813, in his 79th year; with a memoir of that eminent agriculturist.*

If for his tomb, who wrote in blood his name,
Surrounding laurels claim a deathless fame,
And Sculpture's arts, with martial grace, record
The fatal trophies of the Warrior's sword;
Say, should not more unfading wreaths attend
*His memory*, not of man the *Foe*, but *Friend*?
Whose blameless triumphs undefiled appear,
Unstained by blood, unsullied by a tear;
Who gave his useful time, and active mind,
Still to promote the good of human kind;
To improve, with scientific skill, the soil,
By Agriculture's honourable toil,
And, (worthier far, than deeds of splendid strife!)
Increase the comforts, and the means of life.—
Yes! o'er the RURAL PATRIOT's peaceful grave,
Still shall the immortal wreaths of Virtue wave!
While public praise and private grief combine,

To grace, with pure regret, his sacred shrine;
And, for his honoured memory, justly claim
*No undeserved, but high and honest Fame !*

The subject of the above lines was the fourth son of Matthew
Culley, Esq. of Denton in the county of Durham, who was
eminent for the superior cultivation of an estate of his own of
considerable extent. At his decease, it came into the possession of
his eldest son Robert, who being bred to the law, the management
of the estate devolved upon the third and fourth sons, Matthew
and George. The former being somewhat delicate, attended markets and gave the principal directions for carrying on the operations of the farm; the latter being of a hardy, robust constitution
and athletic form, was accustomed to assist in almost every kind
of work that was going forward; in the various branches of which,
he was uncommonly expert. He thus, early in life, acquired an
accurate judgement [of] what ought to be done by servants in the
practical operations of agriculture, which enabled him to teach
those that were not so perfect as they ought to be in their
respective departments.

The father was not only a good cultivator but was also eminent
for his livestock, both of cattle and sheep, and ranked amongst the
first of the district as a breeder and grazier; and the sons, being
constantly in the habit of receiving their father's instructions on
those subjects, were early in life esteemed first-rate judges in
those departments. Having heard of Mr Bakewell's improved
breed of sheep, Matthew went to see them in the year 1762, and
George the year following; and being fully convinced of their
great superiority, they hired a ram, and continued to do so for a
great number of years afterwards. When they hired the first ram
their own sheep were of the Teeswater breed, which weighed
from 40 to 50 lb a quarter. These, in a few years, were reduced to
about half the weight, which fattened at a much earlier age, and of
course a much greater number were kept on the same quantity of
land; yet, notwithstanding so manifest an improvement, so great
is the power of prejudice that few of their neighbours benefited by
their example until some years afterwards.

At this first visit Mr Bakewell took such a particular liking to
George, and entertained so high an opinion of his judgement and
agricultural acquirements, that he seldom made a tour to examine

the different breeds of livestock in various parts of the kingdom without contriving to have him as a fellow traveller; by which means he not only became acquainted with Mr Bakewell's private sentiments respecting the different breeds of animals, but also gained a knowledge of the agricultural practice of almost every part of the kingdom: in short, he became Mr Bakewell's confidential friend and was always considered his favourite disciple.

In 1786 he published his *Observations on Live Stock*, which was the first treatise on the subject that attempted to describe the different breeds of domestic animals found in this island, and containing hints for choosing and improving the most useful kinds. A second edition, much altered and enlarged, was published in 1794, which has been so well received by the public that more editions have been since called for. In 1793, he was appointed by the Board of Agriculture, in conjunction with Mr Bailey of Chillingham, to draw up the Reports for the counties of Cumberland and Northumberland. He was also a frequent contributor to periodical works on agriculture, particularly Young's *Annals*.

With such acquirements, his brother Matthew and he had for some time been anxious to take a farm of greater extent and for a term of longer endurance than could be had in their own county. This they accomplished in 1767 by taking Fenton farm, near Wooler in Northumberland, containing upwards of 1,100 acres. At this period the sheep flocks that were kept on the arable and grazing districts of Northumberland were a large, slow-feeding, longwoolled kind; and a mixed breed, between those longwoolled sheep and the Cheviot. These breeds were rarely got fattened before three years old; but the improved Leicesters (which were first introduced by Messrs Culley) are sold fat at little more than a year old; and though they met with much opposition at their first introduction, there is now scarcely a flock to be found that has not been improved by them.

Before Messrs Culley left the county of Durham they had been in the habit of letting rams; and upon their removing into Northumberland they attempted a similar practice, which at first met with little encouragement, except from a few discerning individuals: But, in a few years, the superiority of this breed having decidedly shown itself, the demand for rams became so great that they let great numbers every year, sometimes to the value of £1,500.

Their breed of shorthorned or Teeswater cattle were also a great acquisition to the district; and the breed of draught horses were considerably improved by their introducing a stallion of Mr Bakewell's. They were always amongst the first to adopt and make experiments of any new mode of culture, new implements of husbandry, or new varieties of grain. Their great attention to minutiae, unremitting industry, and superior cultivation not only raised a spirit of exertion and emulation in the surrounding neighbourhood, but gained them such celebrity as first-rate breeders and agriculturists that they had pupils from various parts of the island, with whom they received considerable premiums, besides being amply paid for their board and instruction. To all those acquirements they added strict economy; the consequence of which was a great accumulation of wealth, which they applied (as occasions offered) to increasing their farming concerns; and this to such an extent that for several years they occupied farms to the amount of about £6,000 a year. The large capital which such extensive concerns required, applied with so much attention and judgement, could not fail of producing the most lucrative effects. The result is that, from a small original capital, their respective families are now enjoying landed property to the amount of nearly £4,000 a year each (besides a very large sum invested in farming)—the well-merited reward of unremitting industry and extensive agricultural knowledge.

The dispositions of the two brothers were peculiarly adapted to the respective departments, of which they each, more particularly, took the charge. Matthew, with a most active mind, was of a grave, thoughtful disposition, and remarkably ingenious in planning and contriving the best and most advantageous modes of arranging and performing the different species of labour, and of laying out fences, drains, roads, and making every kind of improvement, in which he had a particular enjoyment. He was also remarkably fertile in expedients to remedy any accident or unexpected misfortunes that occasionally happened, and was ever ready to try new improvements or to introduce new practices: amongst many others that of watered meadows was his great favourite, which he first introduced into Northumberland and the county of Durham. With such a disposition it was most congenial to him to look after the management of the farms and arrange their particular details; of course, the disposal of the produce fell chiefly to the lot of George, who frequently spent four days a week in attending fairs and markets; and few persons were better qualified for the purpose since to an accurate judgement of the value of stock was joined the most pleasing and conciliating manner and that equality of temper fitted to sustain with calm indifference the ill-natured remarks to which, in the transaction of business, he was inevitably exposed: these were generally answered by a facetious observation or good-humoured jest which disappointed the asperity or malevolence of his opponents and not unfrequently made them his customers and friends. To that gay and good temper, unruffled spirits, and agreeable manner which never fail to please, were added a liberality of sentiment, which made his conversation as inoffensive as delightful. His integrity and judgement were so universally acknowledged that he was generally resorted to as an arbitrator in settling disputes and in valuing livestock and corn crops between off-going and in-coming tenants, and in the division of estates amongst different proprietors. He fulfilled all the relative duties of existence with conscientious propriety; nor, while his charity cheered many a countenance and brightened many a gloomy prospect, was he ever forgetful of those gentle courtesies which dispose the generous spirit 'to shun the guilt of giving needless pain'.

As his life gained him universal respect, his loss is generally felt and lamented; and has occasioned a blank in the society of this district that will not be easily supplied.

# XIX

Liver-rot in sheep was one of the most serious causes of losses of livestock for farmers. While the disease had long been recognized as having an association with wet pastures, its precise cause was unknown and unsuspected, particularly as the destructive liver-flukes (conveyed to the sheep by their eating slugs) could not be found on the ground used by affected animals. The following is an example of the promotion of secret remedies to which the limited state of veterinary knowledge exposed farmers: Oxfordshire County Record Office, document Wi IX/1 (c).

---

## ROT IN SHEEP

An effectual cure and preventative for this fatal disease, which annually destroys so great a number of sheep, is at length so certainly discovered, as to be able to stand the test of the whole world, by

### MR THOMAS FLEET,
#### of Moundsmere Farm, near Basingstoke, Hants,

who will be happy, for the good of the community at large, to make known the remedy on these conditions:

A subscription to be opened, at not less than one guinea each, which, if not found sufficient, to be returned to the different subscribers. There are sixteen of the sheep, for the inspection of the public, at Mr Fleet's at this time.

*Basingstoke, 5 November 1793*
We, whose names are hereunto subscribed, having this day seen sheep, at a meeting held for that purpose at the Angel Inn in this town, with the different persons attending to identify and prove that they were the same delivered to Mr Thomas Fleet in June last, and were then in the last stage of the rot, some of them

nearly expiring; that the sheep here produced are the identical sheep, and are now perfectly sound, healthy, and in as thriving a state as if they had never been affected with the disease, do certify, that one of the said sheep which Mr Fleet bought of Mr John Wythe of Hartley-Row, with some others for one shilling each, was killed, perfectly free from any appearance of the rot; was fat, good-coloured, fine-flavoured, and full of gravy:

| | | | |
|---|---|---|---|
| F. S. Wallace | Rector of Botley | S. Martin | Bradley |
| John Tubb | Sherbourn St | John Bassett | Nutley |
| | John | John Biggs | Woodgarston |
| Nich. Windover | Basingstoke | Tho. Penton | Sherbourn St |
| Cha. Tubb | Sherbourn St | | John |
| | John | Rich. Martin | Ashford |
| F. Vickers | Hatch Warren | Baker | |
| | Farm | J. Smith | Preston |
| Wm. Tubb | Sherfield | | Candover |
| J. Colebrook | Preston | R. Curtis | Angel Inn, |
| | Candover | | Basingstoke |
| J. Carpenter | Bradley | Tho. Garret | Wootton |

The following persons are ready to certify on oath, the identity of the cure of rotten sheep of their own, and under their own inspection during the process:

| | | | |
|---|---|---|---|
| Wm. Poate | Finch Dean | John Wythe | Hartley Row |
| Tho. Padwick | ditto | Rich. Tubb | Sherfield upon |
| Daniel Tubb | Flood Farm, Nr. | | Lodden |
| | Odiham | J. Egerton | Sherbourn St |
| Mr Husband | Dogmersfield | | John |
| | Park | | |

William Poate and Thomas Padwick, the above-named, having a number of sound sheep, grazed them together three successive years. Mr Poate, the first year drenched his, saved all, and fatted them. Mr Padwick's all died rotten. They purchased others the second year, and each pursued the same plan with similar success. The third year the fresh flock of Mr Padwick were drenched, as well as Mr Poate's and all saved and fatted.

Mr Fleet makes the following offer to the public, by way of trial:

Any number of sound sheep shall be put into the most rotting ground possible; one-third shall be treated after his manner, and shall never take the rot; the remaining two-thirds will become rotten, half of which Mr Fleet will then engage to cure; the other half, to which no assistance shall be given, will die rotten. All the sheep shall be together during the experiment and live in the same manner, the drenching only excepted.

The money which shall be subscribed is not to be paid to Mr Fleet until it shall be certified by three magistrates at least, of the counties of Southampton, Wilts, and Berks, or of some or one of the said counties, that they are satisfied of the efficacy of Mr Fleet's specific, both for the prevention and the cure of the sheep; and in default of such certificate within one year from the date hereof, the money subscribed and advanced shall be returned; and in the meantime it shall remain in deposit in the several banking houses appointed to receive the same.

When a sufficient number have subscribed, a book will be delivered to each subscriber, giving every direction necessary to the preparing the medicines, the most proper time to administer them, and every requisite to complete a perfect cure.

Five pounds per hundred is the utmost expense that will be incurred in the completing the cure or preventing the disease.

---

We, whose names are hereunto subscribed, do hereby certify, that on or about 4 September last we attended a Petty Sessions of Justices at the Town Hall at Basingstoke in the County of Hants, and afterwards dined at the Club held at the Crown Inn in the said town, at which time we recollect that (amongst other dishes) a leg of mutton was set on the table, boiled, and some mutton chops by way of trial of a receipt of Mr Thomas Fleet of Moundsmere Farm for curing the rot in sheep which mutton we were well satisfied with, and esteemed it fit, in point of fatness, colour, yielding gravy, and flavour, to be set to any table. We further certify that it was afterwards incontestibly proved to us by Mr Merchant, butcher to Sir Henry St John Mildmay, Bart. of Dogmersfield, that the said mutton was part of a sheep killed by the said Mr Merchant, which the said Mr Fleet had, about six months before, bought for one shilling; the liver of which was then produced and looked sound; though not without a scar or

two, which denoted, as we thought, that it had been infected:
Witness our Hands, this Twenty-first Day of November 1793.

Tho. Hall, Preston Candover

Wm. St John Dogmersfield

Tho. Husker, Chinham

W. Greene, Basingstoke

W. Willson, Crown Inn,
   Basingstoke.

\* Subscriptions will be received at the Oxford Bank.

# XX

Frederick Law Olmstead, an American agriculturist, made a tour of England in 1850. His comments ranged over numerous aspects of the country and covered both technical matters of farming and social conditions, such as the ignorance and conservative outlook of the labourers whom he met. In the following passage he describes the water-meadows he found on the south downs near Warminster, and goes on to mention the use of town sewerage-water as a manure: Frederick Law Olmstead, *Walks and Talks of an American Farmer in England* (first published 1852; reprinted University of Michigan Press, 1969), pp. 258–61.

---

Geologically, [the Downs form] a chalk district, the whole earth, high and low, and to any depth that I saw it exposed, being more or less white, generally grey, but sometimes white as snow. The only stone is flint, which occurs in small boulders or pebbles, cased in a hardened crust of carbonate of lime mingled irregularly with the chalk, more thickly on the hill-tops, and often gathered in beds. The road is made of these flint pebbles, broken fine, and their chalk-crust, powdered by the attrition of wheels, is worked up into a slippery paste during such heavy rains as I was experiencing, and makes the walking peculiarly fatiguing. The soil upon the hills is very dry and thin. In the valleys it is deeper and richer, being composed, in a considerable part, of the wash of the higher country, and the wheat and forage crops are often very luxuriant. Advantage is sometimes taken of the streams to form water-meadows, and the effect of irrigation can often be seen at a considerable distance in the deeper green and greater density of the grass upon them. As these meadows are of great agricultural value, I will describe the method of construction and management of them.

An artificial channel is made, into which the water of a brook may be turned at will. This is carried along for as great a distance as practicable, so as to skirt the upper sides of fields of a convenient surface for irrigation. At suitable intervals there are gates and smaller channels, and eventually a great number of minor ducts, through which the water is distributed. The fields are divided by low walls, so that the water can be retained upon them as long as is desired, and then drawn off to a lower level. Commonly, a series of meadows, held by different farmers, are flooded from one source, and old custom or agreement fixes the date of commencing the irrigation and the period of time at which the water shall be moved from one to another.

The main flooding is usually given in October, after the grass has been closely eaten off by neat stock. It is then allowed to remain resting or quietly flowing over the land for two or three weeks; or for two weeks, and, after an interval of a day or two, for two weeks more. This consolidates the grassy surface, and encourages the growth of roots. The grass springs and grows luxuriantly after it, and, as soon as it is observed to flag, the water is again let in for two or three weeks; it may be twice during the winter. Whenever a scum is observed to form, indicating that decomposition is commencing below, the water is immediately drawn. In warm weather this will occur very soon, perhaps in a day or two. I believe it is intended not to allow the water ever to freeze upon the meadows. In the spring, by the middle of March, sometimes, sheep and lambs are turned on to the grass. After being fed pretty closely, they are removed, and the meadows are left for a crop of hay. They are ready for mowing in less than two months, and are then, after a short interval, pastured again with horned cattle and horses. Some meadows are never pastured, and yield three heavy crops of hay. Mr Pusey (a Member of Parliament) declares, that he keeps sheep upon his water-meadows in Berkshire at the rate of thirty-six an acre, well fed, and intimates his belief that the produce of grass-land is doubled by irrigation. Grass and hay, however, from irrigated meadows are of slightly less nourishing quality. It is generally said, that a single winter's flooding will increase the growth of grass equal to a top-dressing of thirty (thirty bushel) loads of dung.

We may judge somewhat from these facts and opinions of practical men, whether, in any given circumstances, we can afford to construct the dam, channels, gates, sluices, etc., by which we may use this method of fertilizing our meadows. There are millions of acres in the United States that could be most readily made subject to the system. The outlay for permanent works might often be very inconsiderable, and the labour of making use of them, after construction, would be almost nothing. The cost of conveying manure, and its distribution by carts and manual labour, is a very important item in the expenditure of most of our eastern farms; and, though this is felt less here, where labour is cheaper, we may obtain many economical hints with regard to it from British practice. Fields distant from the farmstead, and hill-lands not easily accessible, should nearly always be enriched by bone, guano and other concentrated manures; of which a man may carry more on his back than will be of equal value with many cartloads of dung, or by some other means which will dispense with long and heavy transportation. I have obtained increased crops, with a saving of some hundred dollars a year of expenditure, in this way.

Different streams vary in their value for irrigation. The muddiest streams are the best, as they generally carry suspended a great deal of the fertile matter of the land through which they have flowed; often, too, road-washings, and other valuable drainings, have been taken along with them, and these are caused to be deposited upon the meadow. A perfectly transparent fluid will often, however, have most valuable salts in solution; and I noticed that most of the Wiltshire streams were peculiarly clear, reminding me of the White Mountain trout-brooks. It is said that streams abounding in fish, and which have abundance of aquatic plants and luxuriant vegetation upon their borders, are to be relied upon as the most enriching in their deposit. Streams into which the sewerage of large towns is emptied, are often of the greatest value for agricultural purposes. A stream thus enriched is turned to important account near Edinburgh. Certain lands which were formerly barren wastes, being merely the clean, dry sands thrown up by the sea in former times, having been arranged so that they may be flowed. The expense of the operation was great—about 100 dollars [£20 11s] an acre—and the annual cost of flooding is very much greater than usual—4 or 5 dollars [16s 6d to 20s 7d] an acre; but the crops of hay are so frequent and enormous (ten cuttings being made in a season), that some parts of the meadow rent for 100 dollars a year for one acre, and none for less than 75 dollars!

It is estimated by the distinguished agriculturist, Smith of Deanston, that the sewerage water of a town may be contracted for, to be delivered (sent by subterranean pipes and branches, so that it may be distributed over any required surface) eleven miles out of town, for 4 cents [2d] a ton. Mr Hawksley, a prudent engineer, offers to convey it five miles, and raise it 200 feet, for 5 cents a ton; the expense of carting it to the same distance and elevation being estimated at about 1 dollar [4s 6d]. Another estimate makes the expense of conveying and distributing manure, in the solid form, as compared with liquid, at 15 dollars to 75 cents [£3 1s 9d to 3s 1d], for equal fertilizing values. Professor Johnston estimates the annual fertilizing value of the sewerage of a town of 1,000 inhabitants as equal to a quantity of guano which, at present American prices, would be worth 13,000 dollars [£2,675], Smith of Deanston estimates the cost of manuring an acre by sewerage, conveyed in aqueducts and distributed by jet-pipes, at 3 dollars [12s 4d] an acre, and that of fertilizing it to an equal degree, in the usual way, by farmyard manure, at 15 dollars [£3 1s 9d]. Considering that the expense of conveyance and distribution of solid manure is much greater in America than in England, these figures are not without personal interest to us.

The use of manure-drainings and the urine of the cattle of a farm, very much diluted with spring water, has been found to have such astonishing immediate effects, when distributed over young herbage, that several English agricultural pioneers are making extensive and costly permanent arrangements for its distribution, from their stables, over large surface. It is first collected in tanks, where it is retained until putrefied, and mixed with the water of irrigation. This is then driven by forcing-pumps into the pipes which convey it, so that it can be distributed (in one case, over 170 acres). The pipes are hard-burnt clay pipes, 1 inch thick, joined with cement, costing here about 12½ cents [6d] a yard. The pipe is laid underground, and at convenient intervals there are heads coming to the surface with stop-cocks, where a hose can be attached and the water further guided in any direction. For greater distances a cart like those used for sprinkling the dusty streets of our cities is used. It is conjectured that, eventually, all manure will be furnished to land in a state of solution.

# XXI

Agricultural chemistry, with particular reference to the composition and efficacy of artificial manures, was a major interest of scientifically-minded agriculturists in the middle nineteenth century. Sir John Bennet Lawes and Dr J. H. Gilbert carried out a series of experiments at Rothamsted in order to determine the effects of various fertilizers on crop yields, and in the paper from which these extracts are drawn they published some of their findings and the grounds for their disagreement with the mineral theory advocated by the German authority, Justus von Liebig: *Journal of the Royal Agricultural Society of England*, XII (1851), pp. 1-9.

---

*On Agricultural Chemistry—especially in relation to the Mineral Theory of Baron Liebig.* By J. B. Lawes, of Rothamsted, and Dr J. H. Gilbert.

It was under the auspices of the British Association that Professor Liebig in the year 1840 first promulgated his views on the subject of agricultural chemistry; and however much some may be disposed to differ from him in opinion on special points therein treated of, few we presume will deny that from the appearance of the first edition of Professor Liebig's work on *Organic Chemistry in its relations to Agriculture and Physiology* we may date a spirit of investigation into Agricultural Chemistry such as had not previously been manifested in this country. Indeed, we conceive that in looking back to the words of his preface in 1840, wherein he says, 'I shall be happy if I succeed in attracting the attention of men of science to subjects which so well merit to engage their talents and energies'—in this respect, at least, Professor Liebig must feel that his efforts have been rewarded far beyond what his most sanguine expectation could at the time have led him to hope for. It could scarcely be expected, however, that with the progress of inquiry, such as is here invited, there should not result from time to time some, and perhaps material, modifications on questions which it is admitted the facts already at command were not competent satisfactorily to solve; indeed, if it were not so, if no further facts were requisite, and the views as then put forth were all and in their manifold detail already fully substantiated, where the necessity for further investigation of the subject? Surely it would be labour lost!

Professor Liebig has indeed himself contributed to the development of the subject, in the several succeeding editions of his works; and also in his *Letters on Chemistry*, and in other publications; and he has, in a new and enlarged edition of the second-mentioned work, namely, his *Letters on Chemistry*, published only in May last, given the result of his latest researches in agricultural and physiological chemistry.

Among other labourers in this important field of investigation of late years we may state that one of ourselves was occupied several years, prior to the appearance of the first edition of Professor Liebig's work, in investigating the action of different chemical combinations when applied as manures to the most important crops of the farm; and that since the year 1843 we have been conjointly engaged in systematically investigating the subject of agricultural chemistry in a more extended sense than that alone implied in the question of the action of special substances as manures . . .

What is termed a rotation of crops is at least of such universality in the farming of Great Britain, that any investigation in relation to the agriculture of that country may safely be grounded on the supposition of its adoption. Let us, then, direct attention for a moment to some of the chief features of rotation. What is called a *course* of rotation is the period of years which includes the circle of all the different crops grown in that rotation or alternation. The crops which thus succeed each other, and constitute a rotation, may be two, three, four, or more, varying with the nature of the soil and the judgement of the farmer; but, whatever *course* be adopted, no individual crop—wheat, for example—is grown immediately succeeding one of the same description, but it is sown again only after some other crops have been grown, and at such a period of the rotation, indeed, as by experience it is known that the soil will, by direct manure or other means, have recovered its capability of producing a profitable quantity of the crop in question.

On carefully considering these established and well-known facts of agriculture, it appears to us that, by taking soils either at the end of the rotation, or at least at that period of it when in the ordinary course of farming farmyard manure would be added before any further crop would be grown, we should then have the soils in what may be termed a *normal*, or, perhaps better still, a *practically* and *agriculturally exhausted state*.

Now, if it is found, in the experience of the farmer, that land of any given quality with which he is well acquainted, will not when in this condition of *practical exhaustion* yield the quantity he usually obtains from it of any particular crop, but that after applying farmyard manure it will do so, it is evident that if we supply to different plots of this *exhausted land* the constituents of farmyard manure, both individually and combined, and if by the side of these plots we also grow the crop both without manure of any kind and with farmyard manure, we shall have obtained in the comparative results a far more satisfactory solution of the question as to what constituents were, in this ordinary course of agriculture, most in defect in respect to the production of the particular crop experimented upon, than any analysis of the soil could have given us. In other words, we should have before us very good ground for deciding to which of the constituents of the farmyard manure the increased produce was mainly due on the plot provided with it, in the case of the particular crop: not so, however, unless the soil had been so far exhausted by previous cropping as to be considered *practically* unfit for the growth of that crop without manure. We lay particular stress on this exhaustion, because we believe that the vast discrepancy in the comparative results, with different manures, by different experimenters, arises more from irregularity in what may be called the *floating* capital of the soil than from irregularities in the original character of the soil itself, or from any other cause, unless we include the frequent faulty methods of application.

It is, then, by this *synthetic* rather than by the analytic method that we have sought our results; and in the carrying out of our object we have taken *Wheat* as the type of the cereal crops, *Turnips* as the type of the *root crops*, and *Beans* as the representative of the Leguminous corn crop, since these most frequently enter into rotation; and having selected for each of these a field which, agriculturally considered, was *exhausted*, we have grown the same description of crop upon the same land, year after year, with different chemical manures, and in each case with one plot or more continuously unmanured, and one supplied every year with a fair quantity of farmyard manure.

In this way fourteen acres have been devoted to the continuous growth of *Wheat* since 1843, eight acres to the continuous growth of *Turnips* from the same date, and five to six acres to that of Leguminous corn crops since 1847. Besides these we have made other field experiments—amounting in each year to from thirty to forty on wheat, upwards of ninety on turnips, and twenty to thirty on beans—and also some on the growth of Clover, and some in relation to the chemical circumstances involved in an actual course of rotation, comprising Turnips, Barley, Clover, and Wheat, grown in the order in which they are here stated.

It may be stated, too, that in addition to these experiments on wheat and the other crops usually grown upon the farm as above referred to, we have for several years been much occupied also with the subject of the feeding of animals—viz. bullocks, sheep, and pigs—as well as in investigating the functional actions of the growing plant in relation to the soil and atmosphere; and in connexion with each of these subjects much laboratory labour has constantly been in progress . . .

It has been said that all the experimental fields were selected when they were in a state of agricultural exhaustion. The wheat-field, however, after having been manured in the usual way for turnips at the commencement of the previous rotation, had then grown barley, peas, wheat, and oats, without any further manuring; so that when taken for experiment in 1844, it was, as a grain-producer, considerably more exhausted than would ordinarily be the case. It was, therefore, in a most favourable condition for the purposes of our experiment.

In the first experimental season, the field of fourteen acres was divided into about twenty plots, and it was by the *mineral theory* that we were mainly guided in the selection of manures; mineral manures were therefore employed in the majority of cases. *Ammonia*, on the other hand, being then considered as of less importance, was used in a few instances only, and in these in very insignificant quantities. Rape-cake, as being a well-recognized manure, and calculated to supply—besides some minerals and nitrogen—a certain quantity of *carbonaceous* substance in which both corn and straw so much abound, was also added to one or two of the plots.

The results of this first season (1844) having already been pretty fully detailed in this Journal, we can only give a summary of them in this place:

TABLE I*

Harvest 1844. Summary

| Description of the manures | Dressed corn per acre in bushels and pecks | | Total corn per acre, in lb | Straw per acre, in lb |
|---|---|---|---|---|
| | b. | p. | lb | lb |
| Plot 3. Unmanured | 16 | 0 | 923 | 1,120 |
| ,,   2. 14 tons of farmyard manure | 22 | 0 | 1,276 | 1,476 |
| ,,   4. The ashes of 14 tons of farmyard manure | 16 | 0 | 888 | 1,104 |
| ,,   8. *Minimum* produce of 9 plots with artificial mineral manures: Superphosphate lime 350 lb Phosphate of potass 364 lb | 16 | 1 | 980 | 1,160 |
| ,,  15. *Maximum* produce of 9 plots with artificial mineral manures: Superphosphate lime 350 lb Phosphate magnesia 168 lb Phosphate potass 150 lb Silicate potass 112 lb | 17 | 3¼ | 1,096 | 1,240 |
| Mean of the 9 plots with artificial mineral manures | 16 | 3¾ | 1,009 | 1,155 |
| Mean of 3 plots with mineral manures and 65 lb each of sulphate ammonia | 21 | 0 | 1,275 | 1,423 |
| Mean of 2 plots with mineral manures and 150 lb and 300 lb of rape-cake respectively | 18 | 1¼ | 1,078 | 1,201 |
| Plot 18. With complex mineral manure, 65 lb of sulphate of ammonia, and 150 lb of rape-cake | 22 | 3¼ | 1,368 | 1,768 |

* It should be stated that the terms Superphosphate of Lime, Phosphate of Potass, Phosphate of Soda, and Phosphate of Magnesia, as used in this table, and by which it is convenient to designate the manures, are not to be understood as representing the chemical substances bearing those names. They were formed by acting upon burnt bone-dust by means of sulphuric acid in the first instance; and in the cases of the alkaline salts and the magnesian one by neutralizing the compound thus obtained by means of cheap preparations of the respective bases. The Silicate of Potass was manufactured at

The indications of the table are seen to be most conclusive, as showing what was the character of the exhaustion which had been induced by the previous heavy cropping, and what, therefore, should be the peculiar nature of the supply in a rational system of manuring. If the exhaustion had been connected with a deficiency of mineral constituents, we might reasonably have expected that by some one at least of the nine mineral conditions—supplying in some cases an abundance of every mineral constituent which the plant could require—this deficiency would have been made up; but it was not so.

Thus, taking the column of bushels per acre as given in this summary as our guide, it will be seen that whilst we have without manure only sixteen bushels of dressed corn, we have by farm-yard manure twenty-two bushels. The *ashes* of farmyard manure give, however, no increase whatever over the unmanured plot. Again, out of the nine plots supplied with artificial mineral manures, we have in no case an increase of two bushels by this means; the produce of the average of the nine being not quite seventeen bushels. On the other hand, we see that the addition to some of these purely mineral manures of 65 lb of sulphate of ammonia—a very small dressing of that substance, and containing only about 14 lb of ammonia—has given us an average produce of twenty-one bushels. An insignificant addition of rape-cake too, to manures otherwise ineffective, has given us about 18½ bushels; and when, as in plot 18, we have added to the inefficient mineral manures 65 lb of ammoniacal salts, and a little rape-cake also, we have a produce greater than by the 14 tons of farmyard manure.

The quantities of rape-cake used were small, and the increase attributed to it also small, but it nevertheless was much what we should expect when compared with that from the ammoniacal salts, if, as we believe is the case, the effect of rape-cake on *grain-crops* is due to the nitrogen it contains.

Indeed, the coincidence in the slight or non-effect throughout

---

a glass-house by fusing equal parts of pearlash and sand—a transparent glass, slightly deliquescent in the air, was the result. It was ground to powder under edge-stones. The Sulphate and the Muriate of Ammonia were such as are usually sold for the purposes of manure, and it may be estimated that 1 cwt of them respectively is equal to 100 lb of the pure crystallized salt. The sulphuric acid used was of the specific gravity of about 1·7.

the mineral series on the one hand, and of the marked and nearly uniform result of the nitrogenous supply on the other, was most striking in the first year's experimental produce, and such as to lead us to give to nitrogenous manures in the second season even greater prominence than we had done to minerals in the previous one. This is in some respects, perhaps, to be regretted, as had we kept a series of plots for some years continuously under minerals alone, the evidence, though at present sufficiently conclusive, would have carried with it somewhat more of *systematic* proof.

# XXII

Much of the innovative activity in the eighteenth century was
concerned with developing new designs of existing and essential
implements such as ploughs, rollers, and rakes. Many agriculturists produced their own designs, as did Arthur Young, whose
plough was in wide demand. Few of the new models, however,
were patented and marketed commercially. An exception was the
Rotherham plough, which as the advertisement states, was
patented as early as 1730. It was a swing plough, similar in this
respect to ones introduced into East Anglia from Holland in the
late sixteenth century, but exhibiting important advances in
design and construction, including a winding mouldboard.
Although much more efficient, compact, and manoeuvrable than
existing models, it was many years before its use became widespread. Document from the Oxfordshire County Record Office,
Wi IX/1(a).

---

## THE
## ADVANTAGES
## OF THE
## NEW PATENT PLOUGHS

Whereas his present Majesty King George hath been graciously
pleased to grant his royal Letters Patent for the making and using
a new invented plough: which Letters Patent bear date the 21st
day of September 1730: and are vested in Disney Stanyforth, of
Firbeck in the County of York, Esq.

And whereas many hundreds of the said ploughs have been
tried and approved of, and are now constantly used in several
parts of Yorkshire and other counties and their landlords, by the
use of the said ploughs: which advantages are as follows, viz.

I. These ploughs are worked with more ease, and will plough
more ground in a day, by two or four horses, than the common
sorts by three or six horses, and in many soils by three horses

instead of five, and in several places where they plough double they are worked by two horses instead of four, and in both those cases, where they plough with two horses instead of three or four, they likewise have a driver, whereby one-third, and in some soils, one-half of the charge of ploughing is saved.

II. They being held after a different manner from the common sorts, are at first managed with some difficulty, but when the ploughmen are a little used to them, they are held with much less toil and trouble than the said common ploughs; so that those farmers who use these new ploughs will always command the best ploughmen, who, doubtless, will rather choose to work the said ploughs with ease and pleasure, than to toil like galley slaves at the old ones.

III. They plough the ground fairer to the eye, and (in the judgement of the farmers) better for the preservation of the seed, and increase of corn, than the old sorts: and by cutting a square kirfe [slice], without leaving ridges, and also by laying the furrows rounder and closer than the common ploughs, they have by several farmers been found not only to save ground, but to kill the thistles and other weeds, whereby the charge of weeding (which in many places is equal to the rent of the land) may be often saved; and the land being better ploughed, and the weeds destroyed, the farmers may also expect better corn and larger crops.

IV. They have also been found to plough in a drought, when the common sort of ploughs (with a much greater strength of cattle) have not been able to plough at all which advantage the ploughing and sowing season being thereby saved, may often occasion the saving of a crop. And as they lay the ground fine and close, and will plough shallower and deeper, as occasion requires, they have also been found of advantage for setting potatoes and other vegetables.

V. They clear themselves from the stubble and earth without help, which saves time and the charge of a person to keep them from choking, which many of the common ploughs require; and in a clay soil, after a wet season, when many of the wheel ploughs are useless, these new ploughs perform best, which (by saving the ploughing season) may also frequently prevent the loss of a crop in such clay soils.

VI. Whereas in many places, their work requires two different sorts of ploughs to go through a course of ploughing, these new invented ploughs perform all the orders of ploughing (as breaking up lee [ley], ploughing fallows, stirring, and seed-firring [seed-trenching] without the help of any other sort, which is a further convenience and a less expense.

VII. These ploughs having in them less wood and fewer joints, and their several parts being made by moulds or patterns, and those so mathematically disposed as to support each other, the ploughs are made at less expense, rendered much stronger, require fewer repairs, have no heads or chips [share-beams] to break, and wear out yearly much less iron, than the common sorts of ploughs.

VIII. The said ploughs being made by moulds or patterns as aforesaid, and without heads or chips, the farmers will be always certain of good ploughs, and thereby freed from the frequent disappointments occasioned by bad ones, and from the yearly expense and loss of time occasioned by the frequent breaking the heads or chips of the old sorts.

And the ploughwrights and smiths, by means of said moulds, will make the ploughs in less time, at a greater certainty as to goodness, and with greater profit to themselves, than they can make the common ploughs: nor need they fit every plough to every share as now, by reason that each ploughwright having a plough share by him and fitting his ploughs to the said share, they'll naturally fit all the other shares, tho' never so great a number of each be made at a distance one from the other.

IX. The larger farmers, who choose to keep their usual number of horses may thereby plough their farms in at least two-thirds of the usual time; whereby, in case of unseasonable weather, they may often save a crop, when their neighbours (having for want of time, lost the season for ploughing and getting their seed into the ground) may often hazard it, which has been commonly and fatally experienced.

X. And in the other third of the time they may earn, in some counties, by carriage of goods, 5, 6, 7 to 8 shillings per day, or more, by a draught; which, in case of full employ, may amount from £10 to £20 per ann. for the lucre whereof, and for want of time for such carriage many farmers have neglected their tillage, to the great detriment of their farms, and consequently of their landlords: whereas by means of these new ploughs, they'll have time both for their tillage and carriage of goods.

XI. And, in places where there's want of carriage, they may give their wheat and barley ground one ploughing in every two more than usual, by which means they may frequently save the charge of weeding, and have a chance for better crops.

N.B. And should a crop, by better tilling the ground, produce but one grain in ten more than usual, the farmers in most soils, would gain thereby near ten times the price of their licences. And,

XII. The smaller farmers who in many places are now obliged to borrow strength one of another, will be able, by means of these ploughs, to make up a sufficient draught of their own, whereby the above-mentioned inconveniences, with many others, will be avoided; and such draught may be likewise employed in the better tilling and dunging their lands, in carriage of goods, as above-mentioned, in ploughing for their neighbours for hire, and in doing the other necessary business of their farms besides the several advantages which they'll likewise, by the use of these new patent ploughs, reap in common with other farmers.

# XXIII

Threshing machines began to come into use towards the end of the eighteenth century and spread most rapidly in Scotland and northern England where labour was less plentiful and more expensive. Farmers were presented with a wide variety of designs, and there was much interest in differences in performance and efficiency. Here is an account of a trial of a number of machines worked on farms in Clackmannanshire, printed in the *Farmer's Magazine*, XIV (1814), pp. 178–84.

---

Having often heard various disputes on the quantity of grain threshed in an hour by different threshing-mills, but without any specification of the thickness, length, or weight of the sheaves, I was desirous of having a trial made of some mills in the neighbourhood of Alloa, when these things were particularly attended to. I, therefore, at the close of autumn 1811, gave directions to a very intelligent and attentive head-man of a farm to take two cartloads of strong oats that grew in one field to the several mills; and as I knew how much depended on the feeder, I desired him to feed all the mills himself, and that the same horses should be employed in working them.

The Tables on p. 184 show the result of the trial.

As it was known that this was a trial of different mills, the people employed grew very keen, and everyone exerted himself. The horses could not have continued to work at the same rate for an hour.

If the four horses had threshed 24 bolls, corresponding nearly to 144 bushels, or 18 quarters in four hours, it would have been good work.

Some of the sheaves were 4 feet in length. On a medium, they might be reckoned about $3\frac{1}{2}$ feet. If a threshing-mill puts through 384 sheaves in an hour, the horses would be very warm. Twelve

*A Trial of Threshing-Mills on several farms in The County of Clackmannan*

MILLS of FOUR-HORSE POWER

| NAMES of FARMS | No. of Sheaves | OATS Weight | | | OATS Measure | | | | OATS Weight | | | Weight of chaff | | | Weight of straw | | | Weight of refuse | | | Time in threshing | Quantity threshed per hour | | | |
|---|---|---|---|---|---|---|---|---|---|---|---|---|---|---|---|---|---|---|---|---|---|---|---|---|---|
| | | Cwt | Quarters | Lb | Bolls | Firlots | Pecks | Lippies | Cwt | Quarters | Lb | Cwt | Quarters | Lb | Cwt | Quarters | Lb | Cwt | Quarters | Lb | Minutes | Bolls | Firlots | Pecks | Lippies |
| Hilton | 228 | 19 | – | – | 3 | 3 | 2 | – | 8 | 2 | – | 1 | – | – | 9 | 1 | 22 | – | – | 6 | 15½ | 14 | – | 3 | 2 |
| Alloa Tower | 228 | 19 | 2 | 7 | 3 | 3 | – | 1 | 8 | 1 | 24 | 1 | – | 12 | 9 | 3 | 20 | – | – | 7 | 14 | 16 | – | 2 | 2 |
| Shaw Park | 228 | 18 | 2 | 7 | 3 | 2 | 2 | – | 8 | 1 | 2 | 1 | 3 | – | 8 | 2 | – | – | – | 5 | 13½ | 16 | – | 1 | 3 |
| Total | 684 | 57 | – | 14 | 11 | 1 | – | 1 | 25 | – | 26 | 3 | 3 | 12 | 27 | 3 | 14 | – | – | 18 | 43 | 46 | 1 | 3 | 3 |
| Medium | 228 | 19 | – | 4⅔ | 3 | 3 | – | ⅓ | 8 | 1 | 18 | 1 | 1 | 4 | 9 | 1 | 4⅔ | – | – | 6 | 14⅓ | 15 | 1 | 3 | 3⅔ |

MILLS of SIX-HORSE POWER, worked by FOUR HORSES

| NAMES of FARMS | No. of Sheaves | Cwt | Quarters | Lb | Bolls | Firlots | Pecks | Lippies | Cwt | Quarters | Lb | Cwt | Quarters | Lb | Cwt | Quarters | Lb | Cwt | Quarters | Lb | Minutes | Bolls | Firlots | Pecks | Lippies |
|---|---|---|---|---|---|---|---|---|---|---|---|---|---|---|---|---|---|---|---|---|---|---|---|---|---|
| Parkhead | 228 | 18 | 2 | – | 3 | 2 | 3 | – | 8 | 1 | 7 | 1 | 1 | – | 8 | 3 | 15 | – | – | 6 | 13½ | 16 | 1 | 2 | – |
| King of Muirs | 228 | 20 | 1 | – | 3 | 3 | – | – | 8 | 1 | 7 | 1 | 1 | – | 10 | 2 | 15 | – | – | 6 | 11 | 20 | 1 | 3 | 1 |
| Total | 456 | 38 | 3 | – | 7 | 1 | 3 | – | 16 | 2 | 14 | 2 | 2 | – | 19 | 2 | 2 | – | – | 12 | 24½ | 36 | 3 | 1 | 1 |
| Medium | 228 | 19 | 1 | 14 | 3 | 2 | 3 | 2 | 8 | 1 | 7 | 1 | 1 | – | 9 | 3 | 1 | – | – | 6 | 12¼ | 18 | 1 | 2 | 2½ |
| 3 of 4-horse-power | 684 | 57 | – | 14 | 11 | 1 | – | 1 | 25 | – | 26 | 3 | 3 | 12 | 27 | 3 | 14 | – | – | 18 | 43 | 46 | 1 | 3 | 3 |
| 2 of 6-horse power | 456 | 38 | 3 | – | 7 | 1 | 3 | – | 16 | 2 | 14 | 2 | 2 | – | 19 | 2 | 2 | – | – | 12 | 24½ | 36 | 3 | 1 | 1 |
| Total | 1,140 | 95 | 3 | 14 | 18 | 2 | 3 | 1 | 41 | 3 | 12 | 6 | 1 | 12 | 47 | 1 | 16 | – | 1 | 2 | 67½ | 83 | 1 | 1 | – |
| Medium | 228 | 19 | – | 19⅗ | 3 | 2 | 3 | 3½ | 8 | 1 | 13⅔ | 1 | 1 | 2½ | 9 | 1 | 25⅗ | – | – | 6 | 13½ | 16 | 2 | 2 | 2½ |

of the above sheaves would weigh (straw and grain included) about 1 cwt . . .

The mill at King of Muirs will thresh 8 bolls, corresponding nearly to 48 bushels, or 6 quarters, per hour, with six horses; or 32 bolls, corresponding nearly to 192 bushels, or 24 quarters, in four hours, without overworking the horses.

The diameter of the horse-course at Shaw Park threshing-mill, from centre to centre, is 22 feet 10 inches.

The horses make three turns in a minute.

Revolutions of the feeding rollers $37\frac{1}{2}$ times per minute.

Ditto of the straw-shakers      30     ditto     ditto
Ditto of the drum              300    ditto     ditto

At the above rate the mill would thresh 5 bolls (corresponding nearly to 30 bushels) per hour. This the feeder considers good work; and what four horses could stand to perform each day.

The quantity threshed in four hours 20 bolls, corresponding to 119 bushels; in eight hours 40 bolls, corresponding to 238 bushels. The feeder is of opinion that the above quantity could be done by all the three mills of four horses' power; but not much more, without straining the horses.

The threshing-mill at Parkhead has two pair of fanners, one under the other, driven by the horses. The cleansing fanners of all the rest are placed separately from the first pair, and are generally driven by hand; for though they can be wrought by the machinery, this additional labour is, however, found to be too hard work for the horses to continue at it for any length of time.

The attentive and intelligent feeder preferred the mill at Parkhead (which was erected under old Andrew Meikle's own eye, and perhaps it was among the last, if not the very last, which he wrought at with his own hands), as she has more power of stroke on the grain, which he thinks proceeds from the drum having a quicker motion and likewise 4 inches more diameter.

Some people may think that the larger the diameter of the drum the greater the strain upon the horses; but, although that may be the case, the motion and stroke of the drum must have a great power to thresh faster and clearer. The drum rollers and shakers being each 4 inches shorter, will lighten the horses' draught more than the extra diameter of the drum will add to it. If the mill loses motion, it is soon felt, both by loss of time, and bad threshing: some people imagine that the mill must be thicker fed, being 4 inches shorter in the drum; but these 4 inches upon 4 feet will never be felt. The above motion and diameter of the drum will, in the feeder's opinion, obviate and do more than compensate for this circumstance.

### Number of hands employed at the threshing-mills

| | |
|---|---:|
| The feeder | 1 |
| One man and a woman to hand the sheaves from the mow to the feeder | 2 |
| One man riddling the grain | 1 |
| Men taking away the straw from the shakers, and stacking it up in the barn | 3 |
| A man (or lad) driving the horses | 1 |
| Total people employed | 8 |

The same horses wrought all the mills.

The height, age, and weight of the horses that wrought the mills, were as follows:

| | | Height | Age | Weight |
|---|---|---|---|---|
| 1. | Nancy | 15 hands | 13 years | 12 cwt |
| 2. | Jack | 15¼ | 20 | 10½ |
| 3. | Glasgow | 14¼ | 14 | 9 |
| 4. | Bassy | 14¾ | 5 | 9¾ |

If I had remained in the country I might perhaps have been induced to have had some more accurate trials of these mills, by making the same feeder and the same horses work four hours in each of them.

Four of the aforementioned mills were substantial ones. Only the mill at Shaw Park was intended to be made on an economical plan—a common fundamental error of making the machinery too slight to undergo any extra fatigue, which usually happens in the beginning of harvest, when the straw and grain are in a raw, tough state, and much work is required to be performed in a small space of time. The slight mills usually give way on this pressure of business, which creates great disappointment and an actual loss—probably a greater charge than what would have made the mill of a proper degree of strength at the first. This was ascertained in the mill at Shaw Park; and alterations were then obliged to be made on it in order to stand the ordinary fatigue of work at that season of the year.

One of the best threshing-mills in the country was erected in 1799 by days' work; the cost of which was estimated (wood, iron, and all workmanship included) at £100. It has threshed more than the crops of a farm of 180 acres; and the expense of repairs (including 1 guinea, which was the expense of putting the mill in complete order before the harvest of 1812) did not exceed 5s per annum.

The millwright, some years ago, erected these threshing-mills for £130; and I believe would still undertake to erect one (notwithstanding the great additional price of wood and iron) for £160 or £170. There is little chance of such substantial mills giving way at any time; and they can be depended on threshing completely the grain in a raw state.

The difficulty of immediately stopping the horses when the feeder requires it has been often experienced; but that is easily obviated by hanging a small bell directly over the centre of the horse-course (the bell-rope hangs on one side of the feeding-bench); and the horses in a very short time learn to stop on the ringing of the bell, and that more instantaneously than by the driver's voice; and as quickly resume their labour again on the second ringing of the bell.

*Threshed at Shaw Park, by two men, the following quantity of oats*

| 1812 18 January | | Sheaves | Cwt | Quarters | Lb | Bolls | Firlots | Pecks | Lippies | Cwt | Quarters | Lb |
|---|---|---|---|---|---|---|---|---|---|---|---|---|
| | Oats and straw | 228 | 18 | 2 | 7 | | | | | | | |
| | Oats | - | - | - | - | 3 | 3 | - | - | 8 | - | - |
| | Chaff | - | - | - | - | - | - | - | - | 1 | - | - |
| | Straw | - | - | - | - | - | - | - | - | 9 | 2 | 3 |
| | Refuse | - | - | - | - | - | - | - | - | - | - | 4 |
| | | - | - | - | - | 3 | 3 | - | - | 18 | 2 | 7 |

3 bolls 3 firlots correspond nearly to 22½ Winchester bushels

Two men threshed the above in 8½ hours, and one woman ridding the barn.

The measure of the oats from the flail was much the same as those threshed by the mills, but the weight of them about 30 lb less; which difference was occasioned by the threshing-mills being driven with such great velocity that they sent back most of the shagg amongst the chaff, which made a better and heavier sample of grain.

The men who threshed the oats with the flail were so earnest to have their quantity to measure equal with the oats threshed by the mills that they would not drive the fanners properly; for if the fanners had been driven with equal velocity the quantity threshed by the flail would not have exceeded 3 bolls 2 firlots, or little more than 21 bushels.

# XXIV

The McCormick reaper from America attracted much attention when displayed at the Great Exhibition of 1851. So keen was the interest that Philip Pusey, the editor of the Royal Agricultural Society's *Journal*, hurried to print a brief report on a first trial of the machine: *Journal of the Royal Agricultural Society of England*, XII (1851), p. 160.

---

## ON MR MCCORMICK'S REAPING-MACHINE
### *by Ph. Pusey, M.P.*

Although the Report on Agricultural Implements is not yet drawn up for the Royal Commission, still the new American reaper is so important to farmers, that having, with Mr Miles and Professor Hlubach, myself tried it for the Council medal, I venture to communicate to the Royal Agricultural Society a very brief account of that trial.

The machine, drawn by two horses, and carrying two men, a driver and a raker, cut the wheat about 8 inches from the ground with the utmost regularity. The horses found the work light, though the machine was cutting at the rate of $1\frac{1}{2}$ acres per hour, making 15 acres per day of ten hours. The raker, standing behind the driver to take the cut wheat from the platform, certainly had to exert himself; but it is obvious that he and the driver, who has only to sit on the dicky, might very well exchange places from time to time. As one cannot put a high price on the labour of farm-horses at such a time, it is plain that a great saving must be effected by this machine, and every farmer can calculate it for himself, as he will also see the advantage of being rendered independent of the arrival of strangers to get in his corn, who cannot always be found. This trial was witnessed by many farmers, and no fault was found with the work. The land, I should say, however, being stock land, is even; where ridges and water-furrows exist, some difficulties seem to arise. But, on this level land, it was wonderful to see a new implement working so smoothly, so truly, and in such a masterly manner. The fact is, however, that it is not an untried implement. Though new in this country, it has been used for some years in America, where experience has enabled the inventor to correct in successive seasons the defects invariably found in new implements. It is certainly strange that we should not have had it over before, nor indeed should we have it now, but for the Great Exhibition, to whose royal originator the English farmer is clearly indebted for the introduction of the most important addition to farming machinery that has been invented since the threshing-machine first took the place of the flail.

*Pusey, 20 August 1851*

# XXV

In concluding his report on the implements exhibited at the Royal Agricultural Society's 1851 show, Philip Pusey provided an estimate of the savings on farms which modern implements made possible, and argued that although the speeding up of operations and saving of labour were small by comparison with the revolution in industrial techniques, yet the agricultural implements had the great compensation of cheapness. He went on to point to the further advantages conferred by new implements in reducing the uncertainties of farming, and deplored the limited extent to which farmers had realized their benefits: *Journal of the Royal Agricultural Society of England*, XII (1851), pp. 642–4.

---

It seems proved that within the last twelve years, since annual country shows of implements were established by Lord Spencer, Mr Handley, and others yet living, old implements have been improved, and new ones devised, whose performances stand the necessary inquiry as to the amount of saving they can effect. To ascertain that amount precisely is difficult; but looking through the successive stages of management, and seeing that the owner of a stock-farm is enabled in the preparation of his land, by using lighter ploughs, to cast off one horse in three and by adopting other simple tools to dispense altogether with a great part of his ploughing—that in the culture of crops by the various drills horse-labour can be partly reduced, the seed otherwise wanted partly saved, or the use of manures greatly economized, while the horse-hoe replaces the hoe at one-half the expense—that at harvest the American reapers can effect thirty men's work, while the Scotch cart replaces the old English wagon with exactly half the number of horses—that in preparing corn for man's food the steam threshing-machine saves two-thirds of our former expense—and in preparing food for stock, the turnip-cutter, at an outlay of 1s, adds 8s a head in one winter to the value of sheep—lastly that, in the indispensable but costly operation of draining, the materials have been reduced from 80s to 15s—to one-fifth, namely, of their former cost; it seems to be proved that the efforts of agricultural mechanists have been so far successful, *as in all these main branches of farming labour, taken together, to effect a saving, on outgoings, of little less than one-half.*

This saving of labour or expense, though large for land—a material certainly very intractable—is small as compared with the saving effected in the weaving of calico or the knitting of stockings. But it is important to observe, on the other hand, that the cost of the means which produce the saving is comparatively insignificant. When the distaff and knitting-needle were abolished, huge factories had to be built, and filled with intricate clockwork of spinning-jennies and looms, costing thousands of pounds. In agriculture we buy a few simple durable tools; and it is evident that a farmer setting up now in business, who, instead of the old wagons with three horses each, should buy one-horse carts, and the smaller number of horses required by such carts and by other improved machinery, would find that, without any increase of outlay whatever beyond the old scale, he could acquire all requisite modern machinery, with one exception, indeed—the steam-engine, but the steam-engine is often hired. It is therefore also demonstrated that *the new agricultural machines have, with reference to the amount of saving produced by them, the merit of very great cheapness.*

There is a further effect of machinery upon agriculture which has hitherto been overlooked. The main difficulty of farming has always lain in its uncertainty. Though machinery has not altogether cured, it certainly has much mitigated, this evil. On undrained clays a wet winter may destroy half the yield of the wheat. On the same land drained, the wheat may escape altogether unhurt, and you may also plough heavy land in wet weather when drained, though you could not before. Upon any land wheat may suffer in winter, but in spring the presser settles it in its bed, and the manure distributor with a cheap sprinkling restores it to vigour. In sowing barley earliness may save the crop; but the ground is often too cloddy, though the season is wearing away, and May-drought approaching. This cloddiness may be prevented, as has been said, by the paring plough, or, if it could not be prevented, may be remedied by the clod-crusher, or

Norwegian harrow; and besides these implements, the cultivator does the plough's work in one-fourth of the former time, thus enabling the farmer to profit by the auspicious hour of seed-time. And so too with the turnip: the land, being prepared for it in the previous autumn and winter, is moist to receive the seed; the dry drill, supplying it with superphosphate, saves it almost certainly from the fly; or yet more, the water-drill, anticipating the clouds, makes its seed-time independent of weather, while the horse-hoe afterwards preserves it from neglect in the busiest harvest-time. Again, while machinery remedies the absence, it also guards against the inconvenient arrival of rain, by making our hay and now even reaping our corn while the sun shines. It may be further said then, that *machinery has given to farming what it most wanted, not absolute, indeed, but comparative certainty.*

I wish I could add that the use of machinery has advanced as rapidly as its improvements. Still it has advanced greatly, as is shown by the increase not only of implements but of eminent implement-makers, and the sale has never been so great as it has been this year. Yet even the best new machines are not yet adopted into general use. This incomplete progress may, however, easily be accounted for. The farmer, whose life is secluded, has little opportunity of seeing them, and it is remarkable that nearly all our first implement makers live on the east side of England, in those four counties from which the other great improvements of agriculture have also proceeded. For threshing-machines again, though universal, until very lately no record of their work has been published, so that a farmer in one county, threshing 13 quarters only a day, could not possibly ascertain that in another county three times that amount was the proper work of a day.

But it must be further admitted, that few even of our best farmers, though they may possess the new implements, carry their use thoroughly out. It seems evident that *the new implements require a new system.* As yet many farmers use the drill and do not use the horse-hoe afterwards, the use of which is pointed out by the drill, while most farmers still use the plough previously, which the drill may have rendered superfluous. It is of course very difficult to give up old practices, but the result of the whole inquiry into agricultural machinery appears to be this—that, inasmuch as the new machinery effects a great saving of labour, and is also exceedingly inexpensive, giving also moderate certainty to a business proverbial for its precariousness, farmers ought no longer to bind themselves down by ancient customs in husbandry, but should consider at once how these practices may be reformed altogether, in order thoroughly to carry out the advantages of modern mechanics. They should look as much to a shed furnished with suitable implements as to their stables, remembering that the best of these implements, though it cost as much as a horse, may take the place of a horse, and, furthermore, when once purchased does not, like the horse, entail a weekly expense afterwards. That this extension as well as improvement will come to pass in the mechanics of husbandry there is no reason to doubt, nor that both have been accelerated by the opportunity for careful study of agricultural implements which has been afforded during five months through their exhibition, under your Royal Highness's auspices, among all the other products of human industry.

# XXVI

This further excerpt from the valuable report on the implements
exhibited at the Royal Show of 1851 gives a concise account of the
cheapening of drainage tile production which had been achieved
by improved machines during the 1840's; there is also an account
of the trial of Fowler's improved draining plough, a remarkable
invention which made it possible to bore the tunnel and draw and
lay the pipes in one operation: *Journal of the Royal Agricultural
Society of England*, XII (1851), pp. 638–41.

---

## I. TILE MACHINES

Twelve years ago draining tiles were made by hand, cumbrous
arches with flat soles, costing respectively 50s and 25s per 1,000.
Pipes have been substituted for these, made by machinery, which
squeezes out clay from a box through circular holes, exactly as
macaroni is made at Naples, and the cost of these pipes averages
from 20s down to 12s per 1,000. The old price was almost
prohibitory of permanent drainage, excepting where stones were
at hand: the new invention has reduced this permanent improvement to a rate of £4 or £3 per acre, not exceeding in cost the
manure given to a single turnip crop in some high-farmed
districts. This result has been obtained by a most spirited competition among mechanists, as no less than thirty-four different
tile-machines competed in 1848 at the York meeting. Since then
the struggle has been practically between three only, on which, in
the present year, we have the following report:

> *Trial of tile machinery*—I recommend to the consideration of the
> jury the tile and brick machines of Mr Clayton, Mr Scragg and
> Mr Whitehead.
> I first tested their capacity in screening the earth. The result of
> this trial was that in five minutes
>
> Mr Clayton screened  .  .  327 lb 2 men and boy

Mr Whitehead . . 361 ,, 2 men
Mr Scragg . . . 202 ,, 2 ,,

I give the preference to Mr Clayton's screen, as it clears itself, and the portion rejected consisted almost entirely of small stones, etc.; whereas the screens of Mr Whitehead and Mr Scragg retained a large portion of clay.

In the manufacture of large pipes 9 inches in diameter, by horizontal delivery and the use of a cylindrical horse, the machine of Mr Whitehead was perfect.

Mr Scragg has much simplified the internal arrangement of his machine by substituting a chain for the rack and pinion: the pipes from this machine were not to be surpassed for regularity and uniformity of shape. After a careful examination of the working of these machines, we recommend the *horizontal* delivery of Mr Scragg and Mr Whitehead in preference to the *vertical* delivery of Mr Clayton, but especially call your attention to Roberts's Patent Hollow and Bonding Bricks as made by Clayton's machine.

A. HAMOND

## 2. THE DRAINING PLOUGH

But for the American reapers, Mr Fowler's draining plough would have formed the most remarkable feature in the agricultural department of the Exhibition. Wonderful as it is to see the standing wheat shorn levelly low by a pair of horses walking along its edge, it is hardly, if at all, less wonderful, nor did it excite less interest or surprise among the crowd of spectators when the trial was made at this place, to see two horses at work by the side of a field, on a capstan which, by an invisible wire-rope, draws towards itself a low framework, leaving but the trace of a narrow slit on the surface. If you pass, however, to the other side of the field, which the framework has quitted, you perceive that it has been dragging after it a string of pipes, which, still following the plough's snout, that burrows all the while 4 feet below ground, twists itself like a gigantic red worm into the earth, so that in a few minutes, when the framework has reached the capstan, the string is withdrawn from the necklace, and you are assured that a drain has thus been invisibly formed under your feet. The jury decided as follows:

The implement went through the trial very well, laying in the tiles with great apparent ease, worked by *two* horses, with a

*Fowler's draining plough*

capstan which was firmly and easily fixed into the ground, and afforded a firm traction to the plough by means of a wire rope and pulley. Progress has been made, since the implement was exhibited at Exeter, in rendering the level of the drains in a degree independent of the level of the surface; but there is still room for further improvement in giving to the drain a *uniform* incline.

The award therefore, of the jury was honourable mention. Since that trial I have thought it right to make further inquiry into the work of the draining plough. In the first place, the trial drains were opened and laid bare from end to end. Straightness is of course one requisite, and the pipes were laid straight; closeness of contact another, and they were perfectly joined. In level, the point on which the jury doubted the perfection of the work, there was some deficiency, which, on entirely flat ground such as this, was a decided fault. That fault, however, has since been remedied for clay land at least. As the plough was shown last year at Exeter, it could not possibly lay a level drain, because its under and upper parts being fixed at an unvarying distance, any unevenness of an undulatory surface must be faithfully copied by an undulating drain below. This year the two parts were so connected that the workman, by turning a screw, can raise or lower the underground snout which burrows out the drain. But at the trial the use of this screw depended on the workman's judgement, which cannot give the drain absolute accuracy. A balanced level, however, has now been added to the plough, by which the changes of surface are made plain to his eye. Other improvements have also been made in the implement. The horse-power required has been reduced by a fourth, and the windlass at which the horses work need now be shifted only once in the day. As to the economy of using the draining plough, it is too expensive to purchase, unless for a large landowner, but it may be hired by the year or the month. Its inventor is also ready to execute work at his own risk by contract, at a saving of from one-third to two-thirds on hand-labour, the greater the depth the greater being the saving. I have only seen the actual cost of two drainages that have been made by this plough. They were both without tiles and shallow, being only $2\frac{1}{2}$ feet deep. Taking the highest of them, and adding the cost of tiles, the price of tile-draining land at that depth, and at 33 feet apart, would be 14s only for work, and with $1\frac{3}{4}$-inch pipes, at 15s per 1,000, 18s 9d for tiles—all together £1 3s 9d, including horses and hire of machine. The plough goes as well, however, at a depth of 4 feet, nor could the additional cost be material. The plough has worked on the following farms:

|  | Acres | Depth ft in |  |
|---|---|---|---|
| Mr Fowler, Melksham | 14 | 2 6 | with pipes |
| Mr Newman, do. | 10 | 2 0 | do. |
| Mr Blandford, near do. | 30 | 3 6 | do. |
| Mr Purch, Down Ampney | 100 |  | without pipes |
| Mr Hall, Brentwood | 200 | 2 6 | with and without |
| „ Wormwood Scrubbs | 40 | from 2 ft to 4 ft, with tiles |  |
| Mr Harris, Darlington | now working 3 6 |  |  |

In clay subsoils, with a gentle fall, the success of this new implement seems to be beyond doubt, and in all circumstances the inventor is ready to undertake the risk of the execution.

# XXVII

William Marshall, the well-known writer of the later eighteenth century, had a keen interest in the subject of agricultural education. (His ideas on the training of farmers and his suggestion for a Board of Agriculture are included in Document III.) Here, in his work on the west of England, he discussed the neglect of training of pauper children apprenticed out to farmers, though properly educated they might have proved a valuable source of skilled labour: W. Marshall, *Rural Economy of the West of England* (1796), pp. 110–13.

---

APPRENTICES. It is universal and common practice throughout Devonshire, and, I believe, the West of England in general, to put out the children of paupers, boys more particularly, at the age of seven or eight years, to farmers and others; and to bind them as apprentices until they be twenty-one years of age; and formerly until they were twenty-four! on condition of the master's finding them with every necessary during the term of the apprenticeship.

This is an easy and ready way of disposing of the children of paupers, and is fortunate for the children thus disposed of; as enuring them to labour and industry, and providing them with better sustenance than they could expect to receive from their parents. To the farmers, too, such children, under proper tuition, might, one would think, be made highly valuable in their concerns, and, in the end, would become very profitable.

The contrary, however, is generally the case: an unfortunate and indeed lamentable circumstance which arises, in a great measure, I apprehend, from improper treatment. Instead of treating them as their adopted children, or as relations, or as a superior order of servants, whose love and esteem they are desirous of gaining for their mutual happiness during the long term of their intimate connexion, as well as to secure their services at a time when they become the most valuable, they are treated, at least in the early stage of servitude, as the inferiors of yearly or weekly servants, are frequently subjected, I fear, to a state of the most abject drudgery: a severity which they do not forget, even should it be relaxed as they grow up. The ordinary consequence is, no sooner are they capable of supporting themselves than they desert their servitude, and fill the provincial papers with advertisements for 'runaway prentices'.

There are, no doubt, circumstances under which it were difficult or impossible to render this class of servants either pleasurable or profitable to their masters; such as the naturally bad disposition of the servants themselves, and the more reprehensible conduct of their parents in giving them bad counsel. Nevertheless, it strikes me forcibly that much might be done by a change of *principle* in their treatment.

When the unfortunate offspring of unfortunate parents fall into the hands of men of sense and discretion, they frequently turn out well, and become most valuable members of the community. A more natural seminary of working husbandmen could not be devised; and the progress in life that some individuals of this class have made is a recommendation of the practice; which, under the proper treatment of farmers, the encouragement of landlords, and the protection of magistrates, might be profitably extended to other districts; and become a prolific source of the most valuable order of inhabitants a cultivated country can possess.

# XXVIII

The wages of farm labourers were frequently supplemented by the provision of a free or cheap cottage, fuel, potato ground, and some items of food and drink. A daily allowance of beer or cider, according to the locality, was commonplace, and free beer assumed such importance to the labourers as sometimes to discourage them from leaving the land to seek better employment. In some areas, as Marshall observes in this passage, it was difficult to get men to work at all without an agreed allowance of drink; and, indeed, for many of them it formed an important part of their sustenance: W. Marshall, *Rural Economy of the Midland Counties* (1790), II, pp. 47–9.

---

In this country [district] the waste of malt is beyond measure. Beer and ale are not only brewed unreasonably strong; but the quantity allowed to workmen is unnecessarily great. That which is termed 'beer' or 'small beer' is nearly equal in strength to the harvest *mild ale* of many counties.

In hay and corn harvest the customary allowance is a gallon of beer a man (in hot weather they drink more), and, beside this, mowers expect two quarts of ale, and never have less than one.

Reapers have no regular allowance of ale; but, nevertheless, expect a little 'drink'.

With some difficulty, I got turnip hoers to accept of two quarts of beer and one of ale: they wanted two of beer and two of ale! enough to stupefy any man, and to make a *sober* man drunk from morning to night.

During the winter months, the quantity of small beer drunk is not much less than in harvest. Mr William Moor of Thorp, a leading man in this neighbourhood, allows his labourers a gallon a day the year round! Each man has his gallon bottle filled in the morning, and what he does not drink he takes home to his family. His motive for establishing this custom, I understand, was that of his men, when they had the beer case to go to, or had it given them whenever they asked for it by careless wasteful servants, getting drunk, or becoming so muddled and stupid as to be unfit for their work: and, upon other farms, this it seems is no uncommon case. It is usual in farmhouses to draw beer in a two-quart copper-can; and there are men who will see the bottom single-handed. Two men seldom fail of emptying one of them at a draught. This being the case, it is wise to allowance them; for, under this regulation, they drink no more, probably, than is serviceable to them; carrying home to their wives and children that which, if drunk, would probably have done them harm.

So great a tyrant, however, as custom is said to be, I am of opinion that if the farmers of this country were to pay money out of their pockets for their malt, this shameful waste of it would be put a stop to. And I am persuaded that nothing but the practice of malting their own barley at public malt houses (the prevailing practice of this district) could prolong so extravagant a custom.

# XXIX

Eden's great enquiry into the state of the poor, first published in 1797, has long been a major source for the study of labourers' conditions at the end of the eighteenth century. The following excerpts include some of his general comments, referring especially to differences in living standards between north and south, together with a sample of his detailed reports on individual parishes, that of Kibworth Beauchamp, Leicestershire: Sir Frederic Morton Eden, *The State of the Poor* (ed. A. G. L. Rogers, 1928), pp. 100–9, 225–7.

---

There seems to be just reason to conclude that the miseries of the labouring poor arose less from the scantiness of their income (however much the philanthropist might wish it to be increased) than from their own improvidence and unthriftiness; since it is the fact, and I trust will be demonstrated in a subsequent part of this work, that in many parts of the kingdom, where the earnings of industry are moderate the condition of the labourers is more comfortable than in other districts where wages are exorbitant. It must strike every one who has at all investigated the subject of diet, that there is not only a remarkable difference in the proportion of earnings appropriated to the purchase of subsistence by labourers in the north and south of England, but that their mode of preparing their food is no less dissimilar. In the south of England the poorest labourers are habituated to the unvarying meal of dry bread and cheese from week's end to week's end; and in those families whose finances do not allow them the indulgence of malt liquor, the deleterious produce of China constitutes their most usual beverage. If a labourer is rich enough to afford himself meat once a week, he commonly roasts it, or if he lives near a baker's he bakes it, and if he boils his meat he never thinks of making it into a soup, which would be as nourishing and more palatable. In the north of England, Scotland and Wales the poorest labourers, however, regale themselves with a variety of dishes unknown in the south. To begin with: *hasty pudding*, which is made of oatmeal, water and salt, about 13 oz of meal to a quart of water, which is sufficient for a meal for two labourers. It is eaten with a little milk or beer poured upon it, or with a little cold butter put into the middle, or with a little treacle. A good meal for one person, supposing the price of oats to be 20s the quarter, will not exceed 1d. *Crowdie* is not so generally used as hasty pudding, though it is a very common dish in the north among labourers of all descriptions, particularly miners. It is made with boiling water and oatmeal in much the same proportions as in hasty pudding, and it is eaten with milk or butter. Another sort is made by pouring boiling water on oatmeal; after stirring, a piece of fat is taken from the broth and put on the crowdie instead of butter or milk. This is the kind which is most in use in the north of England.

Furmenty or barley milk as made in the north is barley with the husks taken off, boiled in water nearly two hours, and mixed with skimmed milk. Sometimes a little sugar is added, and it is generally eaten in Cumberland with barley bread. Barley is also dressed by the peasants in Scotland, and in the north of England, for broth or barley milk. In the northern counties oatmeal is made by grinding, and the refuse which remains, after the meal has been sifted and is similar to the bran of wheat, consists chiefly of husks, and is called *seeds*. It is used for *sowens* or flummery, which is almost solid and perfectly smooth, very like what in England is called blancmange. It is eaten with milk, and though only occasionally used in the north of England, in many parts of Scotland, particularly on the north-east coast, it constitutes the invariable dinner of the labourer. *Pease-kail* is made by boiling peas till they are soft; the water is then poured from them and milk is added. Sometimes peas are put into broth and boiled down into a sort of soup. Neither of these dishes, however, is very generally used, nor much to be commended.

Potatoes are not only particularly good in the north of England, but used in various ways. They are sometimes roasted or boiled and eaten with butter, as in the south, but are more commonly boiled (sometimes with the skin on, and sometimes with it taken off), chopped into small pieces and eaten with butter (either cold or melted) or bacon fried; but the principal way in which they are used by labourers' families in the north is by being peeled or rather scraped raw, chopped and boiled together with a small quantity of meat cut into very small pieces. The whole of this mixture is then formed into a hash, with pepper, salt, onions, etc., which when used by sailors is known as *lobscouse*. The very general use which is now made of potatoes in these kingdoms as food for man is a convincing proof that the prejudices of a nation with regard to diet, however deeply rooted, are by no means unconquerable. Within the present [eighteenth] century, potatoes seem to have been considered as fit for only the poorest classes of the community, but from the following instances of the progress which various districts have made in the cultivation of this valuable root, it seems probable that in a very few years the consumption of potatoes in this kingdom will be almost as general and universal as that of corn. 1, in the central Highlands of Scotland potatoes are become the principal food of the people; before their introduction famines were frequent in the Highlands; 2, in the county of Forfar they afford a supply of food for the poor in July, before the corn harvest comes in; 3, in East Lothian they constitute nearly one-third of the food of the labouring people from the first of August to the end of May; 4, in Perthshire it is said to have done more to prevent emigration than any device whatsoever; 5, had it not been in general use in Banff in 1783, many of the inhabitants would probably have perished for want of food; 6, it is a common practice in Devonshire to make bread of potatoes, mixed with flour; 7, in Cardiganshire potatoes with barley bread form the chief sustenance of the poor; 8, it is no uncommon thing in Somerset for a family, consisting of a father, mother, and five or six children, to consume twenty sacks per year, 240 lb the sack, or 20 lb per head per week, allowing twelve weeks' cessation from this food. Indeed, the children nearly subsist on it, and the deprivation thereof would bring the whole family to the parish.

There are many different sorts of bread used in the north of England. In Cumberland it is generally made of barley and baked in unleavened cakes, of about $\frac{1}{2}$ inch thick, and 12 inches in diameter, but more commonly leavened and made into loaves of about 12 lb each. This bread will keep good four or five weeks in winter, and two or three in summer, and is almost the only bread used by the peasantry of that county. Though somewhat sour, and of a darkish hue, it is considered extremely nutritious by those accustomed to it. Mr Ray, in his collection of north country words, mentions five different sorts of oaten bread: 1, *Thar-cakes* (called in Cumberland hard-cakes) which are the same as bannocks; 2, *Clap-bread*, thin hard cakes, in Cumberland frequently made of barley meal; it is unleavened and baked on a 'girdle' over a fire; a labourer in Westmorland will eat 16 lb of meal made into bread in a fortnight, at a cost of about 1s per week; 3, *Kitcheness bread*, described as thin oat cakes made of thin batter; 4, *Riddle cakes*, said to be thick sour cakes, and identical (in name at least) with the bread called in Wales *bara-greiddell*, from its being baked on a girdle or thin iron plate; 5, *Hand-hoven bread*, now more commonly called *hoven bread*, is leavened bread made into cakes; 6, *Jannock* oaten bread, made up in loaves; neither this kind of bread nor its name appear to be common at present. *Bannocks*, which are the common bread in Scotland, are thick cakes of unleavened bread, made only of meal and water. They are generally made of oatmeal and water, but sometimes of barley meal, or peas meal, and sometimes of oatmeal with milk, butter (or cream), eggs and carraway seed.

The principal advantage which the labourers in the north of England possess over their countrymen in the south consists in the great variety of cheap and savoury soups which the use of barley and barley bread affords them an opportunity of making. The cheapness of fuel is, perhaps, another reason why the meals of the northern peasant are so much diversified, and his table so often supplied with hot dishes. One of the usual soups made by labourers' families in Northumberland and Cumberland consists of meat, oatmeal, barley, and potherbs such as onions, chives, parsley, thyme, etc., in the following proportions: beef or mutton, 1 lb; water, 6 qt; barley 3 oz; after the liquor is reduced to about 3 qt by boiling, 1 oz of oatmeal, previously mixed with a little water, and a handful of herbs are added. A pint or a pint and a half make a good supper. The day the broth is made the dinner usually is broth, with part of the meat, bread and potatoes chopped and boiled. The supper is broth and bread; the next day dinner is cold meat from the broth, warm potatoes, broth and bread, the supper bread and broth warmed up but not boiled again. The broth will keep three days if kept cool.

*Boiled milk*, another very common dish in the north is milk boiled with oatmeal, one handful of meal to three pints of milk.

The meal is put into the pot whilst the milk is boiling, and is soon after taken off the fire and eaten with barley bread for breakfast or supper. There is a prejudice against rye bread in the south of England, though in several parts of the kingdom rye and wheat are considered an excellent species of bread. 'In Nottinghamshire (*Annals of Agriculture* XXV, 580) opulent farmers consume one-third wheat, one-third rye, and one-third barley; but their labourers do not relish it, and have lost their *rye teeth*, as they express it.' It must be confessed that bread into which rye enters in any considerable proportion can seldom be made as pleasant and palatable as mixtures of other sorts of grain. The principal consumption of barley in the south of England is in malt liquor, but it may be doubted whether a given quantity of barley and water made into soup does not contain more nourishment than the same quantity converted into beer. It is certain that a person might subsist entirely on barley broth, but it is not probable that porter alone would long support a person in good health. It is not to be expected that milk should ever form a considerable part of the diet of labourers in the south of England until the practice of keeping cows become more general among cottagers than it is at present. In the vicinity of large towns the value of grass land is much too high to enable labourers to rent it to advantage; and in other districts where there is hardly anything but arable land, and the maintenance of a cow depends on straw, turnips, cabbages, or purchased hay, the system of cow-keeping is much too operose for a labourer to engage in. A garden will prove of infinite benefit to a labourer in almost any situation, but more especially in arable countries, where he would find it difficult to procure sufficient pasture to maintain a cow both in summer and winter, and where, though he might be able to cultivate a few acres of arable land for winter food for his cow, he would not always be able to procure hay for summer food from the farmers. Even in London, where milk is extremely dear ($3\frac{1}{2}$d the quart), poor householders might occasionally use it to considerable advantage. A labouring man who thinks he cannot afford milk and therefore obliges his family to drink their tea in a very crude state, by way of economy buys himself a pound of fat bacon (at 10d or 1s the pound) for dinner. This creates such a thirst that he is fain to allay it with no inconsiderable quantity of porter. As for salt fish, it is going very generally into disuse, and is little eaten except on particular occasions. The aversion to broths and soups composed of barley meal or oatmeal is in many parts of the south almost insuperable. Instances occurred during last winter (1794) when the poor were extremely distressed by the high price of provisions; of their rejecting soup which was served at a gentleman's table. Their common outcry was: 'This is washy stuff that affords no nourishment; we will not be fed on meal and chopped potatoes, like hogs.' It is true that a diet consisting entirely of liquids would neither gratify the palate nor enable the body to support violent fatigue. But a south country labourer probably takes more liquid into his stomach than the Cumberland or Yorkshireman. Exclusive of beer, when he can afford it, and spirits, the quantity of water, which with tea forms a beverage which is seldom qualified with milk or sugar, poured down the throats of a labourer's family is astonishing Any person who will give himself the trouble of stepping into the cottages of Middlesex and Surrey at meal times, will find that in poor families tea is not only the usual beverage, in the morning and evening, but is generally drunk in large quantities even at dinner . . .

The difficulty of introducing any species of food which requires much cooking into the south of England arises in a great measure from the scarcity and high price of fuel. Even the labourer's dinner of hot meat on a Sunday is generally dressed at the baker's and his meals during the rest of the week consist almost wholly of bread purchased from the same quarter. It may, however, be doubted whether the same quantity of fuel which is required to boil a tea kettle twice a day is not more than sufficient to dress a potato soup. Count Rumford truly observes that 'their fireplaces are, in general, constructed upon the most wretched principles', and that 'the fuel they consume in them not infrequently renders them really colder and more uncomfortable by causing strong currents of cold air to flow from all the doors and windows to the chimney'. Balls of small coal, mixed with clay, are very much used all over South Wales, particularly in the counties of Pembroke and Carmarthen. They are formed about the bigness of a man's fist, great in the middle and verging smaller towards the end. They are generally made up and put upon the fire quite wet, in the form of a pyramid and, when thoroughly lighted, make a most brilliant appearance. One of these fires, if made up with skill, will last ten or twelve hours.

The diversity is not greater between the labourers in the north and south of England with respect to the manner in which their food is prepared than with regard to the modes they adopt of supplying themselves with clothing. In the midland and southern counties the labourer in general purchases a very considerable portion, if not the whole, of his clothes from the shopkeeper. In the vicinity of the metropolis working people seldom buy new clothes; they content themselves with a cast-off coat, which may be usually purchased for about 5s, and second-hand wasitcoats and breeches. Their wives seldom make up any article of dress, except making and mending clothes for the children. In the north, on the contrary, almost every article of dress worn by farmers, mechanics and labourers is manufactured at home, shoes and hats excepted—that is, the linen thread is spun from the lint, and the yard from the wool, and sent to the weavers and dyers, so that almost every family has its web of linen cloth annually, and often one of woollen also, which is either dyed for coats or made into flannel, etc. Sometimes black and white wool are mixed, and the cloth which is made from them receives no dye; it is provincially called *kelt*. There are, however, many labourers so poor that they cannot even afford to purchase the raw material necessary to spin thread or yarn at home, as it is some time before a home manufacture can be rendered fit for use. It is generally acknowledged that articles of clothing can be purchased in the shops at a much lower price than those who made them at home can afford to sell them for, but that in the wearing those manufactured by private families are very superior both in warmth and durability . . .

KIBWORTH BEAUCHAMP is divided into three townships: 1, Kibworth Beauchamp; 2, Kibworth Harcourt; and 3, Smeaton Westerby. No. 1 comprises 1,300 acres, No. 2, 1,500, and No. 3 1,200. Houses paying tax are No. 1 43, No. 2 41, No. 3 40. Houses exempt are No. 1 50, No. 2 40, No. 3 45. Prices of provisions are: beef, 4½d to 5d per lb; mutton, 5d; veal, 3½d; butter, 9½d and 10d; bread, 3½d per lb, or 4 lb for 1s; coals, 13d per cwt; potatoes, 6d per gallon; milk, ½d per pint, but very little is sold. Wages vary very much. A common labourer in husbandry earns about 8s 6d a week in winter, and from 10s to 12s a week in summer, without victuals. Women can earn 6d to 10d a day spinning worsted. Children of 12 to 14 earn about 6d a day by spinning. There are 8 ale-houses in the parish, and one friendly society with 110 members, whose rules have been confirmed. Average rent about 25s an acre. Farms generally about £100 a year. Nine-tenths of the land pasture, but no common or waste. 3,600 acres were enclosed in 1780, when the rector had one-seventh of the enclosure instead of tithes. The poor are maintained by a weekly allowance or occasional relief at home. In No. 1 18 poor persons receive £2 11s 11½d weekly; in No. 2 20 poor families receive £5 weekly; in No. 3 21 pensioners receive £3 3s 6d weekly. Other persons receive occasional relief.

The following are the earnings and expenses of a labourer: man, 40 years, with wife and 5 children (girls of 14, 12 and 6, boys of 8 and 1½). He said his earnings were so uncertain that he could give no accurate statement of them, but as near as he could calculate they were as follows: half a year's work at the canal, at 2s a day, when weather permitted. When it did not, the parish allowed him 1s 2d a day, or 8s 6d a week for 26 weeks. Succeeding 13 weeks at 9s; the summer quarter 8s 6d a week and victuals, worth 6s a week. Father's earnings, £26 6s 6d. Eldest girl earns by spinning 2s a week, or yearly £5 4s. Total £31 10s 6d. The parish pay his rent, find him coals, and occasionally give him articles of wearing apparel, and for last 2 weeks 2s a week. The family uses 6 lb of bread a day (formerly costing 10d, now 1s 6d, and lately 2s), which is £27 6s for the year. He could say little about his other expenses, but asserts they use little or no milk or potatoes, and no oatmeal. Seldom any butter, but occasionally a little cheese and sometimes meat on Sunday. His wife and daughters consume a little tea. Bread, however, is the chief support of the family, but at present they do not have enough, and his children are almost naked and half starved. He adds he has worked many days with only bread diet, and that many weeks have elapsed since he tasted beer. A great number of cottages owned by the three townships are inhabited by the poor. Others have their house-rent paid. Several have clothes, etc. The poor complain of hard treatment by the overseers, who accuse the poor of being saucy. The rates are said to have been not one-third of their present figure before the enclosures, and the people attribute the rise to the enclosures, for they say 'that before the fields were enclosed they were solely applied to the production of corn; that the poor had then plenty of employment in weeding, reaping,

threshing, etc., and would also collect a great deal of corn by
gleaning, but that the fields being now in pasturage, the farmers
have little occasion for labourers and the poor being thereby
thrown out of employment, must of course be supported by the
parish'. There is some truth in these observations: a third or a
quarter of the number of hands required twenty years ago is
sufficient according to the present system of agriculture to perform all the farming work of the parish. It is probable, however,
that the wool now produced in Leicestershire employs more
hands (though perhaps not in the county) than its arable fields did
formerly; many labourers get work at a canal cutting in the
neighbourhood. Otherwise the rates would have been much
higher. In the winter men are sent out 'on the rounds'. The
housekeeper who employs one gives him his food and 6d a day,
and the parish adds 4d for the support of his family. As work here
is mostly done by the piece, it is not possible to give a correct
statement as to earnings, but a day labourer has 1s a day and
breakfast in winter, and in hay and corn harvest, which is very
short, 1s 2d a day and board. Many complaints are made against
'monopolizing farmers'.

# XXX

In the nineteenth century farm wages in southern England tended to be markedly lower than in the northern half of the country, as Sir James Caird pointed out in 1851. Within the low-wage area of the south there were some severely depressed districts, ones especially remote from major sources of alternative employment, and generally characterized by large-scale arable farming. In this excerpt Caird comments on the over-supply of labour which exacerbated the poverty of the farmworkers of south Wiltshire, those who depended on the great arable farms of Salisbury Plain: J. Caird, *English Agriculture in 1850–51* (1852, new ed. 1968), pp. 84–7.

---

The wages of labour are lower on Salisbury Plain than in Dorsetshire, and lower than in the dairy and arable districts of North Wilts. An explanation of this may partly be found in the fact, that the command of wages is altogether under the control of the large farmers, some of whom employ the whole labour of a parish. Six shillings a week was the amount given for ordinary labourers by the most extensive farmer in South Wilts, who holds nearly 5,000 acres of land, great part of which is his own property; 7s, however, is the more common rate, and out of that the labourer has to pay 1s a week for the rent of his cottage. If prices continue low, it is said that even these wages must be reduced. Where a man's family can earn something at out-door work, this pittance is eked out a little, but in cases where there is a numerous young family, great pinching must be endured. We were curious to know how the money was economized, and heard from a labourer the following account of a day's diet. After doing up his horses he takes breakfast, which is made of flour with a little butter, and water 'from the tea-kettle' poured over it. He takes with him to the field a piece of bread and (if he has not a young family, and can afford it) cheese to eat at mid-day. He returns home in the afternoon to a few potatoes, and possibly a little bacon, though only those who are better off can afford this. The supper very commonly consists of bread and water. The appearance of the labourers showed, as might be expected from such meagre diet, a want of that vigour and activity which mark the well-fed ploughmen of the northern and midland counties. Beer is given by the master in hay-time and harvest. Some farmers allow ground for planting potatoes to their labourers, and carry home their fuel—which, on the downs, where there is no wood, is a very expensive article in a labourer's family.

Both farmers and labourers suffer in this locality from the present over-supply of labour. The farmer is compelled to employ more men than his present mode of operations require, and, to save himself, he pays them a lower rate of wages than is sufficient to give that amount of physical power which is necessary for the performance of a fair day's work. His labour is, therefore, really more costly than where sufficient wages are paid; and, accordingly, in all cases where task-work is done, the rates are higher here than in other counties in which the general condition of the labourer is better. We found a prevalent desire for emigration among the labourers themselves, as their only mode of benefiting those who go and those who remain behind.

A subdivision of the large farms on the downs would tend to increase the demand for labour, and, with a low range of prices, such a subdivision appears inevitable. These thin lands cannot be kept in cultivation except by a liberal expenditure of capital and the utmost economy in the consumption of the produce; and this is scarcely compatible with a holding of 2,000 acres under one management. Very few men, even if they possessed it, would risk a capital adequate for the thorough development of such a farm; and where men of this class are to be found, they would probably get a better return by dividing their land into four or five farms of 400 acres each, with separate bailiffs vieing with each other in the care of the land under their charge, and answerable separately to the capitalist farmer who would superintend and direct the whole. In the dairy and grazing districts the wages are from 7s to 8s a week.

The opinions expressed by the farmers as to what is requisite to be done under present circumstances, and with future prospects, were of a much more practical character than those we heard in

Dorsetshire. In the dairy districts the farmers ask for drainage and better house accommodation, relief from the unequal pressure of poor-rates caused by the present law of settlement, and the consequent obligation to employ the whole labourers of a parish whether their labour is needed or not. The income-tax is also much complained of, being arbitrarily exacted even when the farmer is actually losing money. This is thought an act of great injustice; and it is not easy to see why the farmers alone should be subjected to an arbitrary assessment, as it is not more difficult for them to strike a balance every year in their accounts than it is for a merchant.[1] Indeed the necessity for doing so would introduce a business-like accuracy of accounts which could not fail to be beneficial to the farmer himself.

On the corn farms a reduction of rent is considered indispensable, or a conversion of money into produce-rents. The idea of a return to protection appears to be abandoned; and, in the dairy district especially, it is readily conceded that free-trade has much less seriously affected the farmers than their brethren in the corn districts, though they think it right, nevertheless, as one man said to us, to 'bear their share in the general grumbling'. With the large corn farmers, however, the suffering is very serious, and much individual loss is unavoidable before matters readjust themselves. Their claims on the justice of their landlords are of the strongest kind. As the landlords, in the manner already explained, without any outlay, obtained a large increase to their rental, and by so doing had in some degree become partners in the scheme of extensive corn farming, they, when through unforeseen causes it becomes unsuccessful, cannot honourably withdraw without bearing the same share in the loss as they drew from the profits of the adventure. A deduction of 10 per cent has in the meantime been generally allowed.

---

[1] This has been amended by the legislature since this letter was published, and a farmer who can show that he has not cleared £150 will now be exempted from assessment.

# XXXI

The poverty of many English farm labourers was such that at first sight it is difficult to understand the limited extent of their interest in migration to the towns or in starting a new life overseas. Their poverty was itself a formidable barrier to movement, and further, many were extremely ignorant, parochial in their outlook, and set in their ideas, as these comments by the American visitor, Olmstead, show. Frederick Law Olmstead, *Walks and Talks of an American Farmer in England* (1852; reprinted University of Michigan Press, 1969), pp. 235–9.

---

We were bound for Monmouth that night, and soon after sunset, having one of the farm labourers for a guide, we struck across the fields into another lane. About a mile from the farmhouse, there was a short turn, and at the angle—the lane narrow and deep as usual—was a small, steep-roofed, stone building, with a few square and arched windows here and there in it, and a perfectly plain cube of stone for a tower, rising scarcely above the roof-tree, with an iron staff and vane on one of its corners—'Saint Some-one's parish church'. There was a small graveyard, enclosed by a hedge, and in a corner of this, but with three doors opening in front upon the lane, was a long, crooked, dilapidated old cottage. On one of the stone thresholds, a dirty, peevish-looking woman was lounging, and before her, lying on the ground in the middle of the lane, were several boys and girls playing or quarrelling. They stopped as we came near, and rolling out of the way, stared at us silently, and without the least expression of recognition, while we passed among them. As we went on, the woman said something in a sharp voice, and our guide shouted in reply, without, however, turning his head, 'Stop thy maw—am going to Ameriky, aw tell thee.' It was his 'missis', he said.

'Those were not your children that lay in the road?'

'Yaas they be—foive of 'em.'

... Our guide was a man of about forty, having a wife and seven children; neither he nor any of his family (he thought) could read or write, and, except with regard to his occupation as agricultural labourer, I scarcely ever saw a man of so limited information. He could tell us, for instance, almost no more about the church which adjoined his residence than if he had never seen it—not half so much as we could discover for ourselves by a single glance at it. He had nothing to say about the clergyman who officiated in it, and could tell us nothing about the parish, except its name, and that it allowed him and five other labourers to occupy the 'almshouse' we had seen, rent free. He couldn't say how old he was (he appeared about forty); but he could say, 'like a book', that God was what made the world, and that 'Jesus Christ came into the world to save sinners, of whom he was chief'—of the truth of which latter clause I much doubted, suspecting the arch fiend would rank higher, among his servants, the man whose idea of duty and impulse of love had been satisfied with cramming this poor soul with such shells of spiritual nourishment. He thought two of his children knew the catechism and the creed; did not think they could have learned it from a book; they might, but he never heard them read; when he came home and had got his supper, he had a smoke and then went to bed. His wages were 7s—sometimes had been 8s—a week. None of his children earned anything; his wife, it might be, did somewhat in harvest-time. But take the year through, *1 dollar and 68 cents* a week was all they earned to support themselves and their large family. How could they live? 'Why indeed, it was hard,' he said; 'sometimes, if we'd believe him, it had been as much as he could do to keep himself in tobacco!' He mentioned this as if it was a vastly more memorable hardship than that, oft-times, he could get nothing more than dry bread for his family to eat. It was a common thing that they had nothing to eat but dry bread. He got the flour—*fine, white wheaten flour*—from the master. They kept a hog, and had so much bacon as it would make to provide them with meat for the year. They also had a little potato patch, and he got cheese sometimes from the master. He had tea, too, to his supper. The parish gave him his rent, and he never was called upon for tithes, taxes, or any such thing. In addition to his wages, the master gave him, as he did all the labourers, three quarts either of cider or beer a day, sometimes one and sometimes the other. He liked cider best—thought there was 'more strength to it'. Harvest-time they got six quarts, and sometimes, when the work was very hard, he had had ten quarts.

He had heard of America and Australia as countries that poor folks went to—he did not well know why, but supposed wages were higher, and they could live cheaper. His master and other gentlemen had told him about those places, and the labouring people talked about them among themselves. They had talked to him about going there. (America and Australia were all one—two names for the same place, for all that he knew.) He thought his master or the parish would provide him the means of going, if he wanted. We advised him to emigrate then, by all means, not so much for himself as for his children; the idea of his bringing seven, or it might be a dozen, more beings into the world to live such dumb-beast lives was horrible to us. I told him that in America his children could go to school, and learn to read and write and to enjoy the revelation of God; and as they grew up they would improve their position, and might be land-owners and farmers themselves, as well off as his master; and he would have nothing to pay, or at least but a trifle that he could gratefully spare, to have them as well educated as the master's son was being here; that where I came from the farmers would be glad to give a man like him, who could 'plough and sow and reap and mow as well as any other in the parish', 18s a week—

'And how much beer?'

'None at all!'

'None at all? ha, ha! he'd not go then—you'd not catch him workin' withouten his drink. No, no! a man 'ould die off soon that gait.'

It was in vain that we offered fresh meat as an offset to the beer. There was 'strength', he admitted, in beef, but it was wholly incredible that a man could work on it. A working-man must have zider or beer—there was no use to argue against that. That 'Jesus Christ came into the world to save sinners', and that 'work without beer is death', was the alpha and omega of his faith.

The labourers in this part of England (Hereford, Monmouth, Gloucester, and Wiltshire) were the most degraded, poor, stupid, brutal, and licentious that we saw in the kingdom. We were told that they were of the purest Saxon blood, as was indeed indicated by the frequency of blue eyes and light hair among them. But I did not see in Ireland, or in Germany or in France, nor did I ever see among our Negroes or Indians or among the Chinese or Malays, men whose tastes were such mere instincts, or whose purpose of life and whose mode of life was so low, so like that of domestic animals altogether, as these farm-labourers.

# XXXII

Though much criticized by historians, the Poor Law Report of 1834 remains an important source for our knowledge of conditions in the countryside in the early 1830's. Allowance must be made for the bias of the observers and of the compilers of the Report, but nevertheless there is much valuable information on labourers' conditions, the burden imposed by high poor rates, and the effects of the expedients resorted to for relief of the able-bodied poor. The following extracts deal with some of the devices used for encouraging farmers to increase the numbers employed, the serious effects of the poor rates on the letting of farms and farm profits, and the deterioration resulting from the demoralization of the labour force: *The Poor Law Report of 1834* (Penguin, ed. by S. G. and E. O. A. Checkland, 1974), pp. 110–13, 128–9, 140–8.

---

Mr Richardson states that in Northamptonshire, the plan generally in use in the agricultural villages is, upon the man's applying to the overseer for work, to send him upon some part of the parish roads, where he is expected to work—not the farmer's hours, or anything like them, but to begin at eight, to leave at twelve for dinner, an hour, and to leave the roads finally at four. It is the business of the overseer or the surveyor of the roads, a farmer or a tradesmen, who, paid or not, has his own business to attend to, to see that the men are actually working. While he is present, and the farmers take credit to themselves for riding up once or twice a day to the roads, the men bestir themselves a little; but the moment his back is turned, a man who gives himself any trouble is laughed at by his companions. As the overseer at Kettering told me, their remark is, 'You must have your 12s a week, or your 10s a week, whether you work or not; I would not be such a fool as to work—blast work—damn me if I work,' etc.; and, of course, under these circumstances, they do anything but work; if there is a wood near, as at Glapthorne and some other places round Oundle, they run into the wood to steal firing, which they hide and carry off at a convenient time; and universally they are in the habit of stealing turnips, or posts, or any little thing of that sort that comes to hand.

In short, where there were many able-bodied men employed on the roads, there everybody complained of petty thefts, pilfering, poaching, etc., as the natural consequences.

Whatever the previous character of a man may have been, he is seldom able to withstand the corruption of the roads; two years occasional employment there ruins the best labourers. More-over, in very many instances, the difference between parish pay for pretending to break stones on the road, and the real wages given by the farmer, does not amount to more than 1s a week; and, if the man has a family entitling him to receive a given sum by the scale as head-money, he receives as much from the parish as he would from any other employer. Accordingly, the labourers who are only occasionally employed are nearly indifferent to pleasing or displeasing their employer; they quit with the remark which I heard at least a dozen times from different overseers, 'I can get as much on the roads as if I worked for you.'

The following extracts from Mr Okeden's and Mr Majendie's reports afford examples of all these systems, sometimes separate and sometimes in combination.

At Urchfont, a parish in the district of Devizes, the population of which is 1,340, and the annual poor-rates about £1,450, there are above fifty men out of employ for forty-five weeks every year. To these the parish pays 3s a week each during that time, and inquires no further about their time or labour; thus creating an annual item of expense of nearly £400.

At the parish of Bodicott, in the district of Bloxham, a printed form is delivered to those who apply for work. The labourer takes this to the farmers in succession, who, if they do not want his labour, sign their names. The man, on his return, receives from the overseer the day's pay of an industrious labourer, with the deduction of 2d. The same system takes place in other parishes.

In the parish of Sidford Gore, in the same district, where the poor-rates are under £650 per annum, £114 was paid last year in six months to men who did not strike one stroke of work for it.

At Deddington, during the severe winter months, about sixty

men apply every morning to the overseer for work or pay. He ranges them under a shed in a yard. If a farmer or any one else wants a man, he sends to the yard for one, and pays half the day's wages; the rest is paid by the parish. At the close of the day the unemployed are paid the wages of a day, minus 2d. I could multiply instances of this application of the scale to the super-fluous labourers; but to do so would only waste your time.

At Rotherfield, in East Sussex, 120 men were out of employ in the winter 1831–2, and various modes were attempted to dispose of them. First they were set to work on the parish account; single men at 5s; men with families at 10s per week; the pay being the same as farmers' pay, the men left the farmers in order to get the same pay with less work. Then they were billeted among the farmers at 1s per day from the farmers, and 8d from the parish. This was changed to 1s from the parish, and 8d from the farmer. The men so billeted did not keep the proper hours of work; then the farmers' men, finding that they who worked the regular hours were paid no more than those who were irregular, gave up their employment to become billeted men, and the farmers were induced to throw their men out of employ to get their labour done by the parish purse. The billeting system having failed, a 6d labour-rate was made: it soon failed. Magistrates now recommend 6d in the pound to be deducted from the full rate, and that the occupier should be allowed to pay that proportion of his rate by employment of the surplus hands.

The labourers are much deteriorated. They do not care whether they have regular work or not; they prefer idle work on the roads. The magistrates at the Uckfield bench told the over-seer, the year before last, that if the men made complaint they should be allowed at the rate of 2s 4d per head for each member of the family.

At Burnash, in East Sussex, in the year 1822, the surplus labourers were put up to auction, and hired as low as 2d and 3d per day; the rest of their maintenance being made up by the parish. The consequence was, that the farmers turned off their regular hands, in order to hire them by auction when they wanted them. The evil of this system was so apparent, that some occu-piers applied to the magistrates, who recommended it should be given up. During the last year, the following plan has been adopted: the names of the occupiers are written on pieces of paper, which are put into a bag; the labourer draws out a ticket, which represents 10s worth of labour, at fair wages; next week the labourer draws another master, and this is repeated till the occupier has exhausted the shilling rate. This has continued two winters, much fraud is mixed up with the practice. Some farmers turn off their labourers in order to have ticketed men; other occupiers refuse to pay the rate, and against them it is not enforced.

## The labour-rate system

By an agreement among the rate-payers that each of them shall employ and pay out of his own money a certain number of the labourers who have settlements in the parish, in proportion, not to his real demand for labour, but according to his rental or to his contribution to the rates, or to the number of horses that he keeps for tillage, or to the number of acres that he occupies, or according to some other scale. Where such an agreement exists, it is generally enforced by an additional rate, imposed either under the authority of the 2 & 3 William IV, c. 96 [1832], or by general consent on those who do not employ their full proportion. This may be called the labour-rate system. We shall consider it more at length in a subsequent portion of this Report . . .

It is with still further regret that we state our conviction, that the abuses of which we have given a short outline, though checked in some instances by the extraordinary energy and wisdom of individuals, are, on the whole, steadily and rapidly progressive.

It is true, that by the last Parliamentary Return (that for the year ending 25 March 1832), the total amount of the money expended for the relief of the poor, though higher than that for any year since the year 1820, appears to fall short of the expenditure of the year ending 25 March 1818; the expenditure of that year having been £7,890,014, and that for the year ending 25 March 1832, £7,036,968. But it is to be remembered, first, that the year ending 25 March 1818 was a period of extraordinary distress among the labouring classes, especially in the manufacturing districts, in consequence of the high price of provisions, unaccompanied by a corresponding advance in wages; secondly, that in the year ending 25 March 1832 the price of corn was lower by about one-third than in 1818, and that of clothes and of the other necessaries of life lower in a still greater proportion; so that, after allowing for an increase of population of one-fifth, the actual amount of relief given in 1832 was much larger in proportion to the population than even that given in 1818, which has generally been considered as the year in which it attained its highest amount; and thirdly, that the statement of the mere amount directly expended, whether estimated in money or in kind, affords a very inadequate measure of the loss sustained by those who supply it. A great part of the expense is incurred, not by direct payment out of the rates, but by the purchase of unprofitable labour. Where ratepayers are the immediate employers of work-people, they often keep down the rates, either by employing more labourers than they actually want, or by employing parishioners, when better labourers could be obtained. The progressive deterioration of the labourers in the pauperized districts, and the increasing anxiety of the principal ratepayers, as their burthen becomes more oppressive, to shift it in some way, either on the inhabitants of neighbouring parishes, or on the portion of their fellow-parishioners who can make the least resistance; and the apparent sanction given to this conduct by the 2 & 3 William IV, c. 96 [1832], appear to have greatly increased this source of indirect and unrecorded loss. Our evidence, particularly Appendix D, is full of instances of which we will cite only those which have been drawn from the county of Cambridge, and are to be found in Mr Cowell's and Mr Power's reports. Mr Cowell's report contains the examination of a large farmer and proprietor at Great Shelford, who, on 500 acres situated in that parish pays 10s per acre poor-rate, or £250 a year. In addition, though he requires for his farm only sixteen regular labourers, he constantly employs twenty or twenty-one. The wages of these supernumerary labourers amount to £150 a year, and he calculates the value of what they produce at £50 a year; so that his real contribution to the relief of the poor is not £250, the sum which would appear in the Parliamentary Returns, but £350. In the same report is to be found a letter from Mr Wedd, of Royston, containing the following passages:

An occupier of land near this place told me today that he pays £100 for poor-rates, and is compelled to employ fourteen men and six boys, and requires the labour of only ten men and three boys. His extra labour at 10s a week (which is the current rate for men), and half as much for boys, is £130.

Another occupier stated yesterday that he held 165 acres of land, of which half was pasture. He was compelled to employ twelve men and boys, and his farm required the labour of only five. He is about to give notice that he will quit. Every useless labourer is calculated to add 5s an acre to the rent of a farm of 100 acres . . .

### EFFECTS ON PROPRIETORS

The committee appointed by the House of Commons in 1817 to consider the Poor Laws stated their opinion 'that unless some efficacious check were interposed, there was then every reason to think that the amount of the assessment would continue to increase, until at a period more or less remote, according to the progress the evil had already made in different places, it should have absorbed the profits of the property on which the rate might have been assessed, producing thereby the neglect and ruin of the land and the waste or removal of other property, to the utter subversion of the happy order of society so long upheld in these kingdoms'. In consequence of the recommendations of that Committee, a check was interposed by the 59 Geo. III, c. 12 [1818]. But though that act, by restricting the power of the magistrates to order relief, and by authorizing the removal of the Irish and Scottish paupers, the appointment of representative vestries and of assistant overseers, the rating the owners of small tenements, and the giving relief by way of loan, occasioned during the six years that immediately followed it a progressive diminution of the amount of the Poor Law assessment, its beneficial enactments appear to be no longer capable of struggling with the evil tendencies of the existing system. The year ending 25 March 1824 was the last year of regular improvement. And we have seen that the amount of relief now given, when estimated in commodities, is actually greater, and greater in proportion to our population, than it was when that report was made. It has increased still more when considered with reference to the value of the property on which it is assessed.

We are happy to say that not many cases of the actual dereliction of estates have been stated to us. Some, however, have occurred; and we have given in the extracts from our evidence the details of one, the parish of Cholesbury, in the county of Bucks. It appears that in this parish, the population of which has been almost stationary since 1801, in which, within the memory of persons now living, the rates were only £10 11s a year, and only one person received relief, the sum raised for the relief of the poor rose from £99 4s a year in 1816 to £150 5s in 1831; and in 1832, when it was proceeding at the rate of £367 a year, suddenly ceased in consequence of the impossibility to continue its collection; the landlords having given up their rents, the farmers their tenancies, and the clergymen his glebe and his tithes. The clergyman, Mr Jeston, states that in October 1832 the parish officers threw up their books, and the poor assembled in a body before his door while he was in bed, asking for advice and food. Partly from his own small means, partly from the charity of neighbours, and partly by rates in aid, imposed on the neighbouring parishes, they were for some time supported; and the benevolent Rector recommends that the whole of the land should be divided among the able-bodied paupers, and adds that he has reason to think that at the expiration of two years, the parish in the interval receiving the assistance of rates in aid, the whole of the poor would be able and willing to support themselves, the aged and impotent of course excepted'. In Cholesbury, therefore, the expense of maintaining the poor has not merely swallowed up the whole value of the land; it requires even the assistance for two years of rates in aid from other parishes to enable the able-bodied, after the land has been given up to them, to support themselves; and the aged and impotent must even then remain a burthen on the neighbouring parishes.

Our evidence exhibits no other instance of the abandonment of a parish, but it contains many in which the pressure of the poor-rate has reduced the rent to half, or to less than half, of what it would have been if the land had been situated in an unpauperized district, and some in which it has been impossible for the owner to find a tenant.

Mr Majendie states that in Lenham, Kent, at the time of his visit, some of the land was out of cultivation. A large estate has been several years in the hands of the proprietor, and a farm of 420 acres of good land, tithe-free and well situated, had just been thrown up by the tenant, the poor-rate on it amounting to £300 a year. He mentions another place in which a farm well situated, of average quality, was in vain offered at 5s an acre, not from objection to the quality of the land, but because men of capital will not connect themselves with a parish in which the poor-rates would keep them in a constant state of vexation and anxiety. He states that in Ardingly those farmers who have any capital left withdraw from the parish as soon as their leases expire. One of them admitted to him that it was out of the power of the landlords to relieve them.

Mr Power, after mentioning the universal complaint in Cambridgeshire that substantial tenants cannot be found at the lowest assignable rents, goes on to say that Mr Quintin, a gentleman of considerable landed property in the county, told him that he had a farm at Gransden for which he could not get a tenant even at 5s an acre, though land from which thirty bushels of wheat an acre had been obtained. 'Downing College', he adds, 'has a property of 5,000 acres in this county, lying principally in the parishes of Tadlow, East Hatley, Croydon, and Gamlingay; it is found impossible, notwithstanding the lowering the rents to an extreme point, to obtain men of substance for tenants. Several farms of considerable extent have changed hands twice within the last five years, from insolvency of the tenants in some cases, in others from the terror of that prospect. The amount of arrears at this time is such as only a collegiate body could support. I draw from authentic sources, being myself a fellow of the college.' In the same county Mr Power found that at Soham, a total absorption of the value of the land in twelve or fourteen years was anticipated; and Mr Cowell, that at Great Shelford the same result was expected to take place in ten.

Mr Pilkington's description of several places in Leicestershire is equally alarming. In Hinkley he found the poor-rate exceeding £1 an acre and rapidly increasing, and a general opinion that the day is not distant when rent must cease altogether. On visiting Wigston Magna in November 1832 he was informed that the value of property had fallen one half since 1820 and was not saleable even at that reduction. It does not appear, indeed, that it ought to have sold for more than two or three years' purchase, the net rental not amounting to £4,000 a year, and the poor-rate expenditure growing at the rate of £1,000 increase in a single year. And on his return to that neighbourhood three months after, the statement made to him was that property in land was gone; that even the rates could not be collected without regular summons and judicial sales, and that the present system must ensure, and very shortly, the total ruin of every individual of any property in the parish. We cannot wonder, after this, at the statement of an eminent solicitor at Loughborough that it is now scarcely possible to effect a sale of property in that neighbourhood at any price . . .

## EFFECTS ON EMPLOYERS OF LABOURERS

### [*Agricultural*]

The effects of this system on the immediate employers of labour in the country and in the towns are very different. To avoid circumlocution, we will use the word 'farmers' as comprehending all the former class of persons, and the word 'manufacturers' as comprehending all the latter; and as they are the least complicated, and most material, we will begin by considering the effects produced on the farmers. The services of the labourer are by far the most important of all the instruments used in agriculture. In the management of live and dead stock much must always be left to his judgement. Only a portion, and that not a very large portion, of the results of ordinary farm labour is susceptible of being immediately valued so as to be paid by the piece. The whole farm is the farmer's workshop and storehouse; he is frequently obliged to leave it, and has no partner on whom he can devolve its care during his absence, and its extent generally makes it impossible for him to stand over and personally inspect all the labourers employed on it. His property is scattered over every part, with scarcely any protection against depredation or injury. If his labourers, therefore, want the skill and intelligence necessary to enable them to execute those details for which no general and unvarying rules can be laid down; if they have not the diligence necessary to keep them steadily at work when their master's eye is off; if they have not sufficient honesty to resist the temptation to plunder when the act is easy and the detection difficult, it follows that neither the excellence or abundance of the farmer's agricultural capital, nor his own skill or diligence, or economy, can save him from loss or perhaps from ruin.

Now it is obvious that the tendency of the allowance system is to diminish, we might almost say to destroy, all these qualities in the labourer. What motive has the man who is to receive 10s every Saturday, not because 10s is the value of his week's labour, but because his family consists of five persons, who knows that his income will be increased by nothing but by an increase of his family, and diminished by nothing but by a diminution of his family, that it has no reference to his skill, his honesty, or his diligence—what motive has he to acquire or to preserve any of these merits ? Unhappily, the evidence shows not only that these virtues are rapidly wearing out, but that their place is assumed by the opposite vices; and that the very labourers among whom the farmer has to live, on whose merits as workmen and on whose affection as friends he ought to depend, are becoming not merely idle and ignorant and dishonest, but positively hostile; not merely unfit for his service and indifferent to his welfare, but actually desirous to injure him.

One of the questions circulated by us in the rural districts was whether the labourers in the respondent's neighbourhood were supposed to be better or worse workmen than formerly? If the answers to this question had been uniformly unfavourable, they might have been ascribed to the general tendency to depreciate what is present; but it will be found, on referring to our Appendix, that the replies vary according to the poor-law admini-stration of the district. Where it is good the replies are, 'much the same', 'never were better', 'diligence the same, skill increased'. But when we come within the influence of the allowance and the scale, the replies are, 'they are much degenerated, being generally disaffected to their employers: they work unwillingly and waste-fully': 'three of them would not do near the work in a day performed by two in more northern counties': 'one-third of our labourers do not work at all, the greater part of the remainder are much contaminated; the rising population learn nothing, the others are forgetting what they knew'. 'They are constantly changing their services. Relying upon parish support, they are indifferent whether they oblige or disobey their masters, are less honest and industrious, and the mutual regard between employer and servant is gone'. 'The system of allowance is most mis-chievous and ruinous, and till it is abandoned the spirit of industry can never be revived. Allowance-men will not work. It makes them idle, lazy, fraudulent, and worthless, and depresses the wages of free labour.' 'With very few exceptions, the labourers are not as industrious as formerly; and notwithstanding the low rate of wages now too generally paid, it costs as much money in the end to have work performed as it did sixteen years ago.' 'The

Poor Laws are perhaps better administered in this parish than in many others; but such a resource in view as parish relief prevents the labourer's exertions, and the young men from laying by anything in their youth. The latter marry early, because they can get no relief unless they have children; this, of course, raises the rates. An instance occurred a short time since, of a labourer marrying, and going from the church to the poorhouse, not having money to pay the fees! By old experienced individuals it is supposed one labourer, forty years ago, would do more than two of the present day.'

The reports of the Assistant Commissioners are full of the same evidence. In the pauperized districts we find sometimes the labourers, or rather those who ought to be the labourers, absolutely refusing work; sometimes we find them bribed by additional pay from the parish to take profitable work; but always they are represented as so inferior to the non-parishioners as to render their services, though nominally cheap, really dear, and generally dear in proportion to their apparent cheapness.

Mr Okeden states that in Wiltshire the farmer finds his labourers idle and insolent, and regardless of him, and his orders, and his work. They openly say, 'We care not, the scale and pay-table are ours.' Mr Majendie states that in Ardingly, Sussex:

> Labourers refuse work, unless of a description agreeable to them; they say, 'Why should we be singled out for hard labour, instead of working for the parish?' A winter ago the clergyman offered 2s a day to three labourers; they refused to work unless they had extra pay for remaining after half-past four, saying, that the parish did not require more than that of them. In the last hay harvest a man, inferior to the average labourers, refused 10s a week from a farmer, saying, that he could do better with the parish.
>
> At Eastbourne, in December 1832, four healthy young men, receiving from 12s to 14s per week from the parish, refused to work at threshing for a farmer at 2s 6d and a quart of ale per day. The fishermen, secure of pay without labour, refuse to go out to sea in the winter: one has said, 'Why should I expose myself to fatigue and danger, when the parish supports my family and pays my rent?' The masters are obliged to send to Hastings to get men for their boats. In May 1832 a respectable fisherman said, 'I fear that, like many of my neighbours, I shall be obliged to sell my boat and come upon the parish for want of hands to man her; I cannot get men here, as they like better their allowance from the parish.

I therefore board a Hastings man, and give him as much profit as I get myself, but this ruins me.'

At Rochford, Essex, the overseers make up wages to 1s 9d per head to families, by the magistrate's order, and this the labourers demand as their right. Good ploughmen are not to be found. The labourers say, they do not care to plough, because that is a kind of work which, if neglected, will subject them to punishment, and, if properly done, requires constant attention, and the lads do not even wish to learn. Nine able-bodied young men were in the workhouse last winter; such was their character that they were not to be trusted with threshing.

Mr Power states the evidence of Mr King, the overseer, and a large occupier of land at Bottisham (Cambridgeshire), who refers the increase of rates in that neighbourhood, not to any increase of population, or diminution of demand, but to the effects of the existing system on the habits of the labourers:

He complained of their deficiency in industry, arising from their growing indifference, or rather partiality, to being thrown on the parish: when the bad season is coming on, they frequently dispose of any little property, such as a cow or a pig, in order to entitle themselves to parish wages. That very evening (says Mr Power) on which I saw him, one of his men swore at him, and said he did not want his work or his wages; he could do better on the parish.

# XXXIII

The differences in farm wage levels which distinguished the northern and southern counties of England were analysed in some detail by Sir James Caird in 1851. The labour surplus and immobility which underlay the poor rewards of the southern farmworkers had serious consequences for farming, more evidently in the burden of poor rates, less obviously in the slow adoption of machinery and more efficient methods of working. Here is Caird's discussion of the problem: J. Caird, *English Agriculture in 1850–51* (1852; new ed. 1968), pp. 510–19.

---

The last class of the agricultural body whose interests we have to consider, is the labourer. The disparity of wages paid for the same nominal amount of work in the various counties of England is so great as to show that there must be something in the present state of the law affecting the labourer which prevents the wages of agricultural labour finding a more natural level throughout the country. Taking the highest rate we have met with—15s a week in parts of Lancashire, and comparing it with the lowest—6s a week in south Wilts, and considering the facilities of communication in the present day, it is surprising that so great a difference should continue. To use the words of Adam Smith, 'Such a difference of prices which, it seems, is not always sufficient to transport a man from one parish to another, would necessarily occasion so great a transportation of the most bulky commodities, not only from one parish to another, but from one end of the kingdom, almost from one end of the world, to the other, as would soon reduce them more nearly to a level. After all that has been said of the levity and inconsistency of human nature, it appears evidently from experience that man is, of all sorts of luggage, the most difficult to be transported.'

The table [on p. 234] shows the average weekly wages, in the counties we visited, of the agricultural labourer in 1850–1.

## OUTLINE MAP OF ENGLAND

*Showing the distinction between the corn and grazing counties; and the line of division between high and low wages*

All to the east of the black line, running from north to south, may be regarded as the chief corn districts of England; the average rental per acre of the cultivated land of which is 30 per cent less than that of the counties to the west of the same line, which are the principal grazing, green crop, and dairy districts.

The dotted line, running from east to west, shows the line of wages; the average of the counties to the north of that line being 37 per cent higher than those to the south of it.

We again divide the country into the two divisions of the corn counties of the east and south coast; and the mixed corn and grass of the midland and western counties. The table is so constructed as also to show the wages of the northern counties separately from those of the southern. The black line, dotted on the map, [on p. 233] indicates the limit southwards of the coal formation, within which the great branches of mining and manufacturing enterprise, with the exception of Wales, Somerset, and Cornwall, may be said to be confined.

An examination of this table shows very clearly that the higher

Table showing the Rate of Agricultural Wages in 1850–1

| NORTHERN COUNTIES | | | |
|---|---|---|---|
| Midland and western counties | Weekly wages | East and south coast counties | Weekly wages |
| | s    d | | s    d |
| Cumberland | 13   0 | Northumberland | 11   0 |
| Lancashire | 13   6 | Durham | 11   0 |
| West Riding | 14   0 | North Riding | 11   0 |
| Cheshire | 12   0 | East Riding | 12   0 |
| Derby | 11   0 | Lincoln | 10   0 |
| Nottingham | 10   0 | | |
| Stafford | 9   6 | | |
| **SOUTHERN COUNTIES** | | | |
| Warwick | 8   6 | Norfolk | 8   6 |
| Northampton | 9   0 | Suffolk | 7   0 |
| Bucks | 8   6 | Huntingdon | 8   6 |
| Oxford | 9   0 | Cambridge | 7   6 |
| Gloucester | 7   0 | Bedford | 9   0 |
| North Wilts | 7   6 | Hertford | 9   0 |
| Devon | 8   6 | Essex | 8   0 |
| | | Berks | 7   6 |
| | | Surrey | 9   6 |
| | | Sussex | 10   6 |
| | | Hants | 9   0 |
| | | South Wilts | 7   0 |
| | | Dorset | 7   6 |
| Average of west | 10   0 | Average of east | 9   1 |

|  | s   d |
|---|---|
| Average of all northern counties | 11   6 |
| Average of all southern counties | 8   5 |
| Average over the whole | 9   6 |

wages of the northern counties is altogether due to the proximity of manufacturing and mining enterprise. The difference between the rates in the corn counties of the east, and the mixed husbandry of the midland and western counties, is not so uniform as to warrant any deduction such as showed itself so distinctly in the average rent of those districts.

The influence of manufacturing enterprise is thus seen to add 37 per cent to the wages of the agricultural labourers of the northern counties, as compared with those of the south. The line is distinctly drawn at the point where coal ceases to be found, to the south of which there is only one of the counties we visited in which the wages reach 10s a week, Sussex. The local circumstances of that county explain the cause of labour being there better remunerated; the wealthy population of Brighton, and other places on the Sussex coast, affording an increased market for labour beyond the demands of agriculture.

A comparison with the price of labour in the same counties in 1770 will show this influence clearly. In Cumberland, at that time, the wages of the agricultural labourer were 6s 6d, in the West Riding 6s, in Lancashire 6s 6d; in each of which counties they have since increased fully 100 per cent. In all the northern counties the increase is about 66 per cent. The increase in the eighteen southern counties mentioned by Young is under 14 per cent. In some of them there is no increase whatever, the wages of the agricultural labourer in part of Berkshire and Wilts being precisely the same as they were eighty years ago, and in Suffolk absolutely less. The average wages in 1770 in the northern counties visited by Young were 6s 9d; and of the southern counties 7s 6d.

Nothing could show more unequivocally the advantage of manufacturing enterprise to the prosperity and advancement of the farm labourer. We constantly hear expressions of regret, on the part of those who do not look beneath the surface, that the agricultural labourer, hitherto accustomed to the peace and plenty of his Arcadian lot, is year after year being withdrawn from it by the increasing demands and more tempting wages of the manufacturer. But, when we look to the facts, we find that in the manufacturing districts agricultural rents and wages have kept pace with each other; while in the purely agricultural counties the landlords' rent has increased 100 per cent, and the labourers' wages not quite 14. In the northern counties the labourers are enabled to feed and clothe themselves with respectability and comfort, while in some of the southern counties their wages are insufficient for their healthy sustenance.

But the agricultural labourer in the southern counties, while he derives from his labour the means of a very scanty existence, is almost everywhere felt as a burden instead of a benefit to his employer. To ascertain how far this feeling is well-founded, we have compiled the table on the following page; in which the counties are arranged for comparison in the same order as in our table of wages [p. 234].

Here will be remarked the same broad line of demarcation which was formerly exhibited in our table of wages, between the northern, or manufacturing, and the southern, or agricultural, districts. But there is this striking difference, which is almost invariable, that the counties which stand high in the scale of poor rates, stand low in the scale of wages.

The evil effects remain of an interference by law, in 1782, to fix the rate of wages. In 1795, owing to a rise in the price of corn from 54s to 75s, the magistrates of several of the southern counties issued tables showing the wages which, in their opinion, every labouring man should receive, proportioned to the number of his family, and the price of bread; and the parish officers were instructed to make up the difference between this rate and that paid by his employer! A system akin to this continued to be acted upon, as is well known, down to the passing of the Poor Law Amendment Act, and destroyed, as might have been expected, every feeling of independence on the part of the labourer. But the same system is, in effect, still in existence; for there is little difference in principle between it and that which we have so frequently mentioned as being adopted by the ratepayers of a parish, agreeing to divide amongst them the surplus labour, not according to their respective requirements, but in proportion to the size of their farms. In such a parish, the superior skill of a farmer in economizing one of the chief costs of production is arbitrarily set aside, and he is reduced to the same level with his unskilful neighbours. But it has been also proved to operate in the same disadvantageous manner upon the skilled labourer, whose capacity would enable him to do more work and earn a higher rate of wages, but which he is discouraged from doing, as the effect

Table showing the rates of the amount expended for relief of the poor, 1st per pound on property, 2nd per head of population, and 3rd the percentage of paupers to the population, vagrants excluded, in thirty-one counties, arranged for comparison, of the eastern with the western counties, and the northern with the southern. Compiled from Parliamentary Returns, 1848, No. 735.

| Midland and western counties | Poor relief: Per £ on property | Poor relief: Per head of population | Ratio per cent of paupers to the population | East and south coast counties | Poor relief: Per £ on property | Poor relief: Per head of population | Ratio per cent of paupers to the population |
|---|---|---|---|---|---|---|---|
| **NORTHERN COUNTIES** | | | | | | | |
| | s d | s d | | | s d | s d | |
| Cumberland | 1 1 | 4 3 | 6·2 | Northumberland | 1 2½ | 5 7½ | 6·7 |
| Lancashire | 1 0¾ | 3 7¼ | 7·2 | Durham | 1 3½ | 3 7½ | 5·2 |
| West Riding | 1 5½ | 4 1¼ | 6·0 | North Riding | 1 1 | 5 10¾ | 6·5 |
| Cheshire | 1 0¼ | 3 8 | 5·5 | East Riding | 1 2¾ | 5 10¾ | 7·9 |
| Derby | 1 0½ | 3 8½ | 4·2 | Lincoln | 1 2¼ | 6 7¾ | 7·5 |
| Nottingham | 1 5 | 5 3 | 7·9 | | | | |
| Stafford | 1 1 | 3 8¼ | 4·3 | | | | |
| **SOUTHERN COUNTIES** | | | | | | | |
| Warwick | 1 3½ | 5 1½ | 5 | Norfolk | 2 2 | 9 8½ | 12·8 |
| Northampton | 1 11½ | 9 2¼ | 11·3 | Suffolk | 2 2 | 9 3½ | 13·6 |
| Bucks | 2 4½ | 10 2¾ | 14·6 | Huntingdon | 2 0 | 9 6½ | 11·6 |
| Oxford | 2 5 | 10 4½ | 15·1 | Cambridge | 1 9¼ | 9 1¼ | 10·7 |
| Gloucester | 1 8¼ | 6 10½ | 9·9 | Bedford | 2 0½ | 7 7¾ | 11·6 |
| North Wilts | 2 3¼ | 10 5 | 16·1 | Hertford | 1 8½ | 7 9¼ | 11·3 |
| Devon | 1 11¼ | 7 0½ | 10·6 | Essex | 2 1¾ | 9 9¼ | 14·2 |
| | | | | Berks | 2 2¾ | 9 11¼ | 12·8 |
| | | | | Surrey | 1 11 | 6 9 | 8·8 |
| | | | | Sussex | 2 1¾ | 9 1½ | 12·7 |
| | | | | Hants | 2 2¾ | 8 2¼ | 11·9 |
| | | | | South Wilts | 2 3¼ | 10 5 | 16·1 |
| | | | | Dorset | 2 2¾ | 9 7½ | 15·7 |
| Average of all midland and western counties | 1 9¾ | 6 3 | 8·9 | Average of east and south coast counties | 1 10 | 7 10½ | 10·9 |
| Average of all northern counties | 1 2 | 4 7¾ | 6·2 | Average of all southern counties, reckoning north and south Wilts once only | 2 0½ | 8 8½ | 12·1 |

would be to diminish the employment of others for whom work must be found. The bad labourer is thus paid the same rate of wages as the good, emulation is discouraged, and the standard of skill and efficiency kept down. If a labourer knows that he must be employed at a certain uniform rate of wages, whatever be the quality of his work, he has no motive to improve. But should he, notwithstanding these artificial trammels, feel within himself both the power and the will to do better, the law of settlement tells him that he is not at liberty to carry his skill to a better market except on conditions which are felt to be prohibitory.

There is another evil with regard to the labourer, which is not confined to the southern counties—the system of 'close' and 'open' parishes, by which the large proprietors are enabled to drive the labourer out of the parish in which he works, to a distant village, where, property being more divided, there is not the same combination against poverty. It is the commonest thing possible to find agricultural labourers lodged at such a distance from their regular place of employment, that they have to walk an hour out in the morning, and an hour home in the evening—from forty to fifty miles a week. In one county the farmers actually provide donkeys, on which their labourers ride out and home, to prevent them tiring themselves with walking, that so they may be more vigorous at their work. Two hours a day is a sixth part of a man's daily labour, and this enormous tax he is compelled to pay in labour, which is his only capital. Nor is this the sole evil of the practice, for the labourers are crowded into villages where the exorbitant cottage rents frequently oblige them to herd together in a manner destructive of morality and injurious to health.

Here it appears that, while the average wages of the north are

| | | | | |
|---|---|---|---|---|
| The average wages of the northern counties have been shown to be | 11/6 | | | |
| Their average poor relief per £ on property | — | 1/2 | | |
| — — per head of population | — | — | 4/7¾ | |
| Their rate per cent of paupers to the population | — | — | — | 6·2 |
| *Contrasted with which are:* | | | | |
| The average wages of the southern counties | 8/5 | | | |
| Their average poor relief per £ on property | — | 2/0½ | | |
| — — per head on population | — | — | 8/8½ | |
| And their percentage of paupers to the population | — | — | — | 12·1 |

37 per cent above those of the south, the expenditure in the north for poor relief is about 70 per cent lower on property, and about 87 per cent lower when estimated according to population; and the difference in the percentage of paupers is nearly as one to two.

The redundance of labour which oppresses property and depreciates wages in the south will not only relieve itself as soon as freedom is restored to the labourer *to settle where he will*, but the change, by equalizing the market of labour, will cheapen the cost, and stimulate the progress, of production in the north. It is obvious, however, that a change to mere union settlements would not accomplish these desirable results; since it is found that the marked inequality in wages and poverty is not limited to unions or counties, but bisects the kingdom by unmistakable lines into two great geographical divisions. We may draw a line across the map of England: all to the south of that line we shall have high poor-rates and low wages, and all to the north of it high wages and low poor-rates;—on one side an enforced excess of labour, impoverishing and bearing down the working man, and, by consequence, rates pressing on property with undue severity; on the other a comparative deficiency of labour, raising its price to an unequal average, and operating unfairly on the cost of production;—in these two divisions the same people, the same language, habits, and institutions, with cheap and rapid communication between them, and no obstacle except a law which, aggravating the natural indisposition to move, hinders the working man from carrying his labour to the best market.

It is not our province to discuss the Poor Laws, or to attempt to lay down a remedy for a state of things which is confessedly injurious both to employer and employed. We desire only, as strongly as we can, to direct attention to a system fraught with so many evils,—a law of settlement which binds the labourer to a parish in which his labour is not required, and prevents another, where labour is deficient, from obtaining that supply which would be to all parties so beneficial. The importance of the subject, and the inquiry and discussion it has recently undergone, lead us to hope that some remedial measure will be early introduced by the legislature to enable and encourage the free circulation of labour throughout England. The over supply is, as far as we have seen, apt to be exaggerated. As labourers begin to withdraw, employers will soon discover, under the pressure of higher wages, that the surplus was not so great as they led themselves to believe. The lowest rate of wages we met with in England, 6s a week, was in an agricultural parish in south Wilts, where one large farmer employed the whole labour of the parish, and fixed as he chose the scale of wages; and yet, in this very parish, the resident labourers were insufficient for the regular summer work of the farms, strangers from a different part of the county being introduced for a season to perform the operation of turnip hoeing, and to assist in the hay and corn harvests.

The change in the price of provisions has added greatly to the comfort of the labourer. Within the last ten years the decrease in price of the principal articles of his consumption is upwards of 30 per cent. In 1840 a stone of flour cost him 2s 6d, which he can now purchase for 1s 8d; good Congou tea in 1840 was, exclusive of duty, 2s 6d per lb, and is now only 1s; and the same quality of sugar which then cost him 6d per lb, can be had now for $3\frac{1}{2}$d.

Such a reduction in the price of provisions is a great boon to the labourer, because it gives him the command of additional comforts, and thereby elevates his condition. This is totally different from the effect of resorting to a lower quality of food, such as potatoes, contentment with which lowers the standard of comfort, and debases the condition of the labourer. The sure consequence of such a depression of standard is, that labourers being more cheaply produced, increase in more rapid proportion than the capital for their employment, and, the labour-market being overstocked, wages are lowered. There could no greater evil befall the English agricultural labourer than that any circumstances should compel him to depress his standard of comfort so far as to be content for his principal subsistence with the lowest species of human food in this country, the potato.

In the counties visited by Arthur Young, the rent of the labourers' cottages has increased since his time from 8d to 1s 5d a week, being upwards of 100 per cent; while agricultural wages in the same counties, on the average, have risen in the same period only from 7s 3d to 9s 7d, or about 34 per cent.

The great difference in the rate of wages between the southern and northern counties, is a sufficient proof that *the wages of the agricultural labourer are not dependent on the prices of agricultural produce*. A bushel of wheat, a pound of butter, or a stone of meat, is not more valuable in Cumberland or the North Riding, than in

Suffolk or Berkshire; yet the wages of the labourer in the two former are from 60 to 70 per cent higher than in the two latter counties. The price of bread is not higher in July and August than in May and June; yet, in every agricultural county, the wages of labour during the period of harvest are increased. Nor are better wages directly the effect of capital; for the poor farmer of the cold clays of Durham or Northumberland pays 11s a week, while the large capitalist who cultivates half a parish in south Wilts or Dorset pays only 7s to his labourer. The higher rate is unmistakably due to the increased demand for labour. This has been greatest in the manufacturing and mining districts of the north, and near the commercial towns and great seaports, whose prodigious increase of business has attracted and been followed by a similar increase of wealth and population. The increase of population shown by the census of 1851, during the last ten years, in the twelve counties in the foregoing table where wages are highest, exceeds by 6 per cent the increase of the southern counties during the same period. It thus appears that the welfare of the agricultural labourer is, more than that of any class in the community, dependent on the continued progress of our manufacturing and mercantile industry.

# XXXIV

Although many labourers' cottages were antiquated, cramped and insanitary, this was not universally the case. A large number of new cottages had been built in the later eighteenth and early nineteenth centuries, and some landowners, like the Duke of Bedford, continued to devote attention to what the Duke called this 'very important subject'. The motives for cottage building were partly moral and humanitarian, and partly economic and social—reflecting a concern for the supply of competent labourers and seeing good cottages as a necessary complement to improved farm buildings; they resulted also from a desire to protect the reputation of the estate and its proprietor. The following is part of a paper sent by the tenth Duke of Bedford to the President of the Royal Agricultural Society: *Journal of the Royal Agricultural Society of England*, X (1849), pp. 185–91.

---

## X—ON LABOURERS' COTTAGES. FROM HIS GRACE THE DUKE OF BEDFORD

### To the President

My dear Lord Chichester—Observing in the last volume of the Royal Agricultural Society's Journal that the Council is directing its attention to that very important subject, the improvement of agricultural labourers' cottages, feeling (in common, I have no doubt, with many other proprietors of estates) greatly interested in it, and having bestowed upon it much and anxious consideration, I am desirous of giving to others the benefit of my inquiries and experience, to enable them to follow the system I am adopting, so far as they may think it expedient to do so; and I therefore beg leave to offer to the Society copies of the plans and drawings according to which I have lately erected some cottages, and intend to erect many more, on my Bedfordshire and Devonshire estates.

My inquiries into the condition of the cottages on those estates led me to the conclusion, first, that, notwithstanding a very considerable annual expenditure upon them, many of them were so deficient in requisite accommodation as to be inadequate to the removal of that acknowledged obstacle to the improvement of the morals and habits of agricultural labourers, which consists in the want of separate bedrooms for grown-up boys and girls; and, secondly, that the practice of taking in lodgers had led to still further evils. The improved methods of cultivation, extensive draining, and general improvement in husbandry (requiring additional hands) that are going on, more or less, in all parts of the country, and the breaking up of inferior grass-lands, and converting woodland into tillage (especially since the passing of the Tithe Commutation Act), by giving work to many more labourers than were formerly employed, have caused a proportionate augmentation of their number, and, consequently, an increased want of cottage accommodation. To meet this increased want, and at the same time to improve the habitations of the labourers, I determined to rebuild the worst of my cottages, and to add to their number in those parts of my estate in which it appeared necessary to do so. I therefore directed my surveyor to prepare a series of plans of cottages suitable for families of different sizes and descriptions, sufficient to satisfy the reasonable wants of the labourers and their families, and to be so constructed as that (avoiding all needless expense) the cottages should be substantial, and not subject to premature decay, or likely to require costly repair.

The experience obtained in erecting the new cottages already built on my estate has enabled my surveyor to ascertain the quantities of each kind of material required for the construction, separately, of the cottages shown in these plans; and in the hope that this information may be useful to others, I have directed those quantities to be put in detail upon the plans. I have deemed it best not to have the prices added, because prices vary in different localities, and therefore to furnish the prices of one locality would be useless, and might mislead. The quantities being given, it will be easy to add the prices they bear in other places in which the erection of cottages according to those plans may be desired.

As the cottages of many landed proprietors may be, and probably are, in a state similar to my own, it appears to me that the information, founded on actual experience, which I have obtained on the subject of cottage-building, and which is embodied in these plans, may be acceptable and generally useful.

Cottage-building (except to a cottage speculator who exacts immoderate rents for scanty and defective habitations) is, we all know, a bad investment of money; but this is not the light in which such a subject should be viewed by landlords, from whom it is, surely, not too much to expect that, while they are building and improving farmhouses, homesteads, and cattle-sheds, they will, also, build and improve dwellings for their labourers in sufficient number to meet the improved and improving cultivation of the land.

But in adding to the number of cottages on our estates, there should, of course, be a limit, or we may fall into evils of another kind. That limit may easily be drawn, either by the proprietor himself, or by an intelligent steward, and made to agree with the reasonable wants of the districts or parishes in which his employer's estates are situated.

To improve the dwellings of the labouring class, and afford them the means of greater cleanliness, health, and comfort, in their own homes, to extend education, and thus raise the social and moral habits of those most valuable members of the community, are among the first duties, and ought to be among the truest pleasures, of every landlord. While he thus cares for those whom Providence has committed to his charge, he will teach them that reliance on the exertion of the faculties with which they are endowed is the surest way to their own independence and the well-being of their families.

I shall not dwell, as I might, on the undeniable advantages of making the rural population contented with their condition, and of promoting that mutual goodwill between the landed proprietor and the tenants and labourers on his estate, which sound policy and the higher motives of humanity alike recommend.

Having lately had the pleasure of visiting with you some of the cottages on your estate in Sussex, knowing the interest you take in the subject, and having witnessed your success in carrying into effect the views we alike entertain upon it, it is gratifying to me to be able to address this communication to you as President of the Royal Agricultural Society for the present year.

I remain, my dear Lord Chichester, with sincere regard and esteem, faithfully yours,

BEDFORD

*Woburn Abbey, March 1849*

## PLANS AND ELEVATIONS FOR LABOURERS' COTTAGES.

TWO WITH ONE BED-ROOM EACH.

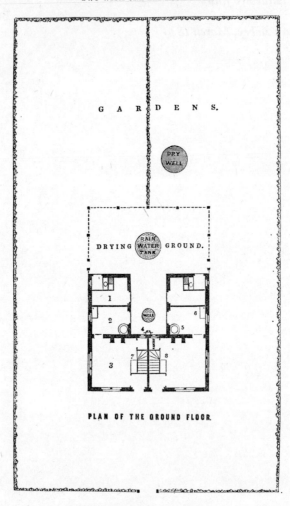

PLAN OF THE GROUND FLOOR.

1. Wood and Coals...10.0 × 6.0  5. Copper.
2. Wash-house......10.0 × 6.0  6. Sink.
3. Kitchen............11.0 × 11.0  7. Dresser.
4. Pump.      - 8. Do.

Scale of Feet.

ELEVATION OF THE FRONT.

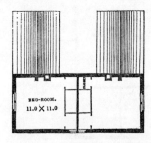

BED-ROOM.
11.0 × 11.0

PLAN OF THE BED-ROOM FLOOR.

ELEVATION OF THE ENDS.

QUANTITIES.

| | | £. s. d. |
|---|---|---|
| 22,950 | Building bricks . . . . . . | |
| 35 lds. | Sand . . . . . . . . . . . | |
| 30 qrs. | Lime . . . . . . . . . . | |
| 10 bus. | Cement . . . . . . . . . . | |
| 1750 | 6 in. paving squares . . . . | |
| 124 | 12 in. shell drain tiles . . . | |
| 54 | 18 in. earthen pipes, 6 ins. diam. . . . . . . . . . . | |
| 7020 | Plain tiles . . . . . . . . | |
| 84 | Valley tiles . . . . . . . . | |
| 44 | 18 in. ridge tiles . . . . . . | |
| 10 bun. | Tiling laths . . . . . . . . | |
| 14 do. | Plastering laths . . . . . . | |
| qrs. lb. 2  0 | Hair . . . . . . . . . . . | |
| 3 | York stones for manholes . . | |
| 4 | Small scrapers and stones . . | |
| 2 | Do. stone sinks with grates, waste pipes, and traps . . | |
| 146 ft. | Cube fir . . . . . . . . . . | |
| 2 ft. 1 in. | Do. oak . . . . . . . . . | |
| 37⅜ | 12 ft. 3 by 9 in. deals . . . . | |
| 10 | Posts to fences and hand gates, 3 ft. out of ground . . . . | |
| 3 | Drying posts, 7 ft. out of grnd. | |
| 8 leng. | Rails and palings, 3 ft. high . | |
| 3 | Hand gates, with hinges and latches . . . . . . . . . | |
| 2 | Solid door-cases, with ledged doors, hinges, and latches, complete . . . . . . . | |
| 6 | Ditto, with stock-locks . . . | |
| 2 | Small louvre frames to privies | |
| 4 | Solid one-light window-frames, with iron quarry lights to open, glazed, complete . . | |
| 5 | Two light ditto, one to open . | |
| 2 | Three light ditto and ditto . | |
| 24 | Iron cloak pins . . . . . . . | |
| 12 prs. | 14 in. cross garnetts . . . . | |
| 12 | Thumb-latches . . . . . . . | |
| 12 | Tower bolts . . . . . . . . | |
| 4 | Chimney-pots . . . . . . . | |
| 2 | Bedroom stoves, and fixed . . | |
| 163 ft. | Iron eaves, gutter, and stack-pipe, fixed, complete . . . | |
| 1 | Double pump, with suctions to draw from well and tank . | |
| 2 | Common closet apparatus, with supply cistern and service from pump to each . . . . | |
| | Nails and screws . . . . . . | |
| qrs. lb. 3  0 | Oil-paint . . . . . . . . . | |
| | Labour . . . . . . . . . . | |
| | Cartage . . . . . . . . . . | |
| | £. | |

**PLANS AND ELEVATIONS FOR LABOURERS' COTTAGES.**

TWO WITH THREE BED-ROOMS, AND ONE WITH TWO BED-ROOMS.

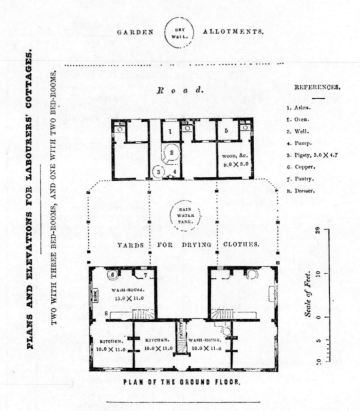

GARDEN ALLOTMENTS.

DRY WELL.

*Road.*

REFERENCES.

1. Ashes.
2. Oven.
3. Well.
4. Pump.
5. Pigsty, 5.0 × 4.7
6. Copper.
7. Pantry.
8. Dresser.

WOOD, &c. 8.0 × 8.0

RAIN WATER TANK.

YARDS FOR DRYING CLOTHES.

Scale of Feet.

WASH-HOUSE. 15.0 × 11.0

KITCHEN. 10.0 × 11.0

KITCHEN. 10.0 × 11.0

WASH-HOUSE. 10.0 × 11.0

PLAN OF THE GROUND FLOOR.

QUANTITIES FOR HOUSES.

| | | £. s. d. | | | £. s. d. |
|---|---|---|---|---|---|
| 38,830 | Building bricks | | 6 | Small one-light solid window-frames, with iron quarry lights to open, glazed, complete | |
| 56 qrs. | Lime | | | | |
| 58 lds. | Sand | | 4 | One-light window-frames, and ditto | |
| 10 bus. | Cement | | | | |
| 3,190 | 6 in. paving squares | | 10 | Two light ditto, one each, to open, and ditto | |
| 12,150 | Plain tiles | | | | |
| 374 | Valley tiles | | 2 | Three light ditto, one each, to open, and ditto | |
| 69 | 18 in ridge tiles | | | Nails and screws | |
| 21 bun. | Tiling laths | | 20 prs. | Cross garnett hinges | |
| 29 do. | Plastering laths | | 20 | Thumb-latches | |
| 2 c. 2 qr. | Hair | | 36 | Iron cloak-pins | |
| 6 | Small scrapers and stones | | 10 | Chimney-pots | |
| 3 | York sinks, with grates, waste pipes, and traps | | 4 | Bedroom stoves, fixed, complete | |
| 245½ ft. | Cube fir | | 3 | Kitchen ditto and ditto | |
| 2 do. | „ oak | | 157 ft. | Iron gutter and down pipes, fixed, complete | |
| 65½ | 12 ft. 3 by 9 in. deals | | 1 c. 2 qr. | Paint | |
| 3 | Solid door-cases and ledged doors, with hinges, latches, and bolts | | | Labour | |
| | | | | Cartage | |
| 3 | Ditto and ditto, with hinges, latches, and stock-locks | | | | |
| | | £. | | | £. |

**ELEVATION OF THE FRONT.**

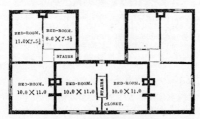

**PLAN OF THE BED-ROOM FLOOR.**

QUANTITIES FOR OUTBUILDINGS, &c.

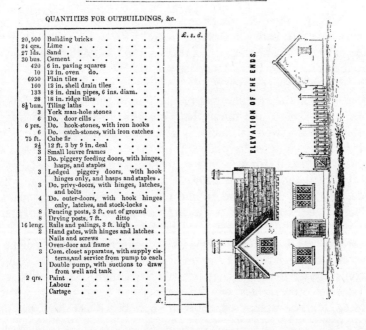

| | | £. s. d. |
|---|---|---|
| 20,500 | Building bricks . . . . . | |
| 24 qrs. | Lime . . . . . . | |
| 27 lds. | Sand . . . . . . | |
| 30 bus. | Cement . . . . | |
| 420 | 6 in. paving squares . . . . | |
| 10 | 12 in. oven do. . . . | |
| 6950 | Plain tiles . . . . . | |
| 160 | 12 in. shell drain tiles . . . . | |
| 133 | 18 in. drain pipes, 6 ins. diam. . . | |
| 28 | 18 in. ridge tiles . . . . | |
| 8½ bun. | Tiling laths . . . . . | |
| 3 | York man-hole stones . . . | |
| 6 | Do. door cills . . . . | |
| 6 prs. | Do. hook-stones, with iron hooks . | |
| 6 | Do. catch-stones, with iron catches . | |
| 75 ft. | Cube fir . . . . . | |
| 2½ | 12 ft. 3 by 9 in. deal . . . . | |
| 3 | Small louvre frames . . . . | |
| 3 | Do. piggery feeding doors, with hinges, hasps, and staples . . . . | |
| 3 | Ledged piggery doors, with hook hinges only, and hasps and staples . | |
| 3 | Do. privy-doors, with hinges, latches, and bolts . . . . . | |
| 4 | Do. outer-doors, with hook hinges only, latches, and stock-locks . . | |
| 8 | Fencing posts, 3 ft. out of ground . | |
| 8 | Drying posts, 7 ft. ditto . | |
| 16 leng. | Rails and palings, 3 ft. high . . | |
| 2 | Hand gates, with hinges and latches . | |
| | Nails and screws . . . . | |
| 1 | Oven-door and frame . . . | |
| 3 | Com. closet apparatus, with supply cis- terns, and service from pump to each . | |
| 1 | Double pump, with suctions to draw from well and tank . . . . | |
| 2 qrs. | Paint . . . . . . | |
| | Labour . . . . . . | |
| | Cartage . . . . . | |
| | | £. |

**ELEVATION OF THE ENDS.**

# XXXV

The following passage is taken from a letter sent to Philip Pusey by Thomas Dyke Acland, a prominent agriculturist of the middle nineteenth century, and deals with an attempt to reverse the decline in the lodging and boarding-in of labourers which had occurred in southern England: *Journal of the Royal Agricultural Society of England*, X (1849), pp. 379–81.

---

*On Lodging and Boarding Labourers, as practised on the farm of Mr Sotheron, M.P.* By THOMAS DYKE ACLAND . . .

When Mr Sotheron took his farm in hand about four years ago, he found, as usual, a barn of double the size required, and divided one end into three compartments, a dining hall, a sleeping room containing six beds, a washing room with a loft over it, for keeping chests of clothes, and a sink communicating with the tank in the yard. The barn doorways are walled up with brick and fitted with glass casements, a large window with a swing sash is opened over the sleeping apartment, one of the threshing floors forms the dais of the dining hall, on which stand a plain large table and some wooden chairs. A lamp, and a long pole for drying clothes, are let down by pulleys from the tie-beams of the roof, a plain hearth and chimney corner have been added at the end, and a cupboard completes the furniture. In this building from five to seven lads have been housed and fed during the last four years. Their wages commence at £4 and rise gradually to £8 10s per annum. They purchase their own clothing out of their wages. The married man is a good workman and manages the steam-engine. Several of the boys have become excellent ploughmen and have won prizes. After work they occasionally amuse themselves with cricket or other games, or with reading and writing, playing the flute, etc. The weekly expenses of their board per head are as follows:

|                  | s | d               |
|------------------|---|-----------------|
| Bread and flour  | I | I               |
| Meat and bacon   | 2 | o               |
| Groceries        | I | o$\frac{1}{2}$  |
| Beer             | I | o               |
|                  | 5 | I$\frac{1}{2}$[1] |

They are allowed to come at sixteen years of age, and remain till they marry or obtain situations. The youngest boy cleans out the room, and they take it in turn to prepare the table for meals, which are cooked by the wife of the bailiff, who lives in an adjoining house and has the assistance of one female servant, who is not allowed to go into the building where the young men live. The bailiff's wife also provides for their washing. The young men are under the superintendence of the bailiff, who presides at their meals, and reads prayers with them morning and evening. A bell rings at meal times, and those who are absent from a meal without leave or good cause, go without it. They are required to observe some rules, few and simple, tending to order and cleanliness—such as to sit down to their meals in clean smock frocks, which they put off when they go out again to work. I ascertained that these

---

[1] The following details are taken from the average of the consumption for several weeks:

|                            | £ | s | d               |
|----------------------------|---|---|-----------------|
| 38 lb   bread at I$\frac{1}{2}$d       | o | 4 | 9               |
| 4$\frac{3}{4}$ lb flour at I$\frac{1}{2}$d   | o | o | 7$\frac{1}{4}$  |
| 9$\frac{1}{2}$ lb butcher's meat at 5d  | o | 3 | II$\frac{1}{2}$ |
| 14$\frac{1}{2}$ lb bacon at 5d          | o | 6 | o$\frac{1}{2}$  |
| 5$\frac{1}{2}$ lb cheese at 6$\frac{1}{2}$d  | o | 3 | o               |
| 2$\frac{1}{2}$ lb sugar at 4d           | o | o | 10              |
| $\frac{3}{8}$ lb coffee at Is 2d        | o | o | 5$\frac{1}{4}$  |
| $\frac{1}{2}$ lb cocoa at 8d            | o | o | 4               |
| 2 lb   rice at 2d          | o | o | 4               |
| Pepper, salt, etc.         | o | o | 3               |
|                            |   |   |                 |
| Board of five boys         | I | o | 6$\frac{1}{2}$  |
|                            |   |   |                 |
| Board of one boy           | o | 4 | I$\frac{1}{2}$  |
| Beer in addition           | o | I | o               |
|                            |   |   |                 |
| Actual food of each boy    | o | 5 | I$\frac{1}{2}$  |

To this must be added a small sum per head for washing, soap, and candles and firing.

rules are in no way irksome to them, but have inspired them with a feeling of self-respect—as their phrase is, they are glad to keep themselves respectable. I sat with them at their breakfast table, and conversed with them while the bailiff was out of the room, and can therefore testify to their demeanour being at once intelligent and respectful. There can be little doubt that such a plan, carried on with kindness and good sense, must tend to the best results, and such in fact have been produced.

Of the total number of youths who have been admitted, two have married, one of whom works on the farm, the other for a neighbouring gentleman; four have been placed out in good situations; three having absented themselves without leave, were not taken back; one left owing to ill health, and afterwards died; five are now at the farm. None have misconducted themselves nor been discharged for any fault.

In connection with these arrangements for the boarding of the farm servants who live in the house, two advantages are provided for the other labourers. A cup of cocoa is given to every person employed on the farm at the time appointed for the beginning of work; and during the winter months nourishing soup is offered to those who choose to pay for it, at the rate of one-halfpenny per quart, which covers the actual cost, and is even more valued than it would be if it were given without payment. The early cup of cocoa is found to have the great merit of allaying the feeling of thirst during the day, which is so great a temptation to labourers: this probably is owing to the irritation of the stomach caused by beginning the day's work fasting being prevented.

The receipt for the soup, which is made *à la Soyer*, is as follows:

|  | s | d |
|---|---|---|
| Meat 2 lb minced | 0 | 9 |
| Sago 6 lb | 1 | 6 |
| Pepper and salt | 0 | 1 |
|  | 2 | 4 |

Making sixteen gallons, which are sold for 2s 8d, leaving 4d to set against the value of the vegetables grown in the garden, fuel, and the time of the servant who makes it.

The merit of these plans, especially of the boarding of the boys, seems to be, that they are natural and simple, in fact a revival of an old English habit, universal some years ago, and still practised, even on very large farms, in the north of England, but driven out in the southern counties partly by the encouragement given to early marriages under the old Poor Law, and partly by the refinement of modern habits, which have banished the labourer from the society of his master, whereas he would derive great advantage from it, and be made a more useful servant.

# XXXVI

In February 1816 the Board of Agriculture, alarmed at the widespread reports of severe agricultural depression, sent out a letter of enquiry to various well-known farmers in England. Extracts from the replies were published later that year, and provided a valuable if rather confused picture of current conditions. Of particular interest are the references to the part played in the farmers' difficulties by the failures of banks and restriction of credit. Following are some samples of letters mentioning this aspect of the problem: Board of Agriculture, *The State of the Kingdom, 1816* (1816, new ed. 1970), pp. 156–7, 363–4.

---

*Thomas Pilley* [Lincolnshire]—Many farms have been given up within the last six months, and a great many more must inevitably be given up, unless some material change takes place; and however well disposed the present Ministers may be to give relief to the agricultural part of the kingdom by reducing their taxation, it will, in my opinion, fall far short of what the country requires; for in consequence of the great failures which have taken place in the country banks and other large commercial concerns in different parts of the kingdom, have so reduced the paper circulation, and given such a shock to public credit, that the farmers have been obliged, a great many of them, to take their corn to market, let the price be what it may; and from the immense quantity of foreign corn imported and on hand in the year 1814, has so overstocked the markets, that scarcely any sale can be obtained for it in many parts of the country; this being the case with corn, stock must of course follow, and although the plough farmers are at present by far the greatest sufferers, yet the breeding-stock farms must eventually be in the same state. If corn remain at the present depressed price, it cannot be grown, the farmer cannot afford to cultivate his land, and the improvements of the country must cease; therefore the labouring poor, which was so usefully and industriously employed before, are now starving for want of employment, and the poor-rates, in consequence, must be very considerably increased. Under these circumstances, which present themselves daily in every part of the kingdom, it is necessary that every effort should be made to alleviate the distressed state of agriculture: many gentlemen have lowered their rents, to what amount I cannot say, but suppose about one-fifth; but the lowering of rents will not afford the relief that is required, even if the landlords would reduce them one-half; the farmer ought, from the produce of his land, to be enabled to employ the labouring poor, or otherwise the country will all be very soon poor together. The taxes may be levied, but they will not long be paid—the farmers, instead of being able to employ and assist the poor, will very soon require support themselves; and it is, I am sorry to say, the case, with a great many at this moment ...

---

*Sir William Strickland*, Bart [Yorkshire].—The distress of the farmers is sufficiently proved by those who have been industrious and careful and hitherto punctual being now unable to pay their rents; by their calling in their capitals, whenever they had any applied in other ways, in order to enable them to live, to pay their rents and taxes; by the diminished energies in the cultivation of their lands; by the extraordinary numbers of farmers that have lately been sold up, and the ruinous prices at which their property has been sold, where so few had the means of purchasing; by the unusual numbers of farms that are advertised to be let, and the backwardness of the tenantry in applying for them; by the number of agricultural labourers now unemployed; and by the greatly diminished trade and business of the shopkeepers, the inferior tradesmen, and mechanics usually employed, and chiefly maintained, by the farmers. Of these facts there can be no doubt.

The produce of arable lands has depreciated about $\frac{2}{3}$, or $66\frac{1}{3}$ per cent; stock between $\frac{1}{3}$ and $\frac{1}{2}$; but this last cannot be ascertained as accurately as the other; some articles of stock farms have not depreciated so much; other articles, as young cattle, and particularly young horses, which are some years distant from the market, are depreciated much more; they are almost worth nothing, they scarcely have a price, for no one can afford to buy or keep what cannot be turned into money in a short time.

All the business of this country is transacted through the medium of paper, almost entirely of the country banks. I have not seen a guinea during several years, and seldom a Bank of England bill. It is to be considered that as all articles have at this time depreciated about two-thirds of their value, the circulating medium to represent them, will diminish in quantity in the same proportion, that is to say, only one-third of the paper will be required to purchase all articles as heretofore, and consequently a greater diminished circulation of paper may be sufficient for the purpose of the country. How far this diminution has taken place is not easily ascertained, but there appears to be sufficient for the circumstances of the country.

# XXXVII

Marshall, in common with other agricultural writers, was hostile to the continuance of antiquated forms of tenure which made for inefficiency and neglect on the part of the farmers. Leases for lives depended on the chance survival of the lives named and on the landlord's willingness in return for a fine, to allow new lives to be put in as the old ones dropped out. Such leases were therefore uncertain as to both duration and the frequency with which fines had to be paid, in contrast to the known duration and fixed rents of leases for terms of years. Most small farms, however, were let on annual tenancies or 'at will', and it is doubtful whether leases for lives were less satisfactory than these more usual forms of tenure. What really mattered in either case was the mutual confidence of landlord and tenant that the property would be adequately maintained and the land properly farmed. In Marshall's day leases for lives were still common in some parts of the country, and here he is remarking upon their prevalence in the west country: W. Marshall, *Rural Economy of the West of England* (1796), I, pp. 43–8.

---

Possessory right, or landed property puts on an appearance here very different from that which it wears in other parts of the kingdom. The fee simple is principally in the possession of men of large property. But instead of *letting* out their lands to tenants, at an annual rent equivalent to their value, they are *sold*, in small parcels or farms, generally for three lives named by the purchaser, or ninety-nine years, provided any one of the parties named survives that period: reserving, however, a small annual rent, together with a heriot or other forfeiture, on the death of each nominee, similar to those attached to the copyhold tenure; which this species of tenancy or tenure, very much resembles: it being usual to put in fresh lives as the preceding ones drop off; receiving a fine or adequate purchase for the addition of a fresh life or lives.

This state of landed property, which is common to the west of England, forms one of the many striking features, which rural economy at present exhibits in this part of the island.

The advantages of this state of landed property are few; its disadvantages many. It is a satisfaction to the purchaser to know that during his own life, and perhaps during that of his son, the land whose temporary possession he has thus purchased will remain in his family; and theory suggests that with such a hold the improvement and enriching of *his own estate*—for as such it is ever estimated—must of course become the great object of his life. But unfortunately for himself and his family, as well as for the community, he has laid out his whole on the purchase and has not a shilling left for improvements: nay, has perhaps borrowed part of the purchase money, and has thus entailed on himself and his family lives of poverty and hard labour. Whereas, had he expended the same money in stocking and improving a rented farm, he might have enriched his family, and have thrown into the markets a much greater proportionate quantity of produce. Besides, the possession depends, perhaps, on his own life, and he has a wife and a young family of children. He dies, and of course leaves them destitute: while, to add to their misfortunes, the bailiff of the manor in the hour of their distress deprives them, perhaps, of the best part of the pittance he has left them.

Another evil tendency of life leases is that of exciting a spirit of speculation and gambling, and of alienating the minds of men from the plain and more certain path of industry. Purchasing a life lease is putting in a stake at a game of chance. An instance fell within my own knowledge in which two sets of lives have ceased and of course the estate has been twice sold, while a woman who was excluded, through a *mere circumstance* from being one of the nominees in the first purchase, is still living. And, on the other hand, there is a well known instance in which the lessee, at the expiration of the term of ninety-nine years, tendered his lease, in person, to the descendant of him from whom his ancestor had received it.

To the proprietor of an estate this is in many respects a disagreeable species of tenancy. His income, as has been shown, is exceedingly uncertain; and, what to a man of sentiment is worse, it literally arises out of the deaths and distresses of the inhabitants of his estate: besides the unpleasant and unprofitable circumstance of having his lands in everlasting bondage. Let them lie awkwardly for the tenants, or intermixed with the lands of others, or in farms of improper sizes, he has no opportunity of adjusting or altering them. He can have no hope of two or three adjoining tenants dying at the same time. Nothing less than the plague, pestilence, or famine can assist him in a measure so salutary, both for himself and the community.

These disagreeable circumstances have induced several men of property to suffer the life leases of their estates to drop in; and afterwards to let their lands for an annual rent, agreeably to the practice of the rest of the kingdom. This desirable change, however, can only be effected by men whose incomes are not wholly dependent on this species of property. Nevertheless, any man who is possessed of such property and is not in distressed circumstances, may release the smaller farms from this unprofitable and impolitic state; and, in the course of two or three generations, the whole might be set at liberty without sensible inconvenience to the proprietors.

It is observable, however, that there is sometimes an inconveniency arises to a proprietor of life leases in suffering his farms to drop into hand, especially when the last life happens to linger. In this case the land is exhausted and the premises stripped: for the property changes with the last breath of the dying nominee.

But, fortunately for both parties, there is an effectual mode of preventing this evil: namely, by granting the lessee or his representative a restrictive lease for a term of three or more years, to commence on the death of the last nominee: a liberal and wise regulation which some few men make, and which common prudence requires. The interests of the landlord, the tenant, and the public are thereby jointly benefited.

# XXXVIII

High farming, as advocated by Caird, was a highly flexible system in which farmers adjusted their production to meet the changing trends in the market. It also involved heavy outlays on manures, cattle food, and improved implements. Hence the growing interest in the nineteenth century in the question of tenant right, the fair compensation of an outgoing tenant for the unexhausted investments already made by him in the land. In this passage Caird argues that either a long lease or a proper system of tenant right was essential for efficient farming. His own preference was for leases with liberal covenants, i.e. leases which allowed the tenant the maximum flexibility in managing the farm, and here he marshals some powerful arguments against the extension of common right throughout the country. However, as he admitted, the long lease was unpopular, and it was the unpopularity of the lease which brought the controversial question of tenant right to the fore: J. Caird, *English Agriculture in 1850–51* (1852, new ed. 1968), pp. 500–9.

---

It would be only repeating what has been much better done by Mr Pusey in the 26th number of the Royal Agricultural Society's Journal, if we were to draw into one view the savings which the modern farmer can effect by the use of improved machines, cheaper feeding stuffs and manures, and more economical and rational processes of husbandry. There is scarcely a single county in which the agricultural reader of these Letters will not find some practice better managed than his own, some process by which he may increase his crops, or fatten his stock, at less expense than it has hitherto cost him. Some counties are much more advanced than others, and accordingly present more numerous examples for instruction; but the careful student will find, in the description of every county, local practices which long experience has brought to a high state of perfection. By combining with his own what he learns of the best, and rejecting the practices of the worst, he may establish for himself a system of agriculture, suited to his particular soil and climate, founded on the experience of successful practical men. He will find that the best farmers have not attained success by blind adherence to a given rotation, but by a constant adaptation of their plans to the growing wants of the country, taking advantage of railway or steam-boat communications to cheapen the cost of transit to the best markets, and of portable manures or cattle food to replace the exhaustion caused by the increasing abstraction of corn and stock from the farm.

The question, what is the best rotation of crops, is so variously answered in these Letters that the reader may have some difficulty in arriving at a satisfactory conclusion. The Norfolk or four-course rotation is undoubtedly the one most generally approved, but it is to its principle of alternate corn and cattle crops, rather than to a strict adherence to its original detail, that this appoval is accorded. In many cases we have inspected farms managed on a strict four-course, to the highest pitch which the land under that system would yield. Do what he could, the farmer was unable to calculate with certainty on the success of each crop in the course. The clover failed, or the turnips were diseased. The barley was too heavy and did not fill, or the wheat lost root and proved thin. Farm as high as he could, his unvarying routine of crops had exhausted something from his light soil which the aids at his command did not exactly replace. He drops the half of the clover from the course and substitutes winter beans. This succeeds, and he is tempted to try again. Mangold is taken instead of a portion of his turnips, and white or yellow turnips are grown where swedes were before. In the next round the position of these crops is reversed. His green crops now flourish, and he turns his attention to the corn. He finds that by enriching his land, he improves the wheat crop but endangers the barley. He cannot grow heavy crops of roots without manure, and he knows that to feed his sheep with profit he must hasten them forward by the aid of corn and cake. The land must therefore be enriched, and as with such high condition the barley might be lost, he sows the ground with wheat. An excellent crop of wheat reduces this condition sufficiently to admit of a safe and productive barley crop, which costs him nothing for manure, and very little for labour. But in this process of improvement the four-course has disappeared and been replaced by a five, so arranged that red clover, white clover and trefoil, winter beans, and mangold, swedes, and turnips, are respectively repeated on the same ground at no shorter intervals than fifteen years. The course then stands thus:

1. One-third Clover, one-third White Clover and Trefoil, one-third Winter Beans.
2. Wheat.
3. One-third Mangold, one-third Swedes, one-third Turnips.
4. Wheat.
5. Barley, in some cases sown after mustard, ploughed in green.

And that in the course of time will without doubt, in its turn, give place to another, under the guidance of further experience. Near a large population, where there is a demand for vegetables and a supply of street manure, the farmer may find himself better paid by green crops than corn. Accordingly we have found the most intelligent farmers in such situations employ two-thirds of their land in growing green crops and one-third in corn. In the western counties the climate exercises a powerful influence, and the successful farmers of Lancashire take two corn crops and two green crops alternately. In short, the detail is everywhere varied by the judicious agriculturist to suit the necessities and advantages of the particular locality, when he is permitted by his agreement and has sufficient skill to pursue a rational system.

The reader will see that no one system or course of husbandry is applicable to every situation. It was not because the four-course was an alternation of corn and cattle crops that it succeeded, though that was itself a great improvement; nor because it produced regularity of system, though that is also of much importance. Nor was it owing to the mere treading of the land by the feet of the sheep, though to that much of the success of the system used to be attributed. It was because it was a step in the right direction, one of those gropings in the dark, by which the man of mere practice occasionally finds the best path. Pursuing it without the guide of science it soon began to fail and lead him astray. There was no virtue in the constant round of crops or regularity of practice to compensate the increased exhaustion occasioned by the sale of larger produce without an equivalent return of manure. It was because it so far fulfilled the principle of keeping the land dry, clean, and rich, that it was in any degree successful.

On a full recognition of that principle rests our future agricultural progress. The landlord and the farmer must both recognize it in their dealings with each other, and with the land. Crops which do not pay the farmer do not suit his purpose, and to restrict him to the growth of such is both impolitic and absurd. His business is to grow the heaviest crops of the most remunerative kind his soil can be made to carry, and, within certain limits of climate which experience has now defined, the better he farms, the more capable his land becomes of growing the higher qualities of grain, of supporting the most valuable breeds of stock, and of being readily adapted to the growth of any kind of agricultural produce which railway facilities or increasing population may render most remunerative. In this country the agricultural improver cannot stand still. If he tries to do so he will soon fall into the list of obsolete men, being passed by eager competitors willing to seize the current of events and turn them to their advantage. The four-course, or any other course when it has served its time, must expand itself to meet the increasing requirements of the day, by appropriating to itself the simultaneously enlarging resources of modern science and enterprise.

This naturally brings us to the statement of a question which we have considered and discussed with intelligent practical farmers in all parts of England—security for the capital of the farmer, whether under the designation of 'compensation for unexhausted improvements', or, more briefly, 'tenant-right'. The investment of a tenant's capital in land seldom contemplates an immediate return. He does not anticipate that a large expenditure in cleaning and enriching worn-out land will be all repaid to him in the first crop. He lays the foundation for a series of good crops, which in the aggregate he expects to repay him with interest. If he drains, makes fences, or other improvements of a more permanent character, a still longer period is requisite to compensate him. But he must either be secured in the possession of his farm for a certain period, sufficiently long to enable him to receive the benefits of his investment, or have some precise agreement under which he is to be repaid, in fixed proportions, for his outlay if his landlord should see fit to resume possession of the farm. Without either the one or the other, an improving tenant has no legal security for the capital he invests in the cultivation of another person's land.

Yet the great proportion of English farms are held on yearly tenure, which may be terminated at any time by a six months' notice on either side. It is a system preferred by the landlord, as enabling him to retain a greater control over the land, and acquiesced in by the tenants in consideration of easy rents. During a period of high prices, moderate rents could be paid without the investment of much capital by the tenant. But low prices and universal competition compel agricultural improvement. We must either farm as well as our neighbours or be undersold by them. The investment of tenants' capital, whether in money, skill, or industry, is now therefore more than ever necessary to success. It may be said with perfect truth that great agricultural improvements have been made, and the most entire confidence subsists between landlord and tenant under this uncertain tenure. That tenants do, in many instances, invest their capital largely, with no other security than their landlord's character, we most willingly testify; and the confidence which subsists between the two classes in England generally is in the highest degree honourable to both. In no country, perhaps, in the world, does the character of any class of men for fair and generous dealing stand higher than that of the great body of English landlords. Yet there are exceptions, and these are unfortunately becoming more numerous. The son does not always inherit the virtues of his father. Necessity or education may make his views different. Family provisions and allowances may leave him less to spend from the same rental. The tenant too, mixing more with the world than he used to do, or being educated at a more advanced period of its progress, begins to dislike the dependence implied in this relation. He knows that he must invest his capital more freely than heretofore in the cultivation of his farm, and in these days of change he feels that he is entitled to ask some effective security for its repayment. That security he may obtain either by being guaranteed by lease in the possession of his farm for such a number of years as will give time for his invested capital to have full effect and be returned to him, or, if the landlord declines to give a lease, by an agreement on a certain basis for compensation for unexhausted improvements when either party wishes to terminate the connection. One or other of these alternatives the improving farmer is fairly entitled to expect, and for the reasons now to be given we most strongly recommend the general adoption of leases in preference to tenant-right.

The only counties in which the custom of tenant-right is fully recognized are Surrey, Sussex, the Weald of Kent, Lincoln, North Notts, and part of the West Riding. In these counties the custom has been so long in operation as to have become binding in law, and they afford us an opportunity of judging whether the system has worked so well in practice as to justify its extension to all the other counties of England. In each of those counties, except the Weald of Kent, which we apprehend to be much the same as the contiguous tract in Surrey and Sussex, we minutely examined the state of agriculture and the relations subsisting between landlord and tenant as affected by this legalized custom, and our impression of each in its place without reference to the other was narrated in our former Letters. In the Wealds of Surrey and Sussex, where the custom is most stringent, we found the state of agriculture extremely backward, the produce much below the average of England, the tenants deeply embarrassed, and the landlords receiving their low rents irregularly; in fact, no men connected with the land thriving, except the appraisers who were in constant requisition to settle the disputed claims of outgoing and entering tenants. We found both farmers and landlords complaining that the system led to much fraud and chicanery, and that an entering tenant was compelled by it to pay as much for bad as for good farming; that intelligent farmers were most desirous that their landlords should buy up the tenant-right, and thus put an end to it, and landlords in many cases were doing so. In Lincolnshire and North Notts we found the great improvement of agriculture of late years attributed to the system of compensation to outgoing tenants; yet, on examining the state of agriculture itself, it seemed to us if not inferior, certainly in no respect superior to the proficiency of the same class of farmers in West Norfolk, whose capital is not protected by any compensation agreements but by a twenty-one years' lease. The indefiniteness of the 'custom' was also much complained of, and its constant liability to increase. Frauds were beginning to creep into the system, and landlords, for their own protection, were obliged to

limit and define the custom by special agreement. In the southern
portion of the West Riding, where tenant-right is very stringent,
it is found to lead to great fraud and abuse, there being instances
of 'smart' men who make it their business to take a farm, hold it
for a year or two, and by 'working up to a quitting', as it is termed
in Surrey, make a considerable profit by the difference which
their ingenuity and that of their appraiser enables them to
demand when they leave, as compared with what they paid at
their entry. Obsolete practices are valued under this system at
their original cost, so that the plan of giving five furrows to a light
soil in preparation for turnips is perpetuated and must be paid
for, though, under the modern system two furrows on such land
at the proper season are known to be not merely more economical,
but really more beneficial.

The amount of these valuations varies between £3 and £5 an
acre. A tenant entering to a farm is thus obliged to pay over a
large sum to his predecessor for operations in the direction and
execution of which he has had no voice. There can be no doubt
whatever that any man would prefer to spend his money in
making improvements according to his own judgement; but the
advance of so much capital over and above the ordinary stock of
the farm either requires tenants of more than the means of
ordinary farmers, or throws the land into the hands of men who,
having expended the larger portion of their ready money in
paying for their entry, are so hampered during their tenancy as to
be unable to do justice to their farms. It is also obvious—for we
are bound to look at the question as it affects both parties—that
such a system offers great facility for combination by the tenants
against their landlord. The owner of say 4,000 acres in such a
district might find it very difficult to refuse the demands of his
tenants, however unjust, if during a period of agricultural depression they offered him the alternative of getting his farms thrown
on his hands, with a tenant-right to be paid down amounting to
four or five years' rental.

Without going further into the question, it must be plain that it
is not the interest of the landlords, if the decision is left with
them, to adopt this system. To legalize it by act of parliament so
as to render its operation general over the kingdom, it would be
necessary to prove that it would promote the public welfare. We
have seen in the counties where it exists that *the agriculture is on*

*the whole inferior to that of other districts,* and in no case, even under the most favourable circumstances, superior to other well-conditioned counties which do not possess this tenant-right. In every county it has led to fraud in a greater or less degree. It perpetuates bad husbandry by stereotyping costly practices which modern improvements have rendered obsolete. It absorbs the capital of the entering tenant, thus limiting his means for future improvement. It unfairly depresses the letting value of land. Perhaps it may be urged that we dwell on the abuses rather than on the fair and legitimate uses of the system. But it is not easy to see where the line of demarcation is to be drawn. The difficulty has already occurred in Lincolnshire, where landlords find it necessary to limit by special agreement the otherwise indefinite and constantly widening objects which this custom may be understood to embrace. With the best and purest intention a farmer may lay out £1,000 in drainage or manures, but, if his investment turns out disadvantageous, is it consistent with common sense that he is to be at liberty to relieve himself from the consequences of his own miscalculations or imprudence by giving up his farm and demanding reimbursement of the 'unexhausted improvement' from his landlord? The same principle too which is applicable to the farmer in his buildings and his farm might be equally claimed by the labourer in his cottage, his garden, and his allotment.

The practical working of tenant-right has thus led us to the conviction (contrary, we admit, to our preconceived opinions,) that it is not desirable to extend it, either legally or conventionally, to other parts of the kingdom. However well it may look in theory, we should find the honest and intelligent farmers of other counties becoming disgusted with its frauds, and, as the same class are now doing in Surrey, North Notts, and the West Riding, demanding its restriction and recommending their landlords to buy it up and get rid of it.

The wish for leases will increase when the tenant at will discovers that security for his capital by tenant-right is neither possible nor desirable. There is a very prevalent dislike of leases on the part of the tenantry of England. To a considerable extent this was occasioned by the uncertainty of the maintenance of protection previous to the free-trade measures, but chiefly from the fact that there was really less change of tenancy and a lower scale of rent under a system of yearly tenure than under lease. If a man improved his farm during a lease, he was obliged to pay an increased rent for it in consequence of that improvement when he renewed it for a second term. If held from year to year he either made no improvement, or, speaking generally, so little that the difference of produce from year to year was so gradual and imperceptible that the farmer kept nearly the whole advantage to himself. In the one case there was a gradual progress caused by a greater exertion on the part of the tenant, and a larger outlay by the landlord, in the advantage of which all parties participated; in the other an encouragement to maintain things as they are that there might be no inducement on the part of the landlord to raise the rent.

# XXXIX

Caird's famous pamphlet on high farming was one of the most influential agricultural publications of the nineteenth century. It represented the view of an experienced capitalist farmer of liberal, free trade leanings, that the loss of protection need not be harmful to farmers who were efficient in farming 'high', and who were flexible in adapting production to meet the needs of the market. Much of the pamphlet was taken up by a description of high farming methods in Scotland, and the following passages express the general argument which he was propounding: J. Caird, *High Farming under Liberal Covenants the best Substitute for Protection* (1848, new ed. 1849), pp. 5–7, 25–8.

---

Anyone who had been long accustomed to lean upon a crutch would feel very uncomfortable if it were suddenly knocked away from him. If he were a real cripple, that would be a very cruel act. If he only fancied himself one, it might be the kindest thing in the world; but, whether a true cripple or a hypochondriac, he would be very angry in the first place. The cripple would fall down from weakness, the hypochondriac would throw himself down in bewilderment and despair. Both would be disposed to cry—'Give me back my crutch!'

This is not unlike the present condition of the British farmer. The crutch of legislative protection has been swept away. No doubt it was first shortened, and then he was allowed to go about with it for two or three years till he could accustom himself to do without it. But it still remains a question among farmers—'Was he an enemy bent on mischief, or a kind of judicious physician, who did this?'

The writer of these pages is himself a tenant-farmer, having no other occupation, and paying a money rent exceeding £1,000 a year; and observing the fears of his brethren, particularly in the south, he is induced to lay before them, without argument, a simple narrative detailing a mode of management in which success is comparatively independent of foreign competition.

Self-reliance is the great secret of prosperity in human affairs, and it is this lesson which it is the practical object of these pages to inculcate. The landlord is the party chiefly interested, and with him therefore any decided improvement ought to originate. An intelligent co-operation on the part of the tenant is equally necessary to ensure success. And it is thought by the writer that an authentic instance of this mutual co-operation may be valuable at present, both to show *by what has been done*, what still remains to do, and also to supply in brief detail a guide for those who may feel the want of one.

The leading principle herein developed will be found to be a greater reliance on *green crops, grass, and forage,* as contradistinguished from *corn*, but by no means exclusive of corn. In connexion with this, the writer desires to direct attention to the prosecution of a high system of farming, which enlarges the field of labour and its remuneration, leads to the accumulation and economy of manure, and affords the means of applying it to the crops in a far more liberal manner than has heretofore been thought either necessary or advantageous. By pursuing this course, the farmers of Great Britain would be naturally brought into a plan of management which the advantages of their position, the favourable nature of the climate, and the wants of a manufacturing population, concur in demanding . . .

The fact that foreign grain can now be imported on equal terms with our own, and the comparative facility with which it can be brought great distances by sea, will more and more press upon us the propriety of turning our attention to that branch of agriculture— the cultivation of green vegetable crops—in which, from their bulk and perishable nature, we are least liable to foreign competition. Other circumstances concur to bring about this change. The abundant supplies of imported manures, for want of which, in former times, such a change would have been impossible; the increase of the population, and the consequent increasing demand for vegetables and dairy produce and the increasing consumption of butcher-meat; the constantly increasing facilities of transport between the different parts of the kingdom by railways and steam vessels which bring the remote parts of the country into the neighbourhood of the large consuming towns—all these circumstances point to an entire change in our general system of farming. The modes of management which have heretofore been confined to farms in the neighbourhood of large towns are now gradually extending into the remoter parts of the country; and the circle is every year widening within which dairy farming, the cultivation of vegetables for sale and for the production of butcher-meat, with a more garden-like management of the soil, are found the most profitable points to which the farmer can direct his labours.

We have seen that in the present case the farmer reaps a very satisfactory return for his capital and skill, and that the landlord has also received an increase of rent. This increase is no more than a fair interest for the capital expended by the landlord in house accommodation and draining. And while it is acknowledged that the farm is moderately rented, it must not be forgotten that under the former management the land was found dear enough— so that if now much more remunerative to the present tenant it has become so as the result of his improvements. At the termin- ation of the present lease the landlord will have it in his power to reap his just share of the benefits accruing from the encourage- ment he has afforded. Still, it cannot be doubted that the moder- ate rent at which the farm is now let operates very favourably for the success of the tenant and of the system on which he has been thereby encouraged to embark.

The increase of rent, however, is only a small part of the benefit likely to accrue to the landlord. This farm is situated near the centre of his very extensive estates. It must be traversed by a large portion of his tenantry every time they go to market; and no men, who are not wilfully blind, can pass through it frequently without acquiring a taste for the like bulky crops and a desire to adopt the means which have effected such manifest improvements.

To the labourer the increase of employment has been threefold; and even on this small farm the demand for extra labourers has been followed by an increase in their individual remuneration. This increase of wages, amounting to about one-fifth, with im- provements in the labourers' domestic accommodation, is no doubt the natural result of increased demand for labour, and is believed to be generally a concomitant of the increasing produc- tiveness of the soil, and in part a natural reflection of the increasing profits of the farmer. However this may be, it is demonstrable that if all the arable land in the same parish were gradually brought into an equally high state of cultivation the demand for labourers would be so increased as to give room for the profitable employment of double its present male adult population.

In a national view the matter becomes very interesting, both as it affects the prospective employment of our increasing population, and the capacity of the land to feed them. We have seen that the increase of the annual produce of this farm has been fourfold; suppose the same system to be gradually extended over the country and we see ample capacity in the soil to keep pace with the population for generations yet to come, even without the aid of any other principles than those which have already been discovered, and carried into successful operation.

# XL

These two maps of Waltham, Lincolnshire (reproduced by kind permission of Mr Rex C. Russell) show in graphic form the dramatic change which enclosure brought to a village where a large area of common land had survived. Points to notice are the growth before the enclosure of small closes round the village itself, the increase in the number of roads after the enclosure, the allocation of land to the Rector in lieu of tithes, and the fact that some of the larger of the new holdings were divided into separate blocks of land at a distance from each other. This last might be due to the proprietors' expressing a preference for particular allotments or to the commissioners' desire to achieve the greatest possible fairness in the allotting of both the quantity and the quality of the land. Taken from Rex C. Russell, *The Enclosures of Holton-le-Clay, 1763–66, Waltham, 1769–1771 and Tetney 1774–1779*. (Workers Educational Association, Waltham Branch, 1972).

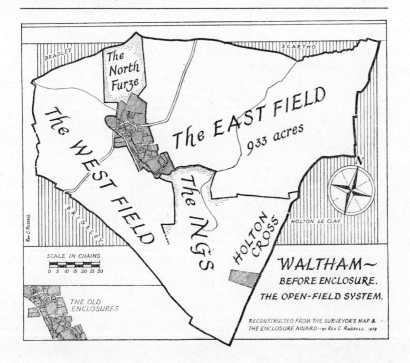

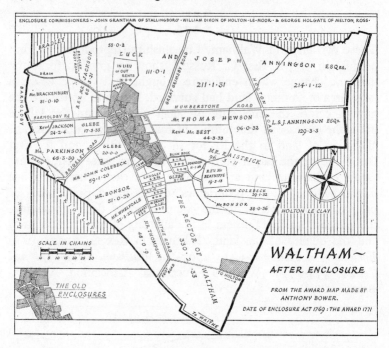

WALTHAM ~

AFTER ENCLOSURE

FROM THE AWARD MAP MADE BY
ANTHONY BOWER.

DATE OF ENCLOSURE ACT 1769 : THE AWARD 1771

THE OLD
ENCLOSURES

# XLI

Although the best farming of the middle nineteenth century was productive and efficient, there were still many instances of outmoded ideas and antiquated techniques. In his tour of English farming Caird noted some examples of the extreme backwardness which sometimes permeated whole districts. Here are his acidic descriptions of the inefficient dairy farming of the Vale of Gloucester, the unproductive arable practices of the unenlightened Surrey farmers, and the ancient wooden ploughs and excessive teams still used for breaking the ground on the Sussex downs: J. Caird, *English Agriculture in 1850-51* (1852, new ed. 1968), pp. 42-3, 122-5, 127-8.

---

A brief outline of the appearance of a Gloucestershire dairy farm may serve to show the present state of the art in that district. January is not the month most favourable for viewing the operations of a dairy, but the management of the cows at this season is of much influence on their yield afterwards. An inconvenient road conducted us to the entrance gate of a dilapidated farmyard, one side of which was occupied by a huge barn and wagon-shed, and the other by the farmhouse, dairy, and piggeries. The farmyard was divided by a wall, and two lots of milch cows were accommodated in the separate divisions. On one side of the first division was a temporary shed, covered with bushes and straw. Beneath this shed there was a comparatively dry lair for the stock; the yard itself was wet, dirty, and uncomfortable. The other yard was exactly the counterpart of this, except that it wanted even the shelter shed. In these two yards are confined the dairy stock of the farm during the winter months; they are supplied with hay in antique square hay-racks, ingeniously capped over to protect the hay with a thatched roof, very much resembling the pictures of Robinson Crusoe's hat. In each yard two of these are placed, round which the shivering animals station themselves as soon as the feeder gives them their diurnal ration, and there they patiently ruminate the scanty contents. A dripping rain fell as we looked at them, from which their heads were sheltered by the thatched roof of the hay-rack, only to have it poured in a heavier stream on their necks and shoulders. In the other yard the cows had finished their provender, and showed their dissatisfaction with its meagre character by butting each other round the rack. The largest and greediest having finished her own share, immediately dislodges her neighbour, while she in her turn repeats the blow on the next; and so the chase begins, the cows digging their horns into each other's sides and discontentedly pursuing one another through the wet and miry yard. Getting over an inner gate we came upon the piggeries, where a dozen well-fed and warmly housed pigs showed by their sleek round sides the benefits of food and shelter. Inquiring of the farmer whether he thought his cows would not be bettered by equally comfortable accommodation, he said they would, but his landlord did not give that accommodation, and he had no security by which at his own cost he could safely make the outlay. Leaving the yard, we passed into the fields, sinking at every step in the sour wet grasslands. Here little heaps of dung, the exhausted relics of the hay from which the cows derive their only support in winter, were being scattered thinly over the ground to aid in the production of another crop of hay. But we need not continue the picture further. The management of the dairy itself did not come under our observation, as nothing is done in it at this season; but it is said to be conducted with great care, cleanliness, and attention ...

In the neighbourhood of Reigate along the valley, the land is of a friable texture, fairly cultivated in some instances, but not, in any one that came under our observation, with that energy and skill which are to be met with in districts of the country which have very few of the advantages enjoyed by this. Four and five horses are frequently used in a plough. The plough itself is of very antiquated construction. As illustrating the prejudices of some of the farmers, we were told of an instance in which a farmer coming here from a 'two-horse country', introduced the two-horse plough, continued to use it for thirty years, turning over on an average an acre a day; and yet his neighbours on both sides of him at the end of that long probation still insist that it is impossible to plough land with only two horses! The course of husbandry followed, where any is adhered to, is the four field; but we were assured on very competent authority—that of an intelligent farmer long resident in the district—that the ordinary farmers have no plan, but usually decide as to the next crop of a particular field according to the opinion of one or two neighbours at their weekly consultations in the alehouse on market-days! The stock kept on the different farms varies with the character of each, some rearing early lambs for the London market, some keeping also a few cattle, and some dairying . . .

That portion of the Weald which we have examined in Surrey is for the most part a stiff wet clay, becoming at intervals more loamy and friable, and rising in some instances to good stock and green crop farms. Being naturally very difficult to manage profitably it has for a series of years been gradually deteriorating under the present management, and while it yields scarcely a subsistence to the cultivator, it affords a scanty rent to the owner and a niggard supply of work to the labourer. The system of cultivation is begun by a bare summer fallow, the ground being as carefully managed as its undrained state admits, and then dunged with such manure as the farm produces and limed, if the farmer can afford the expense. The wheat is then sown, the field being ploughed in 'lands' so as to admit the horses in drawing the harrows to pass up the open furrows without trampling the rest of the land. The crop reaped after this preparation varies from twelve to twenty bushels an acre. Four or five crops then follow, according to the taste of the cultivator, whose study is how to get from the soil at the least expense the different qualities it may have imbibed or accumulated during the year of bare fallow. When it is clearly ascertained that these are thoroughly exhausted, the land is again bare fallowed. Scarcely any stock worth mentioning is kept on these farms. The implements used are of the rudest kind; the barn implements in an especial degree, the use of the common barn winnowing machine being frequently unknown. Its place is supplied by sacks nailed to four horizontal spars which are fixed on a pivot at both ends, and when turned briskly round get up a breeze of wind in which the corn is riddled by hand and the chaff blown away! Under such a system it is quite impossible that this land can long continue in cultivation. The first improvement necessary is thorough drainage, and after that is accomplished we should expect much assistance in the further development of its resources by the facilities of communication afforded by the several lines of railway which traverse it. We should anticipate great benefit to the texture of the soil by heavy applications of chalk, which might be brought along the line from the nearest chalk cuttings, and if the railway companies would co-operate with the farmer it might be worth his while to bring down from London large quantities of the cheapest manure—coal ashes and street sweepings, to be laid on in heavy doses in the hope that by this management the soil might gradually be rendered friable and suitable for the production of green crops as well as corn. This no doubt contemplates much outlay of capital; but when regard is had to the impossibility of things going on as they are at present and to the advantages this tract enjoys in being little more than an hour distant from London, we have no doubt the experiment, in good hands, would prove successful. This soil, if dry, and if its texture can be altered so as to admit of being kept clean under constant tillage, possesses a strength and depth of staple which could not be easily exhausted.

The farms are from 50 to 200 acres in extent, and are let at from 5s to 15s an acre of rent, to a class of men whose families, though they may shift from farm to farm, have been located in the district for many generations. In intelligence and education they are extremely deficient; many of them, as we were told, being scarcely able to sign their own names. The efforts of their landlords, some of whom are anxious to promote drainage and other fundamental improvements, are greatly frustrated by the prejudices of such a class of tenantry. Not a few of them are now two years in arrear of rent, and all are every day becoming less able to meet those increased outlays by which alone larger crops can be produced and diminished prices compensated.

Labourers' wages in Surrey are from 9s to 10s. Taskwork is very common, and 12s a week is often earned. Cottage rents are high, varying from 1s 6d to 3s and 3s 6d a week with very little garden ground. The cottages on farms are sometimes held by the labourers direct from the landlord, in others they go with the farm. Beer is generally given in hay and harvest-time, but there is no rule on the subject. Many farmers are reverting to the custom of keeping the farm servants more in the farmhouse, the low price of corn and meat rendering this the cheapest plan they can now adopt. Besides the facilities which they afford, the railways, by sharing the burden, have exercised a very beneficial influence on the 'rates' of the parishes through which they pass. Poor-rates and highway-rates in some parishes are from this cause extremely moderate.

The chief complaint among the farmers themselves, apart from that of low prices, was the heavy burden of the tithe. The unfair character of some of the payments claimed by the out-going tenant from his successor, which have already been referred to [see Document XXXVIII], was also mentioned as a heavy tax on a farmer's capital. One fact arising from this 'tenant right' in Surrey is that there is less competition for farms and a more moderate scale of rent than we have met with in other counties; but we are bound to add that these advantages have not contributed to better cultivation, as we should have anticipated. Incapable of appreciating the advantages of their proximity to the best market in the world, within a distance varying from ten to thirty miles of London, with railway accommodation if they choose, with a soil and climate adapted for the production of the earliest vegetables of every kind for the use of the table, the great body of the Surrey farmers follow a system suited to farms 500 miles distant from the metropolis, where it is necessary to convert everything the land produces into the least bulky form for cheap transit, so that the produce of two acres of wheat may be condensed into a ton weight, and the whole green crop of the farm be packed up and borne to market, after being digested, in the living bodies of the sheep stock . . .

On the Sussex Downs the cultivation of the soil and the management of stock differ in some points from what we have hitherto met with in the chalk country. On the better lands the four-field course is adopted, and this is extended to a five or even a six field (being laid one to two years to 'rest') where the land becomes thinner and less valuable. Very old-fashioned clumsy ploughs are used, made of wood, with a bit of flat wood for a mould-board, which is shifted from side to side at each turning; the beam, a thick, strong, straight piece of wood, set on to the head of the plough at an angle of 45 degrees, and borne up in front in a very solid and substantial manner on a pair of wheels from $2\frac{1}{2}$ to 3 feet in diameter. This implement is drawn by three or four horses, or six bullocks. Within a couple of miles of Brighton these ploughs may be seen in use every day; and we saw in that neighbourhood a working team, which, for waste of opportunity, of power, and of time, could probably not be matched in any other county in the United Kingdom. At the end of a ploughed field were a lot of bullocks all crowded together, but which we presently perceived were in the yoke, and being turned round. Slowly the crowd separated, each team wheeling about; and steadily advancing up the hill came eighteen heavy bullocks, two and two abreast (six oxen in each plough), drawing three ploughs following each other, one man guiding each plough, while another, armed with a long pliable stick, like a fishing-rod, kept the team under his charge at their duty. The furrow was of an ordinary depth, and the land by no means very steep or heavy to cultivate. On the next farm to this we found that a well-managed dairy cow produced upwards of £20 a year, the milk being sold in Brighton, one of the best markets in England; and here, with the command of the same market, on precisely similar soil, was the keep of six oxen lavishly expended on an operation which could have been infinitely more cheaply executed by one man and two good horses.

# XLII

At the end of his mid-century survey Caird drew up a summary of his findings, drawing comparisons between the conditions of 1850–1 and those described by Arthur Young eighty years earlier. Caird gave particular emphasis to the shift which the market had shown in favour of butter, meat and wool, and he pointed to the advantages which the more easily-cultivated light soils enjoyed over the costly clays. Rents, he noted, reflected the preference which the market gave to grass over arable, and his advice was for the farmer to adapt his output to the market trend: 'Let him produce as much as he can of the articles which have shown a gradual tendency to increase in value'. J. Caird, *English Agriculture in 1850–51* (1852, new ed. 1968), pp. 473–6, 479–81, 482–5.

---

An interval of eighty years affords ample room for denoting with precision the progress of agriculture. Young's 'Tours' conclude with very specific data showing the actual state of rents, produce, prices, and wages in 1770 in the twenty-six counties which he then examined. The information on which his data are based seems to have been the same as ours—personal inquiry from the most trustworthy sources. As regards rent and produce, it is obvious that unless the same farms had been spoken of exactness of comparison is impossible. The figures which we give are therefore not offered as perfectly correct, but as the nearest approximation to correctness in our power. Until Government shall take up the important question of agricultural statistics, we must be content with such broad results as it is in the power of individual inquiry to elicit, conscious though we may be of the comparatively limited data from which we are obliged to generalize.

It thus appears that in a period of eighty years the average rent of arable land has risen 100 per cent, the average produce of wheat

Table showing the rent of cultivated land per acre, the produce of wheat in bushels, the price of provisions, the wages of the agricultural labourer, and the rent of cottages, in 1770 and 1850, in twenty-six of the English counties.

| | Rent of cultivated land per acre | | Produce of wheat per acre | | Price of Provisions | | | | | | Labourers' wages per week | | Cottage rents | |
|---|---|---|---|---|---|---|---|---|---|---|---|---|---|---|
| | | | | | Bread | | Meat | | Butter | | | | | |
| | 1770 | 1850 | 1770 | 1850 | 1770 | 1850 | 1770 | 1850 | 1770 | 1850 | 1770 | 1850 | 1770 | 1850 |
| | s d | 2 d | | | d | d | d | d | d | s d | s d | s d | s d | s |
| Northumberland | 12 6 | 20 0 | 18 | 30 | ¾ | 1¼ | 2½ | 5 | 5 | 10 | 6 0 | 11 0 | 20 0 | 60 |
| Cumberland | 7 6 | 25 0 | 23 | 27 | ¾ | 1¼ | 2½ | 5 | 5½ | 10 | 6 6 | 13 0 | 20 0 | 55 |
| Durham | 21 0 | 17 0 | 25 | 16 | 1 | 1¼ | 3¼ | 5 | 6 | 1 0 | 6 6 | 11 0 | 20 0 | |
| North Riding | 12 6 | 29 0 | 21 | 20 | 1 | 1¼ | 3 | 5 | 5½ | 1 0 | 6 6 | 11 0 | 25 0 | |
| East Riding | 8 0 | 22 6 | 25 | 30 | 1 | 1¼ | 3¼ | 5 | 5 | 1 0 | 7 6 | 12 0 | 27 6 | |
| West Riding | 16 6 | 40 0 | 20 | 30 | 1¼ | 1¼ | 3½ | 5 | 6½ | 1 0 | 6 0 | 14 0 | 30 0 | |
| Lancashire | 22 6 | 42 0 | 26 | 28 | 1 | 1¼ | 3 | 5 | 6½ | 11 | 6 6 | 13 6 | 27 6 | |
| Cheshire | 16 0 | 30 0 | 25 | 28 | 1 | 1¼ | 3 | 5 | 6 | 11 | — | — | 27 6 | 80 |
| Nottingham | 13 0 | 32 0 | 31 | 32 | 1¼ | 1¼ | 3½ | 5 | 6 | 1 0 | 9 0 | 10 0 | 25 0 | |
| Lincoln | 10 0 | 30 0 | 21 | 26 | 1½ | 1¼ | 3¼ | 5 | 6 | 1 0 | 7 0 | 10 0 | 20 0 | 80 |
| Stafford | 17 6 | 30 0 | 23 | 28 | 1 | 1¼ | 3½ | 5 | 6½ | 1 0 | 6 4 | 9 6 | 40 0 | 70 |
| Warwick | 17 6 | 32 6 | 28 | 30 | 1½ | 1¼ | 3 | 5 | 6 | 1 0 | 8 0 | 8 6 | 35 0 | |
| Northampton | 7 0 | 30 0 | 23 | 28 | 1¾ | 1¼ | 3½ | 5 | 6 | 1 0 | 6 6 | 9 0 | 20 0 | 80 |
| Huntingdon | 10 0 | 26 6 | 18 | 32 | 1¾ | 1¼ | 3¾ | 5 | 6 | 1 0 | 7 5 | 8 6 | 30 0 | 70 |
| Norfolk | 11 6 | 25 6 | 24 | 32 | 1¾ | 1¼ | 3¾ | 5 | 6 | 1 0 | 8 0 | 8 6 | 40 0 | 80 |
| Suffolk | 13 6 | 24 0 | 24 | 32 | 1½ | 1¼ | 3¾ | 5 | 7¼ | 1 0 | 7 11 | 7 0 | 40 0 | 80 |
| Bedford | 12 0 | 25 0 | 19 | 25 | 1¾ | 1¼ | 3½ | 5 | 7 | 1 0 | 7 3 | 9 0 | 40 0 | |
| Hertford | 12 0 | 22 6 | 24 | 22 | 2 | 1¼ | 3¾ | 5 | 7 | 1 2 | 7 6 | 9 0 | 42 6 | |
| Essex | 13 6 | 26 0 | 24 | 23 | 1¼ | 1¼ | 4 | 5 | 8½ | 1 0 | 7 9 | 8 0 | 40 0 | 80 |
| Buckingham | 10 0 | 26 0 | 25 | 25 | 1¼ | 1¼ | 4 | 5 | 7 | 1 2 | 8 0 | 8 6 | 42 0 | 42 |
| Oxford | 19 6 | 30 0 | 26 | 25 | 1¼ | 1¼ | 3½ | 5 | 7 | 1 2 | 7 0 | 9 0 | 45 0 | |
| Berks | 19 6 | 30 0 | 28 | 30 | 1¼ | 1¼ | 3¾ | 5 | 7 | 1 2 | 7 6 | 7 6 | 50 0 | 55 |
| Surrey | 15 9 | 18 6 | — | 22 | 1½ | 1¼ | 4¼ | 5 | 8½ | 1 1 | 9 0 | 9 6 | 55 0 | 100 |
| Sussex | 10 9 | 19 0 | 22 | 22 | 1¾ | 1¼ | 4 | 5 | 7 | 1 0 | 8 6 | 10 6 | 60 0 | 100 |
| Hampshire | 12 0 | 25 0 | 20 | 30 | 1½ | 1¼ | 3 | 5 | 6¾ | 1 0 | 8 0 | 9 0 | 40 0 | 100 |
| Wilts | 12 0 | 25 0 | 20 | 26 | 1½ | 1¼ | 2¾ | 5 | 6 | 1 0 | 7 0 | 7 0 | 30 0 | 60 |
| Dorset | 10 9 | 20 0 | 20 | 21 | 1½ | 1½ | 2¾ | 5 | 6 | 1 0 | 6 9 | 7 6 | 30 0 | |
| Gloucester | 10 6 | 28 0 | 20 | 23 | 1½ | 1¼ | 3 | 5 | 6¼ | 11 | 6 9 | 7 0 | 30 0 | |
| Averages | 13 4 | 26 10 | 23 | 26¾ | 1½ | 1¼ | 3¼ | 5 | 6 | 1 0 | 7 3 | 9 7 | 34 0<br>8d per week | 74<br>1s 5d per week |

| | s | d | |
|---|---|---|---|
| In twenty-six counties the average rent of arable land, in 1770 appears from Young's returns to have been | 13 | 4 | an acre |
| For the same counties our returns in 1850–1 give an average of | 26 | 10 | „ |

| | s | d | |
|---|---|---|---|
| Increase of rent in eighty years | 13 | 6 | or 100 per cent |

| | Bushels | |
|---|---|---|
| In 1770 the average produce of wheat was | 23 | an acre |
| In 1850–1 in the same counties it was | 26$\frac{3}{4}$ | „ |

| | | |
|---|---|---|
| Increased produce of wheat per acre | 3$\frac{3}{4}$ | or 14 per cent |

| | s | d | |
|---|---|---|---|
| In 1770 the labourers' wages averaged | 7 | 3 | a week |
| In 1850–1, in the same counties they averaged | 9 | 7 | „ |

| | s | d | |
|---|---|---|---|
| Increase in wages of agricultural labourers | 2 | 4 | or 34 per cent |

| | Bread | Butter | Meat |
|---|---|---|---|
| In 1770 the price of provisions was | 1$\frac{1}{2}$d | 0s 6d | 3$\frac{1}{4}$d per lb |
| In 1850–1 it was | 1$\frac{1}{4}$ | 1 0 | 5 |

| | s | d | |
|---|---|---|---|
| In 1770 the price of wool was | 0 | 5$\frac{1}{2}$ | per lb |
| In 1850–1 it was | 1 | 0 | „ |

| | s | d | |
|---|---|---|---|
| In 1770 the rent of labourers' cottages in sixteen counties averaged | 36 | 0 | a year |
| In 1850–1, in the same counties | 74 | 6 | „ |

per acre has increased 14 per cent, the labourers' wages 34 per cent, and his cottage rent 100 per cent; while the price of bread, the great staple of the food of the English labourer, is about the same as it was in 1770. The price of butter has increased 100 per cent, meat about 70 per cent, and wool upwards of 100 per cent.

The increase of 14 per cent on the average yield of wheat per acre does not indicate the total increased produce. The extent of land in cultivation in 1770 was, without doubt, much less than it is now; and the produce given then was the average of a higher quality of land, the best having of course been earliest taken into cultivation. The increase of acreable corn produce has therefore been obtained by better farming, notwithstanding the contrary influence arising from the employment of inferior soils. The increased breadth now under wheat, with the higher average produce bear, however, no proportion to the increase of rent in the same period; and the price of wheat now is much the same as it was then. We must therefore look to the returns from stock to explain this discrepancy.

While wheat has not increased in price, butter, meat, and wool have nearly doubled in value. The quantity produced has also greatly increased, the same land now carrying larger cows, cattle which arrive at earlier maturity, and of greater size, and sheep of better weight and quality, and yielding more wool. On dairy farms, and on such as are adapted for the rearing and feeding of stock, especially of sheep stock, the value of the annual produce has kept pace with the increase of rent. With the corn farms the case is very different. In former times the strong clay lands were looked upon as the true wheat soils of the country. They paid the highest rent, the heaviest tithe, and employed the greatest number of labourers. But modern improvements have entirely changed their position. The extension of green crops and the feeding of stock have so raised the productive quality of the light lands that they now produce corn at less cost than the clays, with the further important advantage that the stock maintained on them yields a large profit besides. In all parts of the country, accordingly, we have found the farmers of strong clays suffering the most severely under the recent depression of prices . . .

Rent, in so far as regulated by external circumstances, we shall find depends now on other influences than proximity to or distance from the metropolis. To illustrate this among other points, we have prepared the following table, which divides the country into two sections from north to south with reference to climate, the one embracing the eastern and south coast or corn side of the island; the other the midland and western counties, where the system of husbandry is more a mixture of corn, stock, and dairy farming.

The great corn-growing counties of the east coast are thus shown to yield an average rent of 23s 8d an acre; the more mixed husbandry of the midland counties, and the grazing green crop and dairy districts of the west, 31s 5d. This striking difference,

Table showing the average rent of cultivated land, the produce of wheat in bushels, and the weekly wages of the labourer in 1850–1, in the midland and western counties, being the mixed corn and grass districts; and in the east and south-coast counties, being the chief corn-producing districts of England.

| Midland and western counties | Per acre | | Labourers' wages | East and south coast counties | Per acre | | Labourers' wages |
|---|---|---|---|---|---|---|---|
| | Rent | Produce | | | Rent | Produce | |
| | s  d | bush. | s  d | | s  d | bush. | s  o |
| Cumberland | 25 0 | 27 | 13 0 | Northumber- | | | |
| Lancashire | 42 0 | 28 | 13 6 | land | 20 0 | 30 | 11 0 |
| West Riding | 40 0 | 30 | 14 0 | Durham | 17 0 | 16 | 11 0 |
| Cheshire | 30 0 | 28 | 12 0 | North Riding | 29 0 | 20 | 11 0 |
| Derby | 26 0 | 33 | 11 0 | East Riding | 22 6 | 30 | 12 0 |
| Nottingham | 32 6 | 32 | 10 0 | Lincoln | 30 0 | 26 | 10 0 |
| Leicester | 35 0 | 21 | 9 6 | Norfolk | 25 6 | 32 | 8 6 |
| Stafford | 30 0 | 28 | 9 6 | Suffolk | 24 0 | 32 | 7 0 |
| Warwick | 32 6 | 30 | 8 6 | Huntingdon | 26 6 | 32 | 8 6 |
| Northampton | 30 0 | 28 | 9 0 | Cambridge | 28 0 | 32 | 7 6 |
| Bucks | 26 0 | 25 | 8 6 | Bedford | 25 0 | 25 | 9 0 |
| Oxford | 30 0 | 25 | 9 0 | Hertford | 22 6 | 22 | 9 0 |
| Gloucester | 28 0 | 23 | 7 0 | Essex | 26 0 | 28 | 8 0 |
| North Wilts | 35 0 | 28 | 7 6 | Surrey | 18 6 | 22 | 9 6 |
| Devon | 30 0 | 20 | 8 6 | Sussex | 19 0 | 22 | 10 6 |
| | | | | Berks | 30 0 | 30 | 7 6 |
| | | | | Hants | 25 0 | 30 | 9 0 |
| | | | | South Wilts | 17 6 | 24 | 7 0 |
| | | | | Dorset | 20 0 | 21 | 7 6 |
| Averages | 31 5 | 27 | 10 0 | Averages | 23 8 | 26½ | 9 1 |

Average rent of cultivated land in all the counties     27s 2d
Average produce per acre of wheat     26⅔ bushels
Average weekly wages of labourer     9s 6d

being not less than 30 per cent, is explained chiefly by the different value of their staple produce, as already shown: corn, the staple of the east coast, selling at the same price as it did eighty years ago, while dairy produce, meat, and wool have nearly doubled in value. The difference in rent does not arise from a greater fertility of soil, as may be seen by comparing the produce of wheat. The corn counties, in so far as they yield barley and feed or produce cattle and sheep, benefit by the rise in price . . .

An attentive consideration of the above table will strike the careful reader in several new points of view. That the large capitalist farmer of the east coast, possessing the most cheaply cultivated soil and conducting his agricultural operations with the most skill, should not only pay the lowest rent but be the loudest complainer under the recent depression of prices, is to be accounted for by his greater dependence on the value of corn. The moistness of the climate of the west, on the other hand, discouraged corn cultivation and compelled a greater reliance on stock. And, as the country becomes more prosperous, the difference in the relative value of corn and stock will gradually be increased.

The production of vegetables and fresh meat, hay for forage, and pasture for dairy cattle, which were formerly confined to the neighbourhood of towns, will necessarily extend as the towns become more numerous and more populous. The facilities of communication must increase this tendency. Our insular position, with a limited territory and an increasingly dense manufacturing population, is yearly extending the circle within which the production of fresh food, animal, vegetable, and forage, will be needed for the daily and weekly supply of the inhabitants and their cattle; and which, both on account of its bulk, and the necessity of having it fresh, cannot be brought from distant countries. Fresh meat, milk, butter, vegetables, and hay, are articles of this description. They can be produced in no country so well as our own, both climate and soil being remarkably suited to them. Wool has likewise increased in value as much as any agricultural product; and there is a good prospect of flax becoming an article in extensive demand and therefore worthy of the farmer's attention. The manufacture of sugar from beet-root may yet be found very profitable to the English agriculturist, and ought not to be excluded from consideration. Now all these products require the employment of considerable labour, very minute care, skill, and attention, and a larger acreable application of capital than is requisite for the production of corn. So various are the objectives thus requiring attention and economical arrangement that a very large undertaking, such as is now carried on by some of the wealthier farmers of the eastern counties, could not, on this more elaborate system, be profitably conducted under the single superintendence of one person. This will inevitably lead to the gradual diminution of the largest farms and to the concentration of the capital and attention of the farmer on a smaller space.

The individual experience of the agricultural class may be appealed to in support of this opinion. The consumption of bread in a farmer's family is not half so large an item in the annual expenditure of his household as butcher's meat; and milk and vegetables, if they were purchased in the market, would cost him more than bread. If he looks back for thirty years he will find that this difference has been gradually increasing. With the great mass of consumers bread still forms the chief article of consumption. But in the manufacturing districts where wages are good, the use of butcher's meat and cheese is enormously on the increase; and even in the agricultural districts the labourer does now occasionally indulge himself in a meat dinner, or season his dry bread with a morsel of cheese. In a gentleman's family consisting of himself, his wife, six children, and ten servants, the average expenditure for each individual per annum, for articles of food produced by the farmer, is £9 10s for meat, butter, and milk, and £1 2s 4d for bread. In a large public establishment containing an average throughout the year of 646 male persons, chiefly boys, the expenditure per head for meat, cheese, potatoes, butter, and milk is £4 10s 6d, and for bread £2 1s 6d. The price of each article is charged in both cases at the present average rates throughout England. The first example shows an expenditure in articles the produce of grass and green crops nearly nine times as great as in corn; and the second, which may be regarded as more of an average example, also shows an outlay 2¼ times greater on the former articles of produce than the latter. Here we see not only the kind of produce most in demand, but the direction in which household expenditure increases when the means permit. It is reasonable to conclude that the great mass of the consumers, as their circumstances improve, will follow the same rule. And in further illustration of this argument it may be mentioned that the only species of corn which has risen materially in price since 1770 is barley, and that is accounted for by the increasing use of beer, which is more a luxury than a necessary of life.

Every intelligent farmer ought to keep this steadily in view. Let him produce as much as he can of the articles which have shown a gradual tendency to increase in value.

# XLIII

Although the younger Cobbett's book is little known, and is quite overshadowed by the fame of his father's *Rural Rides*, yet it gives a valuable account of conditions in France at a period not long after Waterloo and provides an interesting comparison with Young's accounts of nearly forty years earlier. It is clear that, in general, English farming in 1824 was still very much in advance of that common in France: James Paul Cobbett, *A Ride of Eight Hundred Miles in France* (1824), pp. 111, 178, 186-9.

---

Between this place and Chatillon sur Indre I saw several women *spreading dung with their hands!* I have in many instances in this part of France, seen the hands of the *softer sex* employed in this unbecoming labour: some of the women spreading the dung upon the land, while others of them were *carrying it upon their backs in baskets into the fields!* Many of my readers, even the most credulous among them, will, very probably, give me credit for a little romancing, when I publish such a relation as this. It is, however, nothing more than is strictly true. . . . The principal difference between the ploughs, carts, wagons, harrows, and the like in France, and such implements in England, is that these things seem to be in this country, on account of their comparative rudeness of fashion, about the same as I should suppose must have been used in England a great many years, perhaps a century, ago. The farming implements here are not generally so heavy as ours. They are nothing like so neatly made, but answer their purpose pretty nearly as well as those of English farmers. Some of the ploughs made use of in the neighbourhood of Briarre, and in other places where the land is light and the climate warmer than it is here, have scarcely any thing of a mould-board attached to them. The land is hardly turned over at all. The ploughshare gives it a shallow stir; and the farmer (unlike the farmer in England) seems to place more reliance on the *climate* than he does on the depth of the ploughing which his land receives. The winnowing machine is the most complicated piece of machinery that I see used by the French farmers; and this is not common among them . . .

The neat, the *flower-garden* cottage, is, it would seem, peculiar to England; for, I have always heard of the dunghill door-ways of the dwellings of the Scottish and Irish labourers; and I can myself speak as to those of the United States of America, where the farmer very seldom seems to care a great deal about the neatness of his yard and his garden but where the mere labourer, though he earn a dollar a day and eat meat three times a day, has, in general, a hole to live in that the poorest of our English labourers would be ashamed of. It is generally a '*caban*' made of boards, without any garden, or any thing that seems to say that it is the abode of comfort.

But notwithstanding this slovenliness, the American labourer is much *better off* than ours. And so is the French labourer. His habits are what we call slovenly; but he has never known the contrary. By the side of the obscurest lanes in England you will see the most beautiful flower-gardens, with little gravel or sand walks before little, old, cottages. These gardens are not intended for *show*. They are seen by nobody but the owners. It is taste, it is habit; most admirable, most meritorious, these are; but those to whom they are unknown do not experience the want of them.

The French labourer is better fed than the English labourer now is. He is better clothed too. His stock of clothes is greater. His body is not exposed, as the bodies of a large portion of our labourers now are. He is more dirty but not so ragged; less neat about his dwelling but he has about three times the quantity of food.

I saw today several men and women *digging* together, in the open fields with a spade (the ordinary spade made use of in France), which had a long handle and was very much like the narrow spade which is made use of in draining in England. The women dug uncommonly well: they stuck the spade into the ground without putting their foot upon it at all, and threw over the full spits of this heavy soil as quick and with as much apparent ease to themselves as the men did who worked alongside of them. The ground that these people were digging was a little plat which in exchange for services rendered to the landowner, or a part of the money paid them for such services, they were enabled to rent. It is a common thing here for a labourer to be the renter of a little piece of land in this way. Instead of being employed in such toilsome labour, the women, if they had been the wives or daughters of English labourers, would have been at home, attending to the state of their cottages and preserving that general system of neatness and order which makes so great a difference between the Englishman's *cottage* and the Frenchman's *caban*. Of the food of the French peasant bread is a principal article; and it is, in France, as it appears natural that it should be, the most abundant article in the way of food. All sorts of vegetables in this country, give way to bread. A less quantity of meat is requisite to a French labourer than what labourers (when they can get it) are used to consume in England. The *economy in cooking* here is such that the same quantity of animal food which we eat in England would feed almost double the number of persons in France. Soup is a food of which the French are so fond that they can scarcely bear to go without it. The best soup they like best; but, they like soup in general so much, that even *soup maigre* is better to them than no soup at all. The French do not cook so much meat in large pieces as we do; they cut it up into small bits and stew or fricassée it most frequently. It is this mode of cooking among them, no doubt, which has led to the supposition, which I do not think well founded, that the French are more abstinent with regard to meat than we are.

# XLIV

The contrast between the progressive capitalist farming of Britain and the prevalence over much of France of small-scale peasant production drew a number of comments in the nineteenth century, and became, in fact, one of the spurs to research in agrarian history. Here a prominent French agriculturist, who toured the British Isles shortly after mid-century, gives his views on one factor in the contrast—the far greater influence in Britain of large urban markets, which made it profitable for farmers to engage in production on a commercial scale: Léonce de Lavergne, *The Rural Economy of England, Scotland, and Ireland* (1855), pp. 153–68.

---

Everybody knows what enormous progress the employment of steam as a motive power has effected in British manufactures and commerce during the last fifty years. The principal seat of this amazing activity is in the north-west of England, the county of Lancaster, and its neighbour, the West Riding of Yorkshire. There Manchester works cotton, Leeds wool, Sheffield iron, and the port of Liverpool, with its constant current of exports and imports, feeds an indefatigable production; there an incessant excavation goes on of that subterranean world, appropriately called by the English their Black Indies—an immense reservoir of coal which covers several counties with its ramifications, and throws up in all directions its inexhaustible treasures. The quantity of coal annually raised is estimated at 40 million tons; this, at 10s per ton, is equal to £20 million sterling, which indicates a gigantic manufacturing production since coal is the material of first importance in all manufactures.

Under this impulse, the population of Great Britain, from 10 million in 1801, has risen to 20 million in 1851; that of Lancashire and the West Riding has tripled; there is perhaps no other place in the world where the population is more dense. France can show nothing like it: its total population during the same period has increased not more than a fourth; from 27 million she has reached 36 million, and her most populous departments, those of the Rhone and the Nord (after the Seine, which forms an exception, as well as London) count only two of a population to the hectare.

The more populous the country, the less proportion does the agricultural population bear to the whole mass of the people. Towards the end of the last century the return of the number of agriculturists in England, as compared to the total population, might be about the same as it is at present with us—that is to say, about 60 per cent.

Since then, as population increased, this proportion has become reduced; not that the rural population has decreased, for it has, on the contrary, slightly increased, but because the manufacturing population has increased in a far greater ratio. In 1800 it was reckoned that there were about 900,000 agricultural families in Great Britain; now there may probably be a million. In 1811 the number of non-agricultural families had already reached 1,600,000; in 1821 2 million; in 1841 2½ million; now it may be put down at 5 million. In general the rural population amounts to a fourth of the whole; but in particular parts it is much less. In Middlesex there are two cultivators of the land for every hundred of the population; in Lancashire, six; in the West Riding, ten; in Warwickshire and Staffordshire, fourteen.

In no part of France, not even in the department of the Seine, do we find such a disproportion. For an urban population, what is Paris with its million of souls, compared to the gigantic metropolis of the British empire, which reckons not less than 2½ million of inhabitants? What is Lyons, even with its appendage St Etienne, compared to that mass of manufacturing towns grouped around Liverpool and Manchester, and which form in the aggregate a population of 3 million souls? One-third of the English nation is congregated on these two points—London in the south, and the manufacturing towns of Lancashire and the West Riding in the north.

These human anthills are as rich as they are numerous. Many workmen in England receive from 4s to 8s a day; the average wage may be reckoned at 2s 6d. What becomes of the immense amount of wages paid to this mass of workmen every year? It goes, in the first place, to pay for bread, meat, beer, milk, butter, cheese, which are directly supplied by agriculture, and woollen and linen clothing, which it indirectly furnishes. There exists, consequently, a constant demand for productions which agriculture can hardly satisfy, and which is for her, in some measure, an unlimited source of profit. The power of these outlets is felt over the whole country; if the farmer has not a manufacturing town beside him to take off his produce, he has a port; and should he be distant from both, he brings himself into connection with them by canal or by one or more lines of railway.

These improved modes of transit not only serve to carry off rapidly and at a moderate expense what the farmer has to sell, but they bring him in the same way what he requires—among other things, manures and improvers such as guano, bones, rags, lime, gypsum, soot, oil-cake, etc., all heavy and bulky articles which could not easily be conveyed otherwise, and the abundance of which supposes a very active industrial development. Among these are also iron and coal, which are every day more and more used in agriculture, and which, to a certain extent, represent industry itself. Something more productive still than coal, iron, and animal and mineral substances, namely, the spirit of speculation, travels along with them from the manufacturing centres where it rises, to the fields, where it finds fresh elements to work upon and brings with it capital: a fruitful interchange, which enriches manufactures by agriculture, and agriculture by manufactures.

Notwithstanding the great facility of transport by steamers and railroads, a sensible difference exists in the gross and net agricultural produce between counties which are exclusively agricultural and those which are at the same time manufacturing.

The manufacturing districts *par excellence* commencing with Warwickshire in the south, and ending with the West Riding of Yorkshire, are those in which rents, profits, and agricultural wages rise highest. There the average rent is 30s per acre, and a country labourer's wages 12s a week; whilst in the district exclusively agricultural lying to the south of London the average rent is not more than 20s per acre, and wages 8s a week. The intermediate counties approach more or less to these two extremes, according as they are more or less manufacturing, and everywhere the rate of land and wages is a sure criterion of the development of local industry.

It is pretty generally believed that pauperism prevails more in the manufacturing than in other districts. This is quite a mistake. It is shown from a table published by Mr Caird in his excellent letters upon English agriculture, that in the West Riding, Lancashire, Cheshire, Stafford, and Warwick the poor's-rate is about 1s in the pound, to 3s or 4s a head, and the number of poor 3 to 4 per cent of the population; whilst in the agricultural counties of Norfolk, Suffolk, Bucks, Bedford, Berks, Sussex, Hants, Wilts, Dorset, etc., it exceeds 2s in the pound, or 10s a head, and the number of paupers is 13, 14, 15 and even 16 per cent of the population. The cause of this difference is easily understood; the number of paupers and the cost of their maintenance increases as the rate of wages becomes lower. Although the working population be three or four times more dense in the manufacturing than in other parts of the country, its condition there is better because it produces more.

What has hitherto appeared to us as a series of problems is now, if I mistake not, found to be perfectly explained.

In the first place, as to the organization of farming. What characterizes English rural economy, is, we know, not so much large farming properly so called, as the raising of farming into a business of itself, and the amount of capital at the disposal of professional farmers. These two features are both due to the immense opening found in the non-agricultural population.

If we transport ourselves to France, to the most backward departments of the centre and south where the *métayer* system predominates, what do we there find? A thinly-scattered population, at the most not exceeding on an average one-third that of the English—one head only, in place of three, to five acres—and that population almost entirely agricultural; few or no large towns, little or no manufactures, trade confined to the limited wants of the inhabitants; the centres of consumption distant, means of communication costly and difficult, and expenses of transport equal to the entire value of the produce. The cultivator has little or nothing to dispose of. Why does he work? To feed himself and his master with the produce of his labour. The master divides the produce with him, and consumes his portion: if it is wheat and wine, master and *métayer* eat wheat and drink wine; if it is rye, buckwheat, potatoes, these they consume together. Wool and flax are shared in like manner, and serve to make the coarse stuffs with which both clothe themselves: should there happen to remain over a few lean sheep, some ill-fed pigs, or some calves, reared with difficulty by overworked cows whose milk is disputed with their offspring, these are sold to pay taxes.

Great fault has been found with this system; however, it is the only one possible where markets are wanting. In such a country agriculture can be neither a profession, a speculation, nor an industry. To speculate there must be the means of selling, and that is impossible where there is no one to buy. When I say no one, it is to strengthen the hypothesis, for such an extreme case is rarely met with. There are always in France, even in the most retired districts, some buyers, though limited in number. It is sometimes a tenth, sometimes a fifth, sometimes a fourth of the population who earn a livelihood otherwise than by agriculture; and as the number of consumers increases, the condition of the cultivator improves, unless he himself pays the incomes of these consumers under the form of judicial expenses or usurious interest for money, which some of them at least do; but a tenth, fifth, or even the fourth of a population is not enough to furnish a sufficient market, especially if this population is not itself a producing one—that is to say, engaged in trade or manufactures.

In this state of things, as there is no interchange, the cultivator is obliged to produce those articles which are most necessary for life—that is to say, cereals: if the soil yields little, so much the worse for him; but he has no choice—he must produce corn or die of hunger. Now on bad land there is no more expensive cultivation than this; even on good, if care is not taken, it soon becomes burthensome; but under these conditions of farming no one thinks of taking account of the expense. The labour is not for profit, but for life: cost what it may, corn must be had, or at all events rye. As long as the population is scanty, the evil is not overwhelming, because there is no want of land: long fallows enable the land to produce something; but as soon as the population begins to increase, the soil ceases to be sufficient for the purpose; and a time soon arrives when the population suffers severely for want of food.

Let us now take the most populous and most industrious part of France—the north-west; still we do not find there a population quite analogous to that of the English—two head only per five acres, in place of three. It is double, however, that which we have anywhere else, and one-half of this population give their attention to commerce, manufactures, and the liberal professions. The country, properly speaking, is not more thickly populated than the centre and south of France; but we there find, in addition, numerous wealthy manufacturing towns—and among them is the largest and most opulent of all, Paris. A large trade is there carried on in agricultural commodities: corn, wine, cattle, wool, fowls, eggs, milk, etc., are directed from all parts to the towns, where they are paid for by manufactured goods. Consequently the lease becomes possible, and in fact introduces itself. This is the true cause of the lease; its existence is a sure indication of an economical condition where the sale of commodities is the rule, and where, consequently, farming may become a specific branch of industry.

This industry begins as soon as a regular market for it is opened—that is to say, as soon as the industrial and commercial populations exceed a certain proportion, whether it be immediately on the spot, or at a sufficiently moderate distance, with easy means of communication so that the expenses of transit do not absorb the profits: it becomes more and more flourishing as the market becomes greater and more approachable—that is, the nearer its vicinity to large towns or great centres of manufacture. In that case the market suffices to create profits which rapidly increase capital, farming becomes more and more prosperous, and progresses towards its maximum. This is the case in the departments nearest to Paris. About one half of France is more or less in this position, the other half possesses only uncertain markets: nothing is easier than to distinguish the two at a glance—in the one the lease prevails, in the other the *métayer* system.

In England, the half without markets has long ceased to exist; in all parts the rural population finds itself near another community; everywhere the outlet for its produce is as large as in the best parts of France, and in some places much greater. This makes the difference between the two agricultures. Take those parts of both France and England where the outlet is equal, and of as long standing, because time must be reckoned in the comparison, and you will most certainly find a similar agricultural development, whatever be the conditions otherwise of property and farming. Every other consideration depends upon this.

As soon as the producer finds a large sale for his commodities, his attention is naturally directed to questions to which hitherto he had not paid any attention; for instance, what produce brings the highest price relatively to its cost of production? By what means is the cost of production to be reduced, in order to increase the net profit? In this consists the whole agricultural revolution. The first consequence is the abandonment of those crops which, in a given situation, are not profitable, throwing the attention of the producer upon those which pay best; the second is the discovery of methods for economizing labour, thereby rendering it more productive.

Why does the English farmer, for example, give a preference to the production of meat? It is not only because the animals maintain by means of their manure the fertility of the land, but also because meat is an article very much in demand and which sells with the greatest facility throughout England. If our French producers could all at once furnish as much meat, the price would fall below the expenses of production because the demand is not great enough. Our population at present is not rich enough to pay for meat; we must wait until manufactures and commerce have made sufficient progress to furnish the means of exchange. In proportion as we make progress in these the demand will increase and our producers will then set themselves to supply it; it would be madness to expect them to do it sooner. Without Arkwright and Watt, Bakewell would have been impossible; the latter appeared just at the moment when the impetus given to industrial production rapidly increased the demand for meat. We do not require to go so far as England to see that the production of this food becomes abundant as soon as there is a sufficient market for it. The parts of the country where it is most largely produced with us are those where it is dearest—that is to say, most in demand; it is cheapest in the south, and the south hardly produces any. In 1770 meat sold in England at 3d per lb; the price now, after all that has been done to increase the production of every kind of cattle, is 6d or just double. These figures speak volumes.

With respect to milk, is it surprising that milch cows should be so numerous when milk sells currently in most parts of England

at 2d or 3d per quart? The working classes in England consume a
great deal of milk. Near manufacturing towns the average produce
of a milch cow is valued at £20, and it is not uncommon for some
to yield as much as £40. Butter, which in 1770 sold for 6d per lb,
now sells for 1s—it also has doubled. Put our farmers in a similar
position, and see if they will not have as good and as well-kept
cows. Look what the proximity of Paris has done for the producers of Gournay and Isigny.

The cultivation of wheat in place of rye is another consequence
of the same principle. In the districts of France farthest from
markets the suppression of the rye crop is quite impossible; for,
in the first place, the *métayer* must have food. He must be near a
market to do otherwise than grow rye, even should the land be
unsuitable for cereals and most favourable for other crops, because
there must be the opportunity for selling the new produce in
order to buy corn. The substitution of wheat for rye presents the
same difficulties, for it requires disbursements for lime and other
expenses; and why make the change, if wheat is in little demand,
or not wanted at all? Wherever the demand for wheat is on the
increase—that is, where there is a population which will pay dear
enough for its bread—the transition takes place even in France. It
has already taken place everywhere in England because the
working classes earn sufficient to pay for white bread.

The employment of horses in place of cattle, the use of
machinery to economize manual labour, are all owing to this. The
grand economical principle of division of labour is practised
under every form. The farmer with no market for his produce
seeks, above all, to curtail his expenses, because he lacks the
means of replenishing his purse; the farmer who is sure of a good
market does not shrink from useful expenditure.

The owner of property in this respect is no better off than the
farmer. Where small property is found to be unremunerative, the
absence of a market is chiefly the cause. A man with a small
capital has no inducement to become farmer when the chance of
profit is small and uncertain. His object also is to live so that the
least possible demand may be made upon his purse; and what
better method of securing his subsistence, when opportunities of
interchange are wanting than to invest his little all in a piece of
land and to work it himself? It was so in England before the great
markets were opened. The yeoman did not find it profitable to

turn farmer until the great industrial movement took place. Arthur Young was the theorist, not the actual promoter of this revolution: it was Watt and Arkwright who effected it.

The same causes which enhance profits raise rents. We have, to a certain extent, seen this to be the case when, in the reign of Louis XVI, trade in agricultural produce became free. We have seen rents rise gradually from 3 francs per hectare to 30 francs, according as industrial and commercial wealth progressed. We see it at this day reach 100 francs and upwards in the departments where a non-agricultural population abounds, and fall to 10 in those where it is wanting. If we had everywhere the same outlets as in England no doubt our average rent would very soon be equal to that of our neighbour; that is to say, double what it is now. Only double the rent, and, even without changing the actual condition of property, many of our poor proprietors would become by this means alone rich proprietors. We should immediately have the exact equivalent of the English gentry.

There are, moreover, two kinds of property: the fixed, called in England real property, and the movable or personal property. The income from real property for the three kingdoms is estimated at £120 million sterling, or 3 milliards of francs. Land, properly so called, figures for only half of this: the rest is from house property, mines, quarries, canals, railways, fisheries, etc. The value of house property alone is nearly as much as the land itself. In Great Britain, the income from land is £46 million sterling, while that of houses is £40 million. The income from personal property may, at the same time, be valued at £80 million sterling, or 2 milliards of francs, deducting interest paid to mortgages, already included as income from properties mortgaged. It follows, therefore, that the rent of land, so high relatively, does not amount to a third of the income of English proprietors.

We see now how they come to be, on an average, richer than ours. In the first place, they are proportionately much less numerous; and then again (and this is the main reason) they have a much larger revenue to be divided among them. With us the income from land, which to begin with is proportionately less than the whole rents of land in England, is not very much less than the half of the income from all capital, both fixed and personal together. Small as the distribution of other wealth is in other hands, very little of it is found in the hands of our landed proprietors. In England, on the contrary, there are few landed proprietors who, in addition to the income from their land, have not an equally large, and oftentimes larger income, from houses, railway shares, government stocks, etc. Many of them are proprietors of coal-pits which have yielded them, and every day bring them in, immense sums. Others have property upon which are constructed manufactories, dwelling-houses, canals, or railways, and from which they have profited by a rise in value.

It is well known that the Marquess of Westminster, the Duke of Bedford, and others, own a great part of the land upon which London stands, and which is let upon long leases. And it is the same with almost all the English towns. Since the year 1800, 1,500,000 new houses have been built in England alone, 6,000 miles of railway have been opened, and an enormous number of coal-pits and mines have been set to work. Here are millions annually, the greater part of which goes into the pockets of the landed proprietors; and it is not the great proprietors only who partake in this good fortune, the middling and smaller ones have also their share.

Lastly, there is another means which causes a large portion of the capital created by manufactures to flow towards landed property—and that is the acquisition of estates by wealthy traders. These acquisitions, more numerous than we in France suppose, add greatly to the average wealth of property and contribute to make its possessors more liberal towards the soil. The new proprietors bring into the administration of their country estates an amount of resources and speculative boldness which to the same extent is rarely found among the others; as witness one example among a thousand. Mr Marshall, the son of a rich Leeds manufacturer, purchased, some years ago, 1,000 acres of land, at Patrington, near the mouth of the Humber in the East Riding of Yorkshire. The enormous expense to which we went in rebuilding offices, erecting steam-engines, draining, liming, etc., is well known throughout England.

Such things take place in France every day, but no doubt of a less striking character because industrial pursuits are less productive, though the features and circumstances are the same. What fortunes have been made during the last fifty years on the lands about Paris, and other towns of France! What large indemnities have already been paid for railways, canals, mines, manufactories! What doubling of rents, caused by the opening of new means of communication, or the development of neighbouring large hives of industry! Finally, what quantities of land every day pass from insolvent and poor hands into wealthy ones! It is the natural progressive movement of society, a movement which is accelerated when not hindered by any political catastrophe.

Reduced to these limits, the agricultural question is nothing more than one of general prosperity. If French society, retarded by all the obstacles which itself originated, could ever have fifty years before it such as those which have elapsed from 1815 and 1848, it would no doubt regain in agriculture, as in everything else, the distance which separates it from its rival. The greatest difficulties are passed. We, as well as the English, make use of those powerful means which nowadays increase the power of labour, and which, applied to almost a new field, are capable of advancing to an infinite extent the progress of wealth. Nowhere are railways capable of producing a more thorough and profitable revolution than with us. In England these wonderful roads connect only parts already connected by other means of communication, and whose productions are similar in character. With us their effect will be to unite regions, all differing in climate and productions, which have as yet only imperfect communication one with the other. It is impossible to predict what may result from such a radical change.

It is of consequence, then, that our proprietors and cultivators apprehend clearly the only means of enriching themselves, lest they hinder their own prosperity. Their opposition would not arrest the course of things, but would render it slow and tedious. All jealousy between agricultural and industrial and commercial interests, will only damage both. If you wish to encourage agriculture, develop manufactures and commerce which multiply consumers; improve especially the means of communication which bring consumers and producers nearer to each other; the rest will necessarily follow. Commerce and manufactures bear the same relation to agriculture as the cultivation of forage crops and multiplication of animals do to cereal production. At first they seem opposed to each other, but fundamentally there is such a strong connecting link between them that the one cannot make any considerable progress without the other.

Markets—this is the greatest and most pressing requirement of our agriculture. The proceedings to be adopted in order to augment production do not come till afterwards. I have pointed out the principal methods followed in England, and will shortly point out others. Our agriculture may there find useful examples; but I am far from giving them as models for imitation. Everywhere each soil and climate has its requirements and resources. The south of France, for example, has scarcely anything to borrow from English methods; its agricultural future is nevertheless magnificent. There is only one law which admits of no exception, and which everywhere produces the same results—that is, the law of markets.

# XLV

Sir James Caird is well known today as the leading contemporary expert on nineteenth-century farming in Britain. His works on America and India are much less familiar, but his study of *Prairie Farming in America* was written to encourage British farmers who might think of emigrating, and contains many relevant comments on the differences between British and American conditions, though perhaps with some bias towards the advantages of America. The following excerpts deal with the dramatic rise of the middle-western grain area and its metropolis, Chicago, and his calculation of the costs and benefits of establishing a farm on the rich prairies of Illinois: J. Caird, *Prairie Farming in America* (1859), pp. 31–3, 85–91.

---

I had now reached the new capital of 'that Western World', as Washington described it, which Penn prophesied would yet make a glorious country. The valley of the Mississippi above Cairo, comprising on its eastern bank Illinois and Wisconsin, and on the west, Missouri, Iowa, and Minnesota, embraces probably the greatest tract of fertile land on the surface of the globe. In total extent it exceeds England and France together, with the kingdom of the two Sicilies thrown into the bargain—it is more than equal to Prussia and the whole Austrian empire—even Spain and Turkey combined would require the territory of the Ionian Islands to place them on a par with it. And this vast territory is not only intersected by numerous lines of railroad, which give it direct access to Montreal, New York, and Philadelphia, but on the north, by means of the lakes and the St Lawrence, and on the south by the Mississippi River, it possesses a continuous water communication with the Atlantic.

Nothing can illustrate more forcibly the vast natural abundance and resources of this splendid country than the history of the grain-trade of Chicago. An Indian village in 1820, this place has become a great city with upwards of 120,000 people, with wharves and granaries for miles along the river canal which opens into Lake Michigan, and with streets, public buildings, churches, and private dwellings that may vie with those of London itself. The stores on the principal streets are equal in size and architectural elegance to the new row of fine buildings which leads from Cannon Street into St Paul's Church Yard. There are numerous stands for hackney-coaches, and various lines of omnibuses ply along the streets. And Chicago is actually the centre of more miles of railway, completed and in operation, than London. Yet it is only twenty years since the first shipment of some forty bags of wheat was made from it. In 1837 its exports amounted to about 100 bushels of grain, in 1847 they had reached 2,243,000 bushels, and in 1857 upwards of 18 million bushels. Chicago and all its wealth are in fact a property created by the profits arising in the mere transference from hand to hand of the surplus produce of but a small part of this wonderful country. Looking to Illinois alone, of which Chicago is the commercial capital and outlet, this surplus, great though it is, is capable of being increased tenfold, as only one-tenth of the fertile lands of this State are believed to be yet brought under cultivation.

But while no man who has seen the country can entertain a doubt of its vast capability of further development, it does not surprise me that capitalists in London are disappointed with their railway investments here. In England we make railways to facilitate an existing traffic. Elaborate statistics are furnished to show the extent of the present business of the country proposed to be accommodated. But in the Western States of America railways are made for hundreds of miles through the wilderness, not to accommodate but to create traffic. You may often travel for miles through the open prairie without seeing a living creature, till the shrill whistle of the engine startles a solitary sand-hill crane or a covey of prairie fowl. An Englishman cannot at first imagine the possibility of a traffic to be found in such a country, adequate to the support of a railway. But the experienced American knows better the rapid rate at which population and produce increase in a rich open country, to which access is made. He points to the fact that six years ago there were only forty miles of railway in Illinois, the earnings of which fell short of £8,000 while last year the total earnings of the lines centring in Chicago exceeded £3,700,000 . . .

I have now before me four detailed accounts of farms of eighty acres each, all of which show a profit, besides paying for the land itself, from the first crop. But these cases were instances during the period of high prices in 1855–6. And the same may be said of all the detailed accounts which have been recently laid before the public. I shall therefore offer an estimate based on the probable future range of prices, and, to facilitate calculations, will take 100 acres of land; the first crop wheat, and the following crop Indian corn. The wheat crop shall be cultivated by contract, the land fenced, broken up, sown with wheat, reaped and threshed, and a labourer's house built, during the first eighteen months. The second and following crops can be managed by two resident ploughmen.

| | |
|---|---:|
| Cash price of 100 acres of land | £200 |
| Contract price of fencing, breaking, sowing with wheat, reaping and threshing, and building a labourer's cottage, and stable and shed | £250 |
| Capital invested in the purchase of four horses, implements, and harness | £110 |
| | £560 |
| Second year wages of two men, horse keep, taxes, and accounts | £200 |
| | £760 |

Cr.

| | | |
|---|---:|---:|
| First crop, wheat, 2,000 bushels, at 3s 6d | £350 | |
| Second crop, Indian corn 5,000 bushels, at 1s 8d | £416 | £766 |

Thus repaying, by two crops, the cost of the land, stock, and improvements, and leaving a trifling surplus.

The third year begins by the prairie farmer finding himself the unencumbered *owner* of his land, all fenced and improved, with a stock of horses and implements, and the whole of his original capital in his pocket. He may continue to crop his farm with Indian corn from which he will reap very large returns on his capital.

The foregoing example has reference to a capitalist purchaser, not a working farmer. The 100 acres may be multiplied by any number for which there is adequate capital, and the results ought to be the same in proportion. There appears to be thus a very ample surplus in the way of annual return, whilst the value of the land itself will probably treble within ten years from the mere growth of population.

But a working farmer will not only receive the same annual dividend from his capital, but will also take to himself the full rate of wages which is allowed for hired labour in this estimate. And he may, moreover, avail himself of the credit given by the Illinois Central Railway Company to the purchasers of their lands.

The Illinois Central Railway Company have still 1,300,000 acres of land to sell. It is situated along their line of railway, chiefly within five miles on either side, and affords every variety of soil, climate, and situation to be found in the State of Illinois. They offer their lands at prices which, considering situation, quality, and terms of payment, are the cheapest I met with in America. Every facility for the transport of produce to market is at the command of a settler on their lands. At every nine or ten miles there is a station with an electric telegraph, where the latest news of the markets may be learned; while there is usually a store at the station for the purchase of produce and the sale of necessaries. Their terms of payment for the land are either cash with a discount of 20 per cent in the price, or a long credit with a moderate rate of interest for America. So confident do they feel in the increasing value of their land that they readily leave the entire price of it as a mortgage to be repaid by annual instalments out of the produce of the land itself. Purchasers from them obtain the further important advantage of exemption from all State taxes until the whole instalments of the price have been paid off, and this usually extends over the first seven years. It is an advantage of very great value which can be obtained nowhere else.

Let us consider the advantage of this credit plan to the father of several sons in this country, to whom he may be anxious to give the means of starting in life. If he desires to place one in a farm in England of 300 acres he must provide him with a capital of £2,000. But if instead of making his son the tenant of another man he determines to purchase a farm of the same extent for him on the prairie, he may pay the advance interest of the purchase money of the land, fence it, build on it, stock it, and sow the first crop for less than £600. Two years elapse before the first instalment of the price is due, and by that time, with good management, the land should have yielded enough to pay it besides all the expenses of management. An intelligent, prudent man, with £600 in his pocket, may rely on finding that sum sufficient to start him successfully on 320 acres of rich prairie land if he avails himself of this credit system.

His position will be this. He enters into a contract with the Company for the purchase of 320 acres of their land at the price of 50s an acre. He pays two years' advance interest upon this, but he pays nothing further for two years. His first instalment, one-fifth of the price, then becomes payable, and each year thereafter, till all is paid, another fifth. His account will stand thus:

| | |
|---|---:|
| Two years' advance interest on price of land at 7 per cent | £112 |
| Contract price of fencing 100 acres, breaking it, sowing with wheat, reaping and threshing, and for building a house, stable, and shed | 300 |
| Price of horses, implements, and harness | 110 |
| | 522 |
| Value of first crop | 350 |
| | £172 |
| Second year: contract for fencing another 100 acres, sowing it with wheat, reaping and threshing | 150 |
| Wages paid and horse keep for cultivating 100 acres of Indian corn | 150 |
| | £472 |

His 200 acres of corn crop will now yield him from £600 to £700, thus more than recompensing his outlay, and leaving plenty in hand to pay his first instalment and to proceed with the vigorous cultivation of the land. The same sum which would be needed to start one son as a farmer of another man's high-rented land in England, would thus start three sons as the *owners* of farms, fenced, stocked, and under crop, on the fine prairie soils of Illinois.

Many English emigrants may, however, prefer to pay cash for their land and take the benefit of the large discount allowed. It is a less speculative system, and, where there is capital sufficient to begin with, I should decidedly recommend it as the best and really cheapest mode of making a purchase from the Railway Company. They allow a discount of 20 per cent for full payment in cash. A capital of £4 an acre will be found adequate to all the expenses of buying and stocking one of their prairie farms, the land being paid for, out and out.

The fact that land which would sell for £60 to £80 an acre in England can be bought in Illinois for 40s or 50s—while the population of the United States, already 28 million, is increasing much more rapidly than England, and the facility of transport is equally good—must carry its own weight to the mind of every thinking man who has a family to provide for.

I have in a previous letter pointed out the profitable nature of sheep farming in Illinois, and would again refer to it here, as an object well worthy of the consideration of young emigrant farmers. Merino sheep prove very healthy, and can be kept cheaply on the prairie. Their wool is nearly as valuable in America as in England, and the supply is not adequate to the increasing home consumption of that country. A large stock of sheep may be purchased with a small capital. I cannot help thinking, that the safest speculation for an enterprising immigrant farmer would be the purchase of a section of land in the midst of untouched prairie. He could enclose and crop his own section and winter a large sheep stock on it, which he might graze on the open prairie during the summer at no other cost than that of herding.

The price of the land is the least consideration that a British emigrant need take into his calculations. For if he avails himself of the credit system he may enter on as much or as little as he likes for an immediate payment of only 7s an acre; and his next payment is not due until he has been two years in possession, by which time the produce of the land ought to be much more than sufficient to meet it. The travelling expenses, the expense of maintenance, the building of a house, and the necessary outlays for stock, are nearly as great to start a small farm of forty acres as one of four times the extent. A man with his wife and four children could not transport himself and them from this country to Illinois, and place himself comfortably even on a forty acre farm, for less than £100. But £40 more would suffice to place him in a farm of 160 acres. I cannot, therefore, advise men who are unable to scrape more together than will merely pay their travelling expenses to go to Illinois. And far less can I advise them to go farther west. Suppose they could obtain land in Iowa or Minnesota, 400 miles farther away, at only half the price, the saving of 3s an acre in their deposit would never compensate even the cost of travel for the additional distance, while every article which they require to purchase must bear an enhanced price from the same cause.

But there is one class of our labouring population for whom Illinois offers great encouragement. Young men of intelligence and prudence who have been brought up to agricultural pursuits and are acquainted with the management of land and livestock may do very well by hiring land from the owner. They get the farm fenced, stocked, with necessary buildings, and with all requisites except labour, for carrying it on. They furnish the labour and share the produce with the owner. This is a transaction which is very common in Illinois; it answers the purpose of both parties; and a prudent active man who enters upon it, will generally in a few years realize enough to start himself in a farm of his own. I heard of many instances of great success attending this sort of arrangement, and from my personal knowledge, I am sure that there are many hundreds of our northern agricultural labourers possessed of the requisite skill and prudence to ensure success. To such men, I should be happy to offer any information in my power on application being made to me.

One great advantage which an emigrant of any class possesses in the Western States is the facility with which land may be acquired; not merely its cheapness, but the readiness and simplicity with which it may be legally transferred. Every five pounds that a man saves may at once be invested in land. He needs to run no risk of bank failures; and his landed investment is constantly improving in value though he were to do nothing whatever with it. The same process is going on at home, but the labouring man at home cannot share in an advantage to which he himself contributes as the land is too dear for him, and the cost of transferring a small parcel of it is nearly as great as the cost of the land itself. He is thus shut out altogether from the hope ever of being the possessor of land, and cannot therefore participate in that increasing value which is the good fortune of the rich alone.

Though I have doubts of the success of even prudent men who have no more capital than their wits and no agricultural knowledge or experience, I feel bound to say that such is not the

general opinion of experienced men in Illinois. One gentleman of
high reputation and fortune in Chicago assured me that he knew
innumerable instances of people brought up in towns, with no
knowledge of country life and very limited means, who had
blundered into experience and comfort in a year or two. 'In this
country,' he said, 'every necessary of life is sluttishly plentiful; it
is not possible here to find a man hungry; nature is so abundant
that no prudent man can help becoming rich; and though they
may sometimes have a setback for a time, they will soon rebound
and take a fresh start. There is plenty for all.'

# XLVI

Caird's last major work on British farming was largely concerned with the threatening prospects of increased foreign competition in agricultural produce. In these final excerpts he considers the causes of the depressed conditions at the end of the 1870's, the factors leading to a future rise in imports, and the need for even greater concentration by British farmers on catering for the market needs brought about by rising real incomes—a closer association with those products like milk, fruit and vegetables, which still retained some natural protection from distance and were in rising demand. In the event depression conditions in the next twenty years forced many farmers to observe this advice. J. Caird, *The Landed Interest and the Supply of Food* (1st ed. 1878, 4th ed. 1880, reprinted 1967), pp. 157–64, 169, 175.

---

Since the last edition of this work appeared we have had in the harvest of 1879 the worst crop in the memory of the present generation of farmers. The wheat crop of 1853 was perhaps less in bulk per acre; but it was better in quality, and the extent was one-fourth greater. After deducting seed, it yielded one-half more food than that of 1879, a large proportion of which was unfit for bread. The importations of 1853–4 were 6 million quarters, and the average price 72s. The population was 6 million less than at present, but the quantity available for consumption was only four and a half bushels per head. It has never since fallen so low. After the abundant crop of 1868, when the population was 3 million greater than in 1853, there was over six bushels per head, and the price had fallen to 48s. With the exception of 1870 and 1874, the history of the home wheat crop since 1868 has been one of diminishing acreage, and acreable produce, but attended by such increasing importations as have kept the supply close upon six bushels a head.

Nothing like the present depression among the farmers has

been seen since the repeal of the corn laws. There have not before been so many farms thrown on the market, and never till now in our time have been seen in England farms tenantless and uncultivated. The continued rain and low temperature of 1879 not only acted destructively on the corn and green crops but damaged the hay crop beyond measure, and over many English counties left behind it the seeds of disease, which in the winter and spring carried off by rot many thousands of the sheep stock. The inferior quality of the fodder crops shows itself in the reduced condition of all kinds of live stock. In nine years there have been seven defective harvests, the last culminating in intensity and including in its grasp a portion of the animal in addition to the vegetable produce of the land. It is no comfort to the British farmer to be told that there is similar depression in the agricultural districts of France and Germany, nor is it any satisfaction to him to hear of the rapid growth of agricultural wealth in the Western States across the Atlantic, the competition of which has prevented that rise of price which has hitherto been some compensation to him for unfavourable harvests. In England itself, where the bulk of the wheat crop of the kingdom is grown, there has been lost in the last ten years by unfavourable seasons a fourth more than a whole year's wheat crop; a loss of over £30 million sterling to the British wheat growers which has heavily crippled their resources.

That loss which has been brought upon us by natural causes we may trust to nature with time to repair. But the agriculture of America has been stimulated in an extraordinary degree by the rising demand occasioned by this long-continued diminution in our own crops, and in those of Western Europe generally. The magnitude which this has attained within the last twenty years is shown by the average exports for the first half of that period compared with those of the last. Wheat has increased threefold, Indian corn fourfold. But the increase in the last three years has been unprecedented. The United States have at present ten times the acreage of wheat compared with that of the United Kingdom. They produce double the quantity of corn of all kinds compared with that of England and France together. They have twice the the number of horses, one-third more cattle, and nearly four times more hogs than both countries. The following table shows this in detail:

Produce of corn in bushels, and numbers of live stock in 1878

| | United Kingdom | France | United States |
|---|---|---|---|
| Wheat | 102,000,000 | 240,000,000 | 420,000,000 |
| Barley | 82,000,000 | 52,000,000 | 42,000,000 |
| Oats | 160,000,000 | 210,000,000 | 413,000,000 |
| Maize | — | 216,000,000 | 1,388,000,000 |
| Horses and mules | 2,000,000 | 2,900,000 | 12,651,000 |
| Cattle | 10,000,000 | 11,600,000 | 33,220,000 |
| Sheep | 32,500,000 | 26,000,000 | 38,173,000 |
| Pigs | 3,768,000 | 5,232,000 | 34,734,000 |

In addition to these vast products the people of the United States raise cotton, tobacco, and sugar worth nearly £50 million sterling.

This prodigious development of agricultural wealth has practically an unlimited power of expansion. For, in addition to the vast areas of the United States still untouched by advancing agriculture, there is the great region of Manitoba and the 'fertile belt' of North Western Canada, stretching in a block of fertile land 700 miles westward from the Red River of the north, watered by navigable rivers, in extent many times larger than the British Islands, with abundance of coal, now at last brought into prominent notice by the Canadian Government.

The war in America interrupted progress for a time, but its attractions are now beginning to be realized. A railway from Lake Superior to the Red River is completed, and another in progress which will tap the produce of this vast region, and after a run of 500 miles of land-carriage place it on board large steamers which, traversing the lakes and the St Lawrence, will tranship it to ocean-going steamers for the ports of the United Kingdom. This is rendered practicable by the works now in progress for widening and deepening the canals which pass the navigation clear of Niagara and the lower rapids of the river. And this, with the economy of fuel effected by the improvements in marine engines, has immensely diminished the cost of transportation. The natural protection which the British farmer possessed fifteen years ago in the cost of transport has thus been reduced on the produce of an acre of wheat, from 56s to 26s. This is still nearly equal to the rent, but the land, in this country of old cultivation must be regularly manured and carefully and expensively cultivated; while the farmers of those foreign lands whose virgin soil is rich enough to yield corn for many years in succession without manure, and with little labour, are thereby able to compete successfully with the British farmer in his own market. It is the unexhausted natural fertility of his soil which gives the advantage to the prairie farmer of the north-west, and this is constantly being aided by the increasing ingenuity and enterprise of the engineer, shipbuilder, and shipowner.

And it is not in corn only but also in all kinds of animal produce that this competition has to be met. The imports of animal produce inclusive of wool, last year exceeded £60 million in value, a sum closely approaching to the entire land rental of this kingdom. The imports of corn of all kinds during the last three years give an annual average slightly exceeding £60 million in value. The enormous volume already reached shows at once that this country still affords the best market, but also that in the face of some decline of price there is no cessation of supply, the reduction being met by scientific appliances which minimize the cost of transport and lessen the risk of bringing fresh meat from the great grazing grounds of America, North and South, and the more distant plains of Australia. A recent French patent has proved that, without the direct use of ice the temperature of fresh meat can be kept so reduced that it is beginning to be transported with safety from the most remote fields of production . . .

We must not deceive ourselves. A great change in the agricultural position is impending. The older States on the eastern seaboard of America are rapidly going out of cultivation by the competition of the richer virgin soils of the west. That competition is nearer to our doors now by the cheapening of transport than it was to theirs twenty years ago. The time has come when it must be promptly met, if we would avoid the same fate . . .

Bakers' shops are diminishing, and butchers' shops increasing. Vegetables fresh from our own fields, or brought by fast steamers from the ports of the neighbouring continent, are more and more displacing bread. That proportion which thirty years ago the richer classes in this country alone could afford to spend on other articles of household consumption than bread, is being rapidly reached by the working class. Our agriculture must adapt itself to the change, freely accepting the good it brings, and skilfully using the advantages which greater proximity to the best market must always command.

# INDEX